GAME FACES

SPORT AND SOCIETY

Series Editors
Randy Roberts
Aram Goudsouzian

Founding Editors
Benjamin G. Rader
Randy Roberts

*A list of books in the series appears
at the end of this book.*

publication grant by
Figure Foundation
in league for fact

GAME FACES

SPORT CELEBRITY AND
THE LAWS OF REPUTATION

SARAH K. FIELDS

UNIVERSITY OF ILLINOIS PRESS

URBANA, CHICAGO, AND SPRINGFIELD

Library of Congress Cataloging-in-Publication Data
Names: Fields, Sarah K., 1968– author.
Title: Game faces : sport celebrity and the laws of reputation /
    Sarah K. Fields.
Description: Urbana : University of Illinois Press, 2016. | Series:
    Sport and society | Includes bibliographical references and
    index.
Identifiers: LCCN 2015043809 (print) | LCCN 2015044593 (ebook)
    | ISBN 9780252040283 (hardback) | ISBN 9780252081736
    (paperback) | ISBN 9780252098543 (e-book)
Subjects: LCSH: Privacy, Right of—United States—Cases. |
    Celebrities—Legal status, laws, etc.—United States—Cases.
    | Publicity (Law)—United States—Cases. | Photographs—
    Law and legislation—United States—Cases. | Freedom of the
    press—United States—Cases. | Heroes in mass media. | BISAC:
    LAW / Media & the Law. | LAW / Sports. | LAW / Defamation.
Classification: LCC KF1262 .F54 2016 (print) | LCC KF1262 (ebook)
    | DDC 342.7308/58—dc 3
LC record available at http://lccn.loc.gov/2015043809

In memory and celebration of Junior,
the joyous Sarah

CONTENTS

ACKNOWLEDGMENTS

My academic interest in the tension between celebrities and the press as well as the balance between what is private and what is newsworthy began with a seminar paper I wrote more than twenty years ago as a graduate student for Professor LeRoy Ashby at Washington State University. The concept grew into my master's thesis, and Professors Richard Hume and Lisa McIntyre, along with Professor Ashby, helped me think through the historical evolution of the rights associated with defamation and privacy. Subsequently, I explored the idea in seminar papers in graduate school at the University of Iowa with Professors William G. Buss in the School of Law and Jeffery A. Smith in the School of Journalism and Mass Communications. Although Professor Smith encouraged me to make more of the topic, the project went on the back burner while I explored other matters. The heat, however, was never quite turned off, and the ideas simmered for years while I kept reading books and articles on the topic. After more than a decade of reading and thinking, I was overwhelmed and suspected that the project would never reach fruition.

Enter Willis G. Regier, director of the University of Illinois Press. At a sport history conference, Bill stopped me and insisted that we talk about my next book project. At the time, I didn't really want a next book project, but he listened to my half-formed ideas and suggested that there might be something worthwhile buried inside. He encouraged me to return to the topic. Without his support, I would never have made it through the proposal process, let alone actually written the thing. Bill kept his faith in me as well as in the project; he patiently waited far too many years for me to submit the book. Without Bill and without his impending retirement, I don't know that this would have ever been finished. Thank you, Bill.

After Bill's retirement, the staff at the University of Illinois Press took excellent care of this manuscript, and I am particularly grateful for the remarkable copyediting of Julie Gay. Her careful work saved me from myself on several occasions. Any errors that remain are exclusively mine.

Although writing can be a solitary process, the creation of a book is not. All of my ideas were verbalized (sometimes repeatedly) to some poor sap. My first set of thanks goes to my students and colleagues. My students have patiently read a surprising number of books on celebrity in class as I pondered different ideas and tried to trick myself into writing. Even after their graduation, a number of them still inquired about my progress, helping to motivate me. The students of Communication and Sport in spring 2015 offered title suggestions after everyone agreed that my working title was terrible. I appreciated the creativity of my students, and the final title is a version of what Joe West suggested. My fellow faculty members in the kinesiology section of the Ohio State University for nine years were all wonderfully supportive and good friends, but without Mel Adelman, I'd likely have never gotten anything done. His loyalty and friendship mean the world to me.

This project was briefly sidetracked when I moved to the Department of Communication at the University of Colorado Denver. In this new department, I found colleagues who encouraged me to finish the project and assured me that it had value. As is the case in most universities, my colleagues and friends extend beyond my department, and I deeply appreciate my affiliation with the Women's and Gender Studies Program at CU Denver. I found also a group of fellow writers who offered their comments and support; thanks to the Humanities Writing Group generally and specifically to Michelle Comstock, Amy Hasinoff, Gillian Silverman, and Sarah Tyson, who all gave me detailed feedback on the preface and the first chapter. I must also thank Eric Baker at the Auraria Library for helping me track down sources about the *San Jose Mercury News*.

Jamila Porter and her brother Barry Porter were my research investigators in Atlanta, Georgia. For several months I became obsessed with the mystery of Warren Spahn's Bronze Star, and Jamila and Barry handled the in-person investigation to determine if the Atlanta Braves Hall of Fame did indeed have the medal. Their diligence and persistence proved that there was no Bronze Star of Warren Spahn's in that museum; their patient and careful work saved me a trip to Atlanta at a time I could ill afford to go. Thank you both.

In the wider field of sport, my colleagues at the North American Society for Sport History (NASSH) and the North American Society for Sport Sociology (NASSS) have patiently sat through session after session as I worked through my ideas about privacy, law, and sport. Their comments, questions, and guidance helped move me forward, and thanking them all by name would not be wrong but would be lengthy. Therefore, I am limited to just a few specific thanks with apologies to all who go unnamed but not unappreciated. Dick Crepeau offered comments on the Joe Montana chapter and gave me good advice about additional sources. Chuck Korr served as a commentator for a presentation on the Warren Spahn chapter and later offered remarkably helpful insights as a reviewer for the book manuscript; I appreciate his wisdom and his support. Dan Nathan was another reviewer for the book manuscript, and I am deeply grateful for his careful reading and discerning comments. Sam Regalado is more enthusiastic about my work than I am: his energy and enthusiasm for the intersection of law and sport history drags me back into the field whenever I think about crawling away. Mo Smith has attended countless presentations and conferences with me, and her work on public imagery has helped me think through issues of what is public. After each of my presentations, Ron Smith would stop me and talk about my work; his insights were invaluable, and his stories about Warren Spahn made me restructure some of that chapter. Patricia Vertinsky, as well, asked critical questions that made me think and re-think some of my ideas about privacy and my representation of sport history. Thank you to all my NASSH friends.

My next set of thanks goes to non–sport history friends. Much of this book was written during a difficult period of my life, and without their help and support, I'm not sure the book or I would have fared very well. Janet Buckworth and Chuck Moody were very good friends who offered help and healthy food. Ruth Almén was not just a friend and counselor but an early editor of this manuscript. Thanks to the many, many people who helped in those challenging days.

Thank you to my family. My parents, Wayne Fields and Karen Johnson Fields, became my first editors when I was a child and have not yet stopped reading or critiquing my work. This book is no exception. They read the M.A. thesis in which I first began working through ideas of public and private selves and have encouraged me to continue ever since. Each has read multiple drafts of this book. They taught me that one should never stop learning and never stop trying to become a better writer. They taught me also that family, no matter what its form, is most important. My sister Elizabeth, her husband

Matt, and their children, Jacob and Sarah, showed me more courage and strength than I ever imagined could exist. And just a month before I wrote this, Liz, Matt, and Jake welcomed Mattie to our family. Their resilience inspires me. My brother Aaron, his wife Kathleen, and their children, Bergen and Bode, have faced loss with compassion and always remained hopeful. I admire their quest for happiness. In the midst of chaos, my dad's wife Joni and my sister Ellen showed remarkable grace and kindness, and I appreciate their presence in the family.

Finally, Dawn Comstock, my spouse and partner in all things, has watched this project grow from a seedling. From the moment she told me I had to pay attention to Princess Diana's death and its subsequent coverage because it was relevant to this project, I knew she understood. She has helped me work through different ideas and patiently waited when I disappeared for days on end, writing. She read and critiqued it also—were this a scientific publication, she'd deserve authorship. Instead, she has my deepest gratitude. Beyond being my editor and colleague, though, Dawn is my better half. Without her, not only would this project be less, but I would be as well. Thank you is inadequate.

PREFACE

The United States is a society of contradictions and paradoxes when it comes to information. Americans love celebrities *and* their own privacy; we do not worry much about the privacy of the celebrity, as that would cut into our sense that we know the celebrity, that they are friends we have yet to meet. While we value our own privacy and are offended by those who intrude into it, we are willing to sacrifice that privacy if it leads to our own celebrity. Americans will share family tragedies with morning news shows, place webcams in bedrooms, and eagerly star on reality television programs and undergo humiliating and risky experiences for fifteen minutes of fame. We do so because of the perceived benefits of fame: money, endorsements, special treatment, and adoration. For that, privacy must be sacrificed. Celebrities know this but, at times, resent it.

In the twenty-first century, sporting figures—such as athletes, coaches, and administrators—are often huge celebrities in American society. Sport, as scholar Barry Smart described it, is "at the heart of contemporary culture."[1] In the United States, an estimated 30 million to 45 million children between ages six and eighteen play in at least one community- or school-based athletic program.[2] The United States is the only country in the world that routinely and completely links education and sport: much of organized sport is habitually managed through schools. As a result, huge numbers of children grow up dreaming of being sport stars, and as adults they become sports fans, consuming the sports media, product endorsements, and everything else surrounding their athletic heroes. In total, an estimated $200 billion a year is spent on the sport industry in the United States.[3] Three of the four Super Bowls between 2010 and 2014 set new all-time highs for live viewership in the United States.[4] Sport, commercialism via sponsorships and advertising, and live viewership have intertwined into what scholar David Rowe called the "media sports cultural complex."[5] ESPN, the self-described "Worldwide Leader in Sports," has eight 24/7 cable television stations, various regional and subscription television networks, a syndicated radio network, multiple digital platforms, a magazine and other publishing outlets, and physical sport complexes in Florida. ESPN is not alone, of course, in sport broadcasting; various professional sports and college sports leagues in the United States have their own television networks, numerous magazines are devoted to sport, and it seems that an infinite number of virtual platforms for bloggers, pundits, critics, and fans exists. All these platforms share information. Thus as sport consumers, Americans often feel as if we know these athletes because we watch their games, follow their statistics, are apprised of their personal lives, and often know more about them than we know about our neighbors. Therefore, celebrity sport figures have potentially endless opportunities to profit from their names and images, but they also lose their privacy and face potential damage to their images, reputations, and identities as they present those aspects of themselves to the world.

Sport figures can have all the celebrity perks of other celebrities: high salaries, endorsements, and crossover media exposure from film to music to books. In many ways they become indistinguishable from other celebrities—with one significant difference: sports figures usually become celebrities because of their performance on the field or for their potential for on-the-field performance. That moment of performance (at almost any level of sport) can occur at any instant, and it can immediately garner the performer national or international acclaim for at least a brief time. For example, every year at the National Collegiate Athletic Association (NCAA) men's basketball championship, some team wins a game on a last-second shot, and the shooter becomes instantly—although sometimes briefly—famous. In 1982, more casual basketball fans heard the name Michael Jordan for the first time after he hit the championship-winning shot. In 1998, Bryce Drew, a player on the little-known and thirteenth-seeded Valparaiso University basketball team, put up a last-second shot to beat fourth-seeded University of Mississippi in the first round of the tournament, and for at least a week Drew was a celebrity among basketball fans.

The significance of celebrity status is not always clear. Being a celebrity has potential perks (money, recognition, and privilege), but other jobs have higher salaries and greater privilege. Yet being a celebrity, being famous, seems somehow more important in narcissistic societies than simply being rich. A 2012 study found that children ages ten to twelve aspired to fame more than anything else, including wealth.[6] A 2013 study found that people want to be famous primarily for three reasons: the desire to be seen or valued, the desire for an elite lifestyle, and a desire to use fame to help others or to gain recognition.[7] As much as I would like to *claim* to eschew a desire to be famous, I feel a certain thrill when I do radio interviews and when I see my name in the press, although, for no logical reason, I do try to conceal my face. Perhaps something in our culture makes many of us so self-centered that we want to be recognized for something, and we sometimes care less about what we are known for than simply being acknowledged by a broader community. Further, the size of that broader community is negotiable. Local celebrity can be just as intoxicating as national or international celebrity.

Celebrity, though, is a delicate and sometimes transient condition. Part of being a celebrity is being in the public eye, and the most effective way to be in the public eye is to be in the media—as many different forms of media as possible. Media in the twenty-first century is a profit-driven business, with part of that profit coming from focusing on celebrity information. This means that celebrities need the media to maintain their celebrity and that the media needs celebrities to stay profitable, but that dance of need is fraught with tension. The media and celebrities have a symbiotic relationship with an ongoing struggle over who controls what information, including who actually controls the celebrity's identity and reputation. In the United States, these ongoing struggles often result in lawsuits.

What makes the tension between celebrity and media in the United States particularly unusual and interesting is the tension between the rights of the individual, represented by laws protecting one's reputation and image, and the rights of the larger community in the form of the First Amendment. Legal scholar Lawrence Friedman argued that the loss of privacy for celebrities in the United States has been greater than that in Europe because European law historically better protected honor, dignity, and personal privacy.[8] Sport scholar Andrew Parker asserted that in the late twentieth and early twenty-first century, courts in the United Kingdom seemed reluctant to adopt the right of publicity as it had evolved in the United States.[9] In the United States, if celebrities, including sporting celebrities, feel the media has been overly intrusive or inaccurate, they cite the ancient tort of defamation or the century-old right of privacy, a right created by American jurists. When they believe that someone else has profited unfairly from their image and name, they rely on the more recently developed right of publicity to protect them. All these laws are about protecting one's image. The result has been a recurring battle in the courts between celebrities and those who profit from their status in one form or another.

This book uses the legal and social histories of six sporting figures as a lens through which to examine the changing balance between the First Amendment and the laws of reputation such as defamation, privacy, and publicity. I investigate how celebrity sporting figures in the United States have used the law to regain control over their image—control they have often lost by virtue of their celebrity status. I argue that the line between celebrity and privacy is translucent and that the U.S. courts have not yet clearly determined how best to balance the privileges of celebrity with the price of fame. By placing the lawsuits in a legal, historical, and cultural context, I explore the costs to the individual athletes who may have felt they have lost something (and sometimes everything), including their dignity, identity, and money. The study concludes that the evolving laws of reputation have a potentially profound impact on all Americans as both future celebrities and constant consumers.

Chapter 1 introduces the concept of celebrity and the rise of the sporting celebrity. It also explains the evolution of the laws of reputation, specifically defamation, the rights of privacy, and the right of publicity. It provides the legal and cultural backdrop to understand where these cases fit in the history of celebrity and law.

Chapter 2 explores the lawsuit that Wally Butts, a member of the College Football Hall of Fame, filed against the publisher of the *Saturday Evening Post* in 1963.[10] *Butts v. Curtis Publishing* changed the standards of libel law in America. Ultimately, the United States Supreme Court reviewed the case and decided it in conjunction with a parallel case, *Associated Press v. Walker*.[11] The *Butts* lawsuit began when the former head football coach of the University of Georgia (UGA) sued the publishing company for libel after its magazine published a story accusing him of fixing the 1962 UGA–Alabama football game with the help of legendary University of Alabama football coach Bear Bryant. This case marked the first time the United States Supreme Court concluded that a sporting figure was a public figure, that a former football coach was a celebrity, and that to win a defamation suit, public figures needed to prove actual malice (that the publisher had knowledge the statement was false or published it with reckless disregard of its falsity). Thus in 1967, for the first time in law, celebrity was fused with sport. It is intriguing to note that one of the justices who agreed that Butts was a public figure was Justice Byron White, a member of the College Football Hall of Fame himself, who had also played professional football for several years while in law school. Butts successfully fought to defend his tarnished reputation.

Chapter 3 explores Warren Spahn's lawsuit against a publishing house in *Spahn v. Julian Messner, Inc.*[12] Born in 1921, Spahn played twenty-four seasons of professional baseball and served in the U.S. Army during World War II. He was voted into fourteen All-Star games and was inducted into the Baseball Hall of Fame in his first year of eligibility in 1973. In 1964, Julian Messner Inc. published a child-targeted biography (called in the business at the time, a juvenile biography) of the man, and Spahn sued to stop publication on the grounds that it violated all four of the tenants of privacy: invasion, false light, private facts, and appropriation. *The Warren Spahn Story* told the story of the perfect man: a good son, a good baseball player, a good husband, and a good soldier.[13] The author of the book admitted that his research consisted of looking at a few magazine stories and clippings and that he had made no effort to speak with Spahn himself, his family, his teammates, or any of his friends or acquaintances. To make the book more entertaining, the author made up dialogue and attributed emotions and reactions to Spahn that had no grounding in reality. Spahn testified at trial that a number of segments of the book were complete fiction, including the report that he had been awarded the Bronze Star for his military service. While it made for a better story and a more clear-cut hero, the book clearly had many fictional elements. Spahn won an injunction against future distribution of the book and $10,000 in damages. Ultimately, the U.S. Supreme Court ordered the case re-tried using the actual malice standard of the *Butts* case, and Spahn won again. The decisions concluded that Spahn, a celebrity athlete, had the right to demand that the basic facts of his life be told accurately, and it required authors of biographies to make a good faith effort to represent their subjects truthfully. Spahn had the opportunity to set the record straight about his identity.

The subject of chapter 4 is Joe Montana and his lawsuit against the *San Jose Mercury News*.[14] Montana was one of the best quarterbacks in the history of the National Football League (NFL). In San Francisco, he led four teams to victory in the Super Bowl and was named the Most Valuable Player of three of those games. His success was legendary and his status, particularly in the Bay Area of California, iconic. After each Super Bowl victory, the local newspaper, not surprisingly, ran stories about Montana and the team and included photographs. These stories and photographs were clearly protected as documenting newsworthy events under the First Amendment. After the fourth Super Bowl victory, however, the *San Jose Mercury News* released and sold a poster that included photos of Montana from all four Super Bowls. Montana felt that the use of his photograph in the poster was a violation of his right of publicity (an evolution of the right of privacy)—that the newspaper had used his image without his permission and profited from it. Montana sued but was unsuccessful. His lawsuit highlighted the question of what was newsworthy and thus protected by freedom of speech and how long that newsworthy privilege lasted. Montana's case also reflected the shift in laws of reputation from protecting dignity to protecting the celebrity's financial interest in his image.

Newcombe v. Coors Brewing is the focal point of chapter 5.[15] Don Newcombe played in the Negro baseball leagues until 1949, when the Brooklyn Dodgers signed him after Jackie Robinson broke the color barrier in 1947. He had a stellar career, winning the Most Valuable Player award, the Cy Young Award, and the Rookie of the Year award. Unfortunately, his career in Major League Baseball was cut short in 1960, in part because of a continuing battle with alcohol. Eventually, Newcombe acknowledged his problem, and, as a recovering alcoholic, he served as a spokesman for the National Institute on Drug and Alcohol Abuse for thee different U.S. presidents. As an anti-alcohol advocate, Newcombe was shocked when he discovered an advertisement for Killian's Irish Red Beer (a brand produced by the Coors Brewing Company) that featured a drawing of an old-time baseball game in which the pitcher was a recognizable version of Newcombe. He promptly sued Coors for a violation of his right of publicity and lost in the federal district court. Despite that decision, the Ninth Circuit of the U.S. Court of Appeals agreed with Newcombe and overturned the lower court, establishing that celebrity athletes had the right to choose how their image was used in advertising and allowing them to disassociate themselves from products they found distasteful.

Chapter 6 explores the lawsuit Tiger Woods filed against the artist Rick Rush.[16] In 1997, the young, multiracial golfer made history, winning the prestigious Masters tournament for the first time and doing so by a record twelve strokes. Woods's victory inspired many fans, including Rick Rush, an artist specializing in sports memorabilia. Rush created a serigraph of Woods's driving the ball while flanked by his caddie and his opponents' caddie. Floating in the sky above the scene were the faces of Jack Nicklaus, Arnold Palmer, and other legendary golfers. The painting was then reproduced as a lithograph and five thousand copies were offered for sale. When Woods learned of the artwork, he sued Rush for violating his right of publicity. Rush argued that his work was protected under the First Amendment as art, while Woods argued that the work was merely sports merchandise like a poster and that it was subject to the right of publicity. The court agreed with Rush and said that regardless of the multiple copies, it was still art and deserved full First Amendment protection. Woods's case differed from Montana's because the question for the court was about whether Rush's images were art, not whether they were newsworthy. After losing the case, one of Woods's attorneys, Mark S. Lee, drafted a law-review article articulating what he believed was a much better test for the right of publicity.

Chapter 7 involves a case in which Mark Lee's article was the basis for the court's decision.[17] Tony Twist played in the National Hockey League between 1988 and 1999. He had a reputation of being a tough-guy enforcer and was exceedingly popular with the St. Louis community, where he played for the Blues and hosted the Tony Twist radio show. Todd McFarlane was a hockey fan who created the comic book *Spawn* in 1992. *Spawn* is a dark, surreal fantasy about a CIA assassin who dies, goes to hell, and returns to earth as an agent of the devil, wreaking havoc and violence. In 1993, his evil hench-man and enforcer, Anthony Twistelli (called Tony Twist) was introduced. The only thing the character and the hockey player had in common was the name and the reputation of being an enforcer, although MacFarlane admitted in notes to the readers at the end of one issue that he named his character after the hockey player. The real Tony Twist sued for appropriation of his image, and the initial jury awarded him almost $25 million dollars in dam-ages. The trial court, though, threw out the verdict, concluding that Twist had not proven appropriation, because it was the use of his name and not his identity. On appeal, the Missouri Supreme Court ruled that Twist's name was part of his identity and that the predominant purpose, a test articulated by Tiger Woods's attorney, of naming the character after the hockey player was commercial: the court believed McFarlane hoped to profit from Twist's name and not simply to create art.

The concluding chapter explores the interconnectedness of the six lawsuits and how these paragons of sport attempted to protect their images and their identities either because of their principals, for profits, or some combination of the two. Celebrity athletes' lawsuits for defamation and violations of their rights of privacy and publicity will no doubt continue in the future, and it is possible that some day the law will consider every American athlete a celebrity.

Missing from these lawsuits are women. Although issues of race are pres-ent and explored in these lawsuits and their broader contexts, all of the lawsuits that I selected involve men. The reason for this is simple: as of 2015, no female sporting figure had taken a lawsuit protecting her image through trial and appeals to the point that the legal decision has been published. I limited myself to published legal decisions, as these have more legal signifi-cance than nonpublished decisions, such as state trial courts. Why are there no significant legal cases involving female athletes or coaches? Elite sport, even today, is still largely a man's game, thus the athletes who have the most brand value still tend to be men. According to Forbes.com, of the one hundred highest-paid athletes (combining salary/winnings and endorsements) from June 1, 2014, through June 1, 2015, only two were women, and both were tennis players. Maria Sharapova earned $23 million in endorsements alone (ranking as the twenty-sixth-highest-paid athlete), and Serena Williams ranked forty-seventh and earned endorsements of $13 million. None of the highest-paid athletes age twenty-five or younger were women, and Li Na, a tennis player who retired midway through the examined period after earning $13 million, was the only woman on the highest-paid-retired-athlete list. Every other retired athlete on the list had been retired for at least five years.[18] Perhaps because of the lesser premium on female athletes as endorsers, fewer women's images have been appropriated or, alternatively, fewer females have pursued expensive lawsuits through an appeals process.

Maybe as women's sports become more popular and financially viable, female sporting figures will face the same struggle to protect their images as male athletes have, but for now, any appropriation of their image seems not to have been dealt with in the U.S. courts. This is not to say that these female athletes have been able to control their identities, their reputations, or their faces any more effectively than male athletes. On the contrary, female athletes have struggled to control how they are represented in the media, as they have frequently, when represented at all, been portrayed as lesser athletes than men.[19] The failure to see lawsuits from the women may be a matter of choice or financial necessity, an unwillingness or inability to pursue legal action when their reputations have been damaged. The lack of right of publicity cases might be a reflection of the lack of financial value that their names and faces have compared with their male counterparts—a reflection, in turn, on the unfortunate lesser role of female sport in American society.

This book should remind the reader that legal history, like sport history, is not just about the laws and the legal mechanisms of a case, but is about the individuals involved. Warren Spahn thought a book that made him out to be a hero was fundamentally wrong and did a disservice to real heroes. Tony Twist feared having a villain named after him would somehow make him into one. All of these individuals have a story, and this book strives to tell these stories where they intersect with the laws of defamation, privacy, and publicity. Their stories and lawsuits affect all of us as consumers of sport, the athletes, and the endorsements that are almost unavoidable in American society. But the lawsuits might someday affect us as potential celebrities, when we have our fifteen minutes of fame and control of our own image is at stake.

1

THE HISTORY OF CELEBRITY AND THE LAWS
OF REPUTATION AND SPEECH

Celebrities and the media have a complex relationship. Both need the other to maintain their status: being a celebrity of significant stature without any media attention in the twenty-first century is difficult, if not impossible. At the same time, in our "Peeping Tom society," the public seems fascinated by stories about celebrities. As legal scholar Lawrence A. Friedman argued, the twenty-first century has pushed the bounds of what has historically been considered personal information, of interest only to the person and close friends and family. In today's society, very little is viewed as being off limits to the media when it comes to the lives of celebrities.[1] Thus, media of all sorts have chosen to capitalize on the public interest in celebrities by giving us what we want, because almost all Americans in this modern world consume and retain information about celebrities, whether we want to or not. That said, the concept of celebrity, just like the status itself, is fluid and ever changing. Furthermore, the media and its role in building celebrity also fluctuate over time. The background to the relationship, the law, which mediates their disputes, is no more static than celebrity or media. The evolution of defamation, the rights of privacy, the right of publicity, and the First Amendment are key to the battle that celebrities face when trying to use the law to regain control of their image.

EXPLORING CELEBRITY AND ITS COSTS AND BENEFITS

In 1961 historian Daniel Boorstin offered a now-classic definition of celebrity as "a person who is known for his well-knownness."[2] In many ways this definition remains unchanged after all these decades and is my own definition of celebrity generally. Celebrity sport figures can be different in that they are usually famous initially for their sporting exploits, whether for their great successes or great failures. But winning a major championship or making a spectacular play is not enough to make an athlete a celebrity; it is only enough to make that athlete a winner. On the flip side, crashing at a ski jump contest only gives the ski jumper fame when the ABC network television show *Wide World of Sports* showcases it weekly on the program's opening reel for more than twenty years as the exemplar of the "agony of defeat." To be a celebrity, the athlete must be known beyond the sporting world, to have name recognition among people beyond sports trivia buffs. The true celebrity sport figure must be famous for being who they are. Their name and image must be part of the cultural zeitgeist, and they must be present in cyberspace and dominate social media. In 2015 celebrities could be identified in part (but only in part) because they had a Wikipedia and Facebook page, a significant number of followers on Twitter, regular postings on Instagram, and enough fame to be known by only one name, like Tiger, LeBron, or Serena.[3] In perhaps one of the most remarkable examples of the brightness of the celebrity spotlight, in July 2010 almost ten million Americans watched an hour-long television special on the sports network ESPN called *The Decision*, in which National Basketball Association (NBA) star LeBron James announced which team he would sign with as a free agent. The audience was one-third the size of the viewing audience for game seven of the NBA championships the previous month.[4]

In the late 1970s scholar/journalist James Monaco categorized celebrities into three groups—categories into which modern athletes can be placed, as well as a starting point for considering the social significance of and fascination with celebrities.[5] The first group contained "celebrity-heroes" who gained their status through what they do rather than what they appear to be. He noted that few true (or actual) heroes exist, and he did not list athletes among them.[6] Boorstin, in fact, warned that "our contrivance to provide substitute heroes finally produces nothing but celebrities."[7] In the sports world, however, some celebrities are heroes; for example, when Michael Jordan hit the championship-winning shot in the NBA finals in 1998, he was a hero to his fans. In 2001 sociologist Chris Rojeck called this "achieved celebrity [that] derives from the perceived accomplishments of the individual in open competition."[8] Sporting heroes, though, are lesser heroes than those who save lives or who take truly heroic and self-sacrificing actions to make life better for others, which is the kind of hero celebrity Monaco defined.

Monaco then classified a second subcategory of celebrities as "stars" who gain their status for what and who they are rather than for what they have accomplished. An athlete such as former tennis star Anna Kournikova, who signed lucrative endorsement deals and whose actions on and off the court were closely covered by even nonsporting media, despite never winning a major singles championship, would be an example of a star.

Kournikova might also fall into Monaco's third category of celebrity: quasars who are celebrities for what the public thinks or assumes they are. Despite her lack of singles championships, Kournikova alone received one-third of the coverage of all of women's sport in British tabloids in the summer of 2000.[9] Such invasive media coverage likely meant that many Kournikova fans were fans of the Kournikova they constructed and not necessarily fans of the actual Kournikova. When fans or media take control of the image of a quasar, celebrities lose control, to at least some degree, but they often gain in celebrity status.

In 2006 Ellis Cashmore, professor of culture, media, and sport, argued that all celebrities lose control of their image, collapsing Monaco's distinctions about the degree of celebrity. Referring to the work of Michel Foucault, Cashmore argued "celebs must surrender themselves to life in a kind of virtual Panopticon,"[10] a space in which the celebrity is constantly under public surveillance. With that surrender comes a loss of control yet, almost paradoxically, an increase in visibility and thus in celebrity status. The circle of exchanging power and control for celebrity status in the twenty-first century can be a rapid one, and with the presence of the 24/7 media cycle, reality television programming, social networking sites, and other forms of mass communication, almost anyone can enter the Panopticon of celebrity, at least briefly. The challenge is for longevity, maintaining celebrity status long enough to reap the rewards and move beyond that simple fifteen minutes of fame that artist Andy Warhol, in 1968, predicted everyone in the future would enjoy.

If the cost of sporting celebrity is the loss of control of one's image, reputation, and privacy, one major benefit is the financial reward both from the sporting field and the endorsement arena. On the one hand, this gives some degree of power to consumers, who can decide with their money whom they will support; if athletes behave badly, they might lose endorsements, much as football player Michael Vick did in 2007 when he was charged and later pled guilty to dog fighting and animal cruelty. The more than 165,000 messages sent to Nike through the Humane Society helped persuade the company to suspend Vick's endorsements.[11] On the other hand, endorsement deals can also allow the celebrity to help craft his own mediated image through commercials, such as the 1990s Hanes commercials starring basketball legend Michael Jordan, several of which included Jordan's family and emphasized his commitment to family.[12] Endorsements, for however long they last, can vastly augment an athlete's income and image.

Cashmore recognized the tie between consumer and celebrity when he argued that the purpose of celebrity might be to keep consumers spending. He explained this by suggesting "we don't buy to possess the same kind of products as celebrities so much as to be more like them."[13] Sport Studies scholars David Andrews and Steven Jackson acknowledged the cash value of celebrity as well as the iconic role celebrities play when they defined celebrity "as a product of commercial culture, imbued with symbolic values, which seek to stimulate desire and identification among the consuming populace."[14] Therefore, from a commercial and sociological standpoint, the image of the celebrity athlete has great value, but that value must be protected—otherwise, the celebrity athlete cannot benefit from his or her image.

Loss of control of one's image and economic value are not the only costs of celebrity. Some deranged members of the public believe that the celebrity "belongs" to them, and this can be far more dangerous to the celebrity than any misrepresentation or loss of an endorsement. One example of the dangers of a fan believing that he had a personal relationship with an athlete resulted famously and tragically in the stabbing of tennis player Monica Seles in 1993. Seles, the top-ranked women's tennis player at the time, was seated during a changeover at a match in Germany when a fan of her rival Steffi Graf came down from the stands and stabbed her in the back. He apparently thought that by removing Seles from the field, Graf would regain the number-one ranking. Many other athletes, including figure-skating champion Katarina Witt, have avoided physical harm yet have suffered the psychological stress of persistent stalkers.[15]

The link between sport figures and celebrity is not a twenty-first- or even a twentieth-century phenomenon. Scholar Barry Smart argued that W. G. Grace, the great cricket player of the second half of the nineteenth century, was one of the first celebrity athletes. Utilizing C. L. R. James's work, Smart maintained that by transforming the game of cricket and endearing himself to cricket fans as a popular culture icon of the era, Grace was a celebrity. Smart suggested that Grace was not alone. From reports about British soccer players in the late nineteenth century, the players were better known than local politicians and even received ovations on the street loud enough to "turn the head of a Prime Minister," which suggested they were celebrities.[16]

In the United States at the beginning of the twentieth century, heroes of the Golden Age of Sport, including Babe Ruth, Red Grange, and Jack Dempsey, held similar celebrity status. Smart ascribed the growth of communications methods and the increase in advertising opportunities with helping to give rise to the modern sports agent; he credited Christy Walsh, a former sport reporter who worked as the agent for Babe Ruth, with transforming Ruth's celebrity sport-figure status into an economic powerhouse. Ruth endorsed products ranging from sports equipment to shoes to cars, and he earned appearance fees for speeches and other public appearances.[17] In short, Ruth capitalized on his fame in many of the ways a twenty-first-century athlete does.

Long before basketball star Michael Jordan became immortalized by his namesake Air Jordan basketball shoes, retired tennis stars René Lacoste and Fred Perry created their own lines of sporting gear. Lacoste, a Frenchman who won the French Championships in 1925, 1927, and 1929, was nicknamed the Crocodile, and his signature logo was a miniature crocodile on the crest of his shirts, which began selling in 1933. Perry, an Englishman who won the Wimbledon singles title in 1934, 1935, and 1936, followed Lacoste's path and lent his name to a line of tennis clothing he helped design in the early 1940s. Both clothing lines were still in existence long after the men's deaths in 1996 and 1995, respectively, although the marketing of each line had moved away from sportswear toward more casual wear. Lacoste and Perry provided a model for late-twentieth-century athletic apparel giant Nike to follow when it began signature lines of clothing for athletes such as Michael Jordan and Tiger Woods.

Sporting celebrity intensified both in terms of the number of celebrities and in terms of their economic, social, and sometimes political power throughout the twentieth century. The rise of sporting celebrity can be partly credited to the increase in the sheer number of media outlets and to their need to broadcast something. Excluding internet and print publications and focusing only on television stations, the increasing numbers of sport-centered media outlets have risen almost beyond imagination. In 1979 ESPN began broadcasting on cable television; it was the first television station to focus on sports all day, every day. By 2014 one satellite television distributor offered multiple sports packages: league passes give access to all professional games in that league, a regional package offered thirty-five additional channels with constant sports coverage, and an international package covered foreign sporting events. Those options did not include the almost twenty other sports channels that come with various tiers of program packaging. By giving athletes, coaches, agents, and sometimes owners, constant exposure, the media helped to feed their celebrity status—status that could result in cash.

In today's society, even before athletes achieve success in the professional realm, they can cash in on their celebrity exposure. In 2005, when golfer Michelle Wie turned professional just before her sixteenth birthday, she signed endorsement deals with Nike and Sony worth an estimated $10 million.[18] She did not win her first professional golf tournament until 2009 and would not win her first major tournament until 2014. Nike and Sony had offered the young woman endorsement deals not simply because the companies thought she would be a good golfer but because she had already established herself as a media darling who was able to attract crowds whenever she played. Those endorsers hoped that Wie's celebrity would cause those crowds and those who saw her through the media to purchase the products she endorsed. The fact that she did not actually win any tournaments in the early years of her career was less important than her potential as both a golfer and a celebrity.

With cash and celebrity status comes at least a certain degree of power as well. Scholar P. David Marshall argued that "within society, the celebrity is a voice above others, a voice that is channeled into the media systems as being legitimately significant."[19] Some celebrity athletes such as boxer Muhammad Ali have used their voices for political purposes. Ali refused to enter the military after being drafted in 1967 because of his personal and religious opposition to the Vietnam War. After the Justice Department denied his claim to be a conscientious objector, he was prosecuted, lost his heavyweight title, and was banned from professional boxing for three years. His consistent opposition to the war cost him in terms of public support.[20] Years later he would regain his popularity in American society and was chosen to light the torch at the 1996 Olympic Games in Atlanta, Georgia, revealing how fickle celebrity can be.

Perhaps learning from what Ali lost by speaking his political mind, Michael Jordan chose not to endorse Harvey Gantt, an African American politician who was running for the North Carolina U.S. Senate seat in 1990 against the conservative Jesse Helms. Helms had run several racially tinged ads and had a history of being a segregationist. When the race was close just before the elections, Gantt's people asked native son Michael Jordan to endorse him. Jordan refused, apparently stating, "Republicans buy sneakers too."[21] Gantt lost the election. Even though Jordan was heavily criticized for not taking a political stand, his endorsement value remained strong.

Times change, and in 2014, following a series of grand jury decisions not to indict white police officers after the deaths of unarmed black men, dozens of athletes chose to speak out in protest. Professional and collegiate athletes, including basketball superstar LeBron James, appeared on national television wearing T-shirts calling for justice for the dead men; although they faced some social criticism, sponsors such as Nike and Adidas supported their athletes' rights to political speech.[22]

The sporting celebrity stands on a razor's edge of complications and tensions. Twenty-first-century sporting celebrities can cash in on their sports performances, but the greater potential for income lies in endorsement deals. This means that sporting celebrities must remain in the public eye to maximize their status; to achieve this, they need media attention. The media also need the celebrity and information about the celebrity in order to maximize their profits; however, in the short run, whether the celebrity information is positive or negative is less important to the media than to the celebrity. O. J. Simpson, the Professional Football Hall of Fame running back of the 1970s, was charged with murdering his ex-wife and her friend in 1994. Prior to the accusation, Simpson had successfully transitioned from star running back to celebrity actor and product endorser. His previous television presence, though, could not compare with the national coverage of his low-speed car chase leading up to his arrest and his subsequent trial and acquittal. The media coverage of the chase even interrupted national television coverage of game five of the NBA championship series. Simpson's personal reputation and his endorsement value never recovered from the murder charges, even before he was convicted and jailed in 2008 for kidnapping and armed robbery (Simpson claimed he was trying to recover his own property from sports memorabilia distributors). Simpson's murder trial did make many of those involved in the case, including police officers and lawyers, celebrities in their own right, at least briefly.

From celebrities' perspective, the modern media cannot be trusted to show them in the best light. The whetted appetite of the media and intense desires of the fans for more information can mean that many facts and innuendoes the celebrity would like to keep private are brought to light. Often, inaccurate stories are circulated. The perceived identity of the celebrity can be at stake. Chris Rojeck explained that each celebrity has a "split between a private self and a public self" and that "the public presentation of self is always a staged activity."[23] Although most celebrities welcome the press with their public selves, they usually would prefer to keep their private selves private. This tension raises the question: Which aspects of a celebrity are public and which are private? Additionally, the celebrity's image and name have commercial value, and sometimes others profit from that without the celebrity's consent. The media and those who use the celebrity's image rely on the First Amendment to protect their use.

THE FIRST AMENDMENT

The First Amendment to the United States Constitution is the shield that purveyors of speech of all sorts (from newspapers and magazines to artists and authors) rely on for protection. Adopted in 1791 as part of the Bill of Rights, the First Amendment pronounced that "Congress shall make no law . . . abridging the freedom of speech, or of the press."[24] Despite the arguments of Supreme Court Justice Hugo Black, who served on the Court from 1937 to 1971, that the First Amendment was absolute and without limitation,[25] the Supreme Court has set limits on what kind of speech is and is not protected. For example, Supreme Court Justice Oliver Wendell Holmes famously wrote in 1919 that the First Amendment did not allow a person to "falsely shou[t] fire in a theatre and caus[e] a panic."[26] But the Constitutional protection afforded by the First Amendment has shifted through the centuries of interpretation.

Early Supreme Court decisions focused on political speech, which has historically been the most protected form of speech. Supreme Court Justice Louis Brandeis wrote in his concurrence to *Whitney v. California* in 1927 that the founders of the United States

> believed that freedom to think as you will and to speak as you think are means indispensable to the discovery and spread of political truth; that without free speech and assembly, discussion would be futile; that, with them, discussion affords ordinarily adequate protection against the dissemination of noxious doctrine; that the greatest menace to freedom is an inert people; that public discussion is a political duty; and that this should be a fundamental principle of the American government.[27]

Even political speech had limits if the speaker advocated a threat to the government or called for violence. Determining what kind of language presented a threat to the government or of violence was another challenge for the Court. In 1919 Supreme Court Justice Oliver Wendell Holmes concluded that speech posing a "clear and present danger" to the government could be restricted.[28] In 1969 the Supreme Court narrowed the test for clear and present danger, concluding that the government could not "forbid or proscribe advocacy of the use of force or of law violation except where such advocacy is directed to inciting or producing imminent lawless action and is likely to incite or produce such action."[29]

The founders' focus on political speech is logical, given the historical underpinnings of the U.S. Constitution and the First Amendment. Under English common law, the foundation of U.S. law, the idea behind freedom of the press was to stop the government from limiting what the press was allowed to publish. For example, Sir William Blackstone's *Commentaries*, a cornerstone of English common law and hence American common law, had this to say about free speech in 1766:

> The liberty of the press is indeed essential to the nature of a free state; but this consists in laying no *previous* restraints upon publications, and not in freedom from censure for criminal matter when published. Every freeman has an undoubted right to lay what sentiments he pleases before the public: to forbid this, is to destroy the freedom of the press; but if he publishes what is improper, mischievous, or illegal, he must take the consequence of his own temerity.[30]

This articulation of free speech intends to prohibit censorship and prior restraints (prior restraint prevents the original publication of a document). This interpretation of free speech would hold the speaker responsible for the contents of the publication after it occurred. The U.S. Constitution went further, however, protecting the contents of political speech and not just the right to publish. Consider the example of a writer who criticized the actions of the government during a war. Blackstone's interpretation of free speech protects the right for the criticism to be published, but it would also allow the government to prosecute the writer. The U.S. Constitution protects both the publication and the writer from prosecution after publication.

Commercial speech, which includes things like advertisements, has not received the same protection as political speech. In 1942 the United States Supreme Court rejected the argument that the First Amendment protected distribution (on public streets of New York City) of handbills advertising the opportunity to buy tickets to visit a submarine.[31] Eventually, the Supreme Court began to offer some protection to commercial speech. In 1976 the Court concluded that a Virginia statute prohibiting pharmacies from advertising the prices of prescription drugs was unconstitutional because of the varying prices of medications among different pharmacies and the public's need for information.[32] Over time, the Court seemed to offer commercial speech some protection but less protection than political speech.[33]

Thus the First Amendment has been deemed to offer broad protection for political speech and less, but still some, protection for commercial speech. Speech, though, can be more personal than political and commercial speech;

it can be about an individual's reputation. If a speaker advocated rejecting a legislative bill, that speech is protected as political speech. If a pharmacy wanted to advertise a sale via a flyer sent through the U.S. mail, that speech is likely protected as commercial speech. But what if the writer published an article attacking the character of another? Does the U.S. Constitution protect such an attack?

Relatively little evidence exists about the nation's founders' attitudes on the matter of reputation. Thomas Jefferson, who drafted the Declaration of Independence, and James Madison, who inserted the First Amendment to the Constitution, both seem to have opposed the English common law of seditious libel. Seditious libel referred to any words (whether true or false) that undermined the people's confidence in government.[34] But Benjamin Franklin said in 1789 that the liberty of the people to discuss "public measures and political opinions" should be unrestricted, yet that if free speech meant "the liberty to calumniate another, there ought to be some limit,"[35] suggesting Franklin supported laws prohibiting false statements against one's fellow citizens. Consequently, in the early years of American history, how much the First Amendment protected statements that damaged the reputation of another was unclear.

THE ORIGINS OF DEFAMATION

When one person communicates untruths about another person, thereby undermining the reputation of the second person, the first person has committed defamation. If the communication is oral, this is slander; and if the communication is written, this is libel.[36] In English law prior to 1500, Church courts heard commoners' complaints about defamation and could sentence the offending party to various acts of penance, but if the defamation involved a temporal matter, like crimes against an individual or the state, the Church could not act. The idea was that hurt feelings and damaged reputations were a matter of immorality but that criminal acts were for the secular courts.[37] The reputations, however, of society's leaders were protected by the state. Because the feudal order relied heavily on personal ties based on honor and loyalty, when one lord defamed another, the defamed lord tended to reply with violence rather than going to his parish priest. The concern was that the attack on a lord was a rift in the feudal society; thus, *De Scandalis Magnatum*, making defamation against the leading men of England a crime, was enacted in 1275 and periodically renewed. Over time the much-maligned, but perhaps misunderstood, Court of Star Chamber (the court where the elites were prosecuted) tried cases of seditious libel (where truth was not a defense),[38] but by 1641, with the abolition of the Court of Star Chamber, common-law courts heard criminal libel cases. These common-law courts had begun to accept jurisdiction in some defamation cases by the mid-sixteenth century. By the seventeenth century, common-law courts awarded cash damages for defamation against the commercial elite. Over time, truth became an absolute defense to civil defamation charges.[39]

The U.S. legal system imported many of the English common-law claims, including defamation, but determining how the First Amendment freedom of speech clause affected defamation was unclear even to the founders. Much of the debate focused on comments regarding political figures, particularly politicians. This is not to say that private defamation cases had not occurred in the colonies: in New York City in 1713 a woman sued a man for calling her a prostitute and asked for damages of 200 pounds. Although the jury ruled in her favor, she was awarded only 20 shillings. In that same time period, a clothier successfully sued a man who had stated that the clothier had defrauded him, and the clothier was awarded 12 pounds. Historian Norman L. Rosenberg attributed that distinction to the greater protection for tradesmen over neighborhood relations.[40] Few of the founders seemed to have believed that the First Amendment was absolute and without limitation. Benjamin Franklin pointed to the system of checks and balances and believed the press could similarly be checked.[41] Alexander Hamilton disliked the very inclusion of the First Amendment because of the potential for invasion into privacy, criticizing parallel clauses in state constitutions in 1787: "What signifies a declaration that the liberty of the press shall be inviolably preserved? What is the liberty of the press? Who can give it any definition that would not leave the utmost latitude for invasion?"[42]

By the early nineteenth century, civil defamation cases became more common as personal attacks against politicians became more frequent. In 1786 Thomas Jefferson and John Jay argued that public officials must simply tolerate attacks on their character as part of the price of holding public office. In the early nineteenth century, politicians fought back via libel suits. For example, in the 1820s the New York courts repeatedly upheld the monetary damages awarded to Erasmus Root, the former lieutenant governor of the state. Root had sued a newspaper for defamation after the paper reported he had often presided over the state senate while drunk.[43]

Thus courts in America quickly carved out defamation exceptions to the First Amendment. In 1940 the Supreme Court Justice Owen J. Roberts wrote, "Resort to epithets or personal abuse is not in any proper sense communication of information or opinion safeguarded by the Constitution."[44] Two years later the Court reaffirmed the limits on free speech, when Justice Frank Murphy wrote:

> There are certain well-defined and narrowly limited classes of speech, the prevention and punishment of which have never been thought to raise any Constitutional problem. These include the lewd and obscene, the profane, the libelous, and the insulting or "fighting" words—those which, by their very utterance, inflict injury or tend to incite an immediate breach of the peace. It has been well observed that such utterances are no essential part of any exposition of ideas, and are of such slight social value as a step to truth that any benefit that may be derived from them is clearly outweighed by the social interest in order and morality.[45]

In 1964 the Supreme Court, in *New York Times Co. v. Sullivan*, reconsidered its attitudes about the link between defamation and the First Amendment, ultimately concluding that, as Justice William J. Brennan wrote, "libel can claim no talismanic immunity from constitutional limitations. It must be measured by standards that satisfy the First Amendment."[46] The Court changed the burden of proof for a public official to recover for defamation. *New York Times Co. v. Sullivan* and its significance for celebrities will be discussed in more detail in chapter 2.

In the twenty-first century the elements of defamation in U.S. law remain similar to its English common-law roots. Essentially, to win a libel or slander case, the plaintiff must prove that the defendant published false statements about the plaintiff to a third party, statements that injured the plaintiff's reputation. Truth is an absolute defense, and if the plaintiff is a private figure, the burden of proof is lower. Public figures, as will be discussed in chapter 2, have a more difficult burden of proof. The tort of defamation, though, is but one weapon in the celebrity's arsenal to protect his or her image; the torts of privacy are even larger, more versatile weapons.

THE EVOLVING RIGHT TO PRIVACY

In the United States, the notion of a right to privacy for individuals was first formally articulated in 1890, when lawyers Samuel Warren and Louis Brandeis published an article on the topic in the *Harvard Law Review*. (In 1916 Brandeis was appointed to the United States Supreme Court, perhaps giving the right of privacy even more weight.) The article called for tort protection of individuals from the intrusion of the press into private aspects of life.[47] In the article, the two writers basically created an American right to privacy, seeing it as an extension of the right to life that includes the right to enjoy life and thus "the right to be let alone."[48] Reputation is protected because it is an intangible possession and thus is a kind of property right. Warren and Brandeis envisioned the right to be let alone as a culmination of other common-law torts, including defamation, which protected reputation and, by implication, an individual's privacy. They argued that defamation alone, however, is not enough to protect privacy because it does not sufficiently guard people from the damages of emotional distress. Instead, defamation requires that the injury be to one's reputation: emotional distress can occur even if one's reputation is unharmed. Defamation also fails to protect people from publication of facts that an individual would prefer to keep quiet. The common law of property and copyright secures the right of each individual to determine "to what extent his thoughts, sentiments, and emotions shall be communicated to others."[49] Copyright law, however, cannot protect one from the publication of photos to which one never consents or to the stories one never authorizes. Warren and Brandeis claimed that it was really the right to be let alone that grew from the right to privacy. They saw the explosion of the press in the late nineteenth century as a threat to that right to be let alone and believed that the press's "gossip" was a further infringement upon that right. They noted that to "satisfy a prurient taste, the details of sexual relations are spread broadcast in the columns of the daily papers."[50]

Warren and Brandeis did limit their explication of the right to privacy: it would not apply to a "matter which is of public or general interest" because the goal of the right was to protect the "privacy of private life, and to whatever degree and in whatever connection a man's life has ceased to be private, before the publication under consideration has been made, to that extent the protection is likely to be withdrawn." They added, "Some things all men alike are entitled to keep from popular curiosity, whether in public life or not."[51]

Warren and Brandeis's tort proposal was problematic, leaving more questions than answers. Of course, that which is not public is private, but the article offers very little toward determining how to distinguish between the two areas of one's life. It left open, for example, the question of whether discussing a private matter opens the door to public interest. While the caveat that "some things all men alike are entitled to keep from popular curiosity" seems intuitively fair and reasonable, it lacks any possibility of consistent practical application. What "some things" are goes undefined. In their article, the authors warn against the "prurient taste" the press has for "details of sexual relations"; 125 years later, we see how the U.S. public reveled in the scandalous details of golfer Tiger Woods's alleged sexual affairs with an untold number of women. As explored in chapter 6, Woods's sex life became part of the American conversation in 2009, despite Woods's repeated pleas that the press and the public respect his privacy and that of his family. The distinction between public and private remains blurred to this day, with shifting lines over time and circumstance. Generally, most of us have something we want kept private at some time, but whether the public and the press must respect that remains murky.

Warren and Brandeis might have been sympathetic to Woods's predicament. Louis Brandeis's biographer wrote that the *Saturday Evening Gazette* had reported, in "lurid detail," on Warren's marriage to a Delaware senator's daughter and their subsequent social engagements, including a series of parties they had hosted. The newspaper had filled its pages with graphic stories about the gatherings, including details the Warrens and their guests found embarrassing. Warren shared his frustration with his law partner, Brandeis, and the foundation of the privacy article was laid.[52] In the late nineteenth century, the social elite emphasized discretion to the point that even marriages were not announced in certain newspapers, including the *Saturday Evening Gazette.*[53]

Warren and Brandeis published their article at a time when American culture was changing. After the Civil War, more and more Americans moved to urban areas in the hopes of finding work in the newly industrialized cities. The shift from a primarily rural community to a primarily urban one resulted in a loss of physical and personal privacy for many people, especially for the poor and working class. The loss of personal space in the shift from a farm to an urban tenement or apartment may have increased both the investment in protecting one's own personal privacy and the interest in the private lives of others.

Just as the demographics of the country were changing, so, too, were the opportunities for the press. The federal government eliminated postage for newspapers so that circulation opportunities expanded. At the same time, the number of newspapers and the competition for readers increased. Papers suspected that the average working-class reader whose own life might have seemed mundane and work centered would be curious about the lives, activities, and scandals of those most unlike themselves, the wealthy and the elite. Press coverage of these individuals increased, much to the consternation of the wealthy scions who had heretofore guarded their privacy from the masses.[54] In the twentieth century and early in the twenty-first, this interest in the wealthy continues, as represented by such long-running television shows as *Lifestyles of the Rich and Famous* (1984–1994) and *MTV Cribs* (2000–2010), both of which took viewers into the homes of wealthy celebrities. Reflecting the evolution of goals of the wealthy, some rich people have courted media—a concept that would have appalled the wealthy in Warren and Brandeis's day. The Kardashian family was reportedly worth millions before they began filming their reality television show *Keeping Up with the Kardashians* in 2007. The show continues through 2016 and has resulted in several spin-off reality shows following individual family members. Similarly beginning in 2006, the various *Real Housewives* reality series have traced the lives of affluent women in a number of cities.

Embedded in the Warren and Brandeis article are ideas about who should enjoy privacy protection and for whose amusement the press invades privacy. The two authors had in mind protection for themselves and other elite individuals who were not intentionally public figures, and they expressed concern for the minds of the lower-class readers. They warned that interest in other people's lives "usurps the place of interest in brains capable of other things. Triviality destroys at once robustness of thought and delicacy of feeling. No enthusiasm can flourish, no generous impulse can survive under its blighting influence."[55] By distinguishing between the elite (whose lives profited the press) and the working class (whose willingness to read about the elite profited the press), Warren and Brandeis identified a troubled relationship between celebrities and their fans, exacerbated by a press looking to make money. In the twenty-first century, the interest in seeing and being seen seems to be shared by many: anyone who can claim celebrity status seems happy to do so, and almost everyone in America consumes information about those celebrities through multiple media. Not knowing about the "private" lives of truly famous celebrities is almost impossible, given how pervasive the media is and how much the media reports on these individuals.

In 1954 legal scholar Melvin B. Nimmer revisited the Warren and Brandeis article and expanded on it. Warren and Brandeis had been worried about protecting the rights of reputation and dignity when they drafted their article in 1890, but, by the 1950s, Nimmer argued that the rise of Hollywood and of the value of celebrities had changed the needs of that population: "Although the well known personality does not wish to hide his light under a bushel of privacy, neither does he wish to have his name, photograph, and likeness reproduced and publicized without his consent or without remuneration to him."[56] He noted that advancement in technology and communication, unimaginable when Warren and Brandeis wrote their article, had opened the doors for financial gain for celebrities. Throughout his article, Nimmer noted lawsuits in which athletes and other celebrities had tried to use a right of privacy to recover for the unauthorized use of their images; often, they lost those lawsuits, and Nimmer argued that the right of publicity could help expand the protections promised by the tort of privacy broadly. Nimmer's articulation of the right of publicity indicated a shift in the laws of reputation from protecting dignity and personal information to protecting one's image and name for pecuniary gain.

In 1960 the esteemed legal scholar William L. Prosser refined and separated the tort into four parts, and his ideas became, over time and with adoption by various courts, firmly entrenched as the torts of privacy in American law.[57] The first component of privacy was the right to prevent widespread publicity concerning personal information; this was the private facts tort. An example of this would be publication of true but private information—perhaps information about family health history. To win a private facts lawsuit, the plaintiff must establish that the defendant disseminated personal information that a reasonable person would find to be highly offensive and not of public interest. A reasonable person is a legal construct describing a hypothetical person who exercises average care, judgment, and skill. Newsworthiness is the best defense, but the definition of what is newsworthy has never been clearly articulated or consistently applied because most courts use it on a case-by-case basis. The second component was the right to be free from intrusions into one's solitude, which would include the right to assume that no infrared cameras are pointed into one's bedroom or that no reporter has sneaked into one's home and bugged it. Physical invasion of one's space to acquire the intrusive material would be trespass. Newsworthiness is not usually a successful defense for intrusion. Another component was the right to be free of publicity that cast a person in a false light—that is, publicity that told a version of the truth but was presented in such a way as to have the same effect as a lie. False light differs from defamation in that a statement might be true or neutral, but it embarrasses the plaintiff. An example of this is a magazine photo spread describing a family held hostage in their home by escaped convicts.[58] The photo spread reported a harrowing tale with implications of violence and extreme terror—when the family felt no such thing. The report (a family was held hostage by criminals) is accurate, but the perception on the part of the viewer that the family suffered physical harm is inaccurate. The final privacy prong was the right of publicity or the tort of appropriation: this meant that one has the right to control one's own name and image for commercial enterprises. In some ways this is the most important right for a celebrity's finances. The right of publicity (which is related to copyright and trademark) means that the producer of Smith's Widgets cannot use Celebrity Sue's name and image for its own profit without Celebrity Sue's consent.[59] As will be discussed throughout subsequent chapters, whether or not the plaintiff is a public figure affects the burden of proof the plaintiff carries.

A NATURAL RIGHT VERSUS A FUNDAMENTAL RIGHT

In 1905 the Georgia Supreme Court acknowledged the conflict between an individual's interest in privacy and the public's interest in newsworthy matters. Justice Andrew J. Cobb wrote in *Pavesich v. New England Life Insurance Company* that the right of privacy was recognized as a "law of nature" but that enforcing that right would "inevitably tend to curtail the liberty of speech and of the press," one of the fundamental rights of Americans. Adding that the "right of privacy must in some particulars yield to the right of speech and of the press,"[60] Justice Cobb anticipated the tension between the two and the constant balancing act that would ensue when the two came into conflict, but he failed to offer a way to balance them. He probably could not have anticipated that, more than one hundred years later, so much of the trappings of celebrity—money, power, image, and so forth—would depend on striking a balance between the right of privacy and the right of the press.

Celebrities in the early twenty-first century are still well known for being well known. Even sport celebrities, who are often helped along the road to fame by their successful athletic performances, are not known solely for their exploits on the field or court. They are famous every moment, and—because they are celebrities—members of the media stalk them and report on their every step and misstep. The media needs celebrities, and celebrities need the media. But periodically the two conflict over who really controls the image of the celebrity. The following chapters explore six court cases in which celebrity sport figures used the law to regain control of their respective images, images they had lost by virtue of their status as celebrities. These cases tell the stories of sporting figures who tried to manage their reputations, to restore or protect their honor, dignity, and self-image, as well as those who attempted to protect their names and images for financial reasons. Each case is part of the evolution of the relationship between the First Amendment and the laws of reputation.

2

LIES, LIBEL, AND FOOTBALL:
COACHES AS PUBLIC FIGURES
BUTTS v. CURTIS PUBLISHING (1967)

Butts v. Curtis Publishing changed libel law in America.[1] The lawsuit began when Wally Butts, athletic director and former head football coach at the University of Georgia (UGA), sued the *Saturday Evening Post* (a magazine owned by Curtis Publishing) for libel in 1963 after the magazine published a story accusing him of "fixing" the 1962 UGA–Alabama football game with University of Alabama coach Paul "Bear" Bryant. As coaches and colleagues, Butts and Bryant had long been linked. When they separately but simultaneously sued the publishing company for libel, their names would be forever linked in the law, and their personal relationship as well as their personalities would be examined publicly. Butts's lawsuit had a convoluted legal history, and ultimately the United States Supreme Court rendered a verdict on it. The Court, however, was unable to agree upon a single majority opinion; multiple justices wrote their own opinions, creating a plurality opinion from the statements they each agreed upon. Five justices agreed that proving defamation (libel and slander) for public figures (celebrities) should be more difficult than for the average private citizen. They believed that this would give greater protection to the First Amendment and the press. The idea was that if private citizens were libeled, they would face greater challenges in telling their stories than celebrities would. Thus, celebrities, in order to win a defamation suit, needed to prove that the speaker who made the false statement knew or should have known that it was false. The *Butts* decision represented the first time the U.S. Supreme Court concluded that a sporting figure was a public figure, that a former football coach was a celebrity.

THE LIFE OF WALLY BUTTS

James Wallace "Wally" Butts was born on February 7, 1905, near the small southeastern Georgia town of Milledgeville. He was relatively short and squat (as a coach his nickname would be the descriptive "Little Round Man"), but he was a strong, three-sport high school athlete who earned scholarships in football, basketball, and baseball. He enrolled at Mercer University in Macon, Georgia, where he was an All-Southern Conference defensive end on the football team. In 1929, his senior year, he married his high school sweetheart, Winifred Taylor, with whom he later had three daughters. After graduating from Mercer, Butts became a high school football coach, serving successfully at a variety of schools across the Southeast. In 1938, Coach Joel Hunt hired him as an assistant coach for the University of Georgia "Bulldogs" football team; the following year, Butts replaced Hunt and was also named athletic director for the university. He remained at UGA until 1963.[2]

As a football coach, the Little Round Man was remarkable. Although his first season was less than successful, with five wins and six losses, he would not coach a team with a losing record again until 1949. Part of his success came with a commitment to the passing game, something new to the Southeastern Conference (SEC). After the 1941 season he led the Bulldogs to their first-ever bowl game—the Orange Bowl on New Year's Day—beating Texas Christian University, 40–26, less than a month after the bombing of Pearl Harbor. The next year UGA won the SEC title, the Rose Bowl (9–0), and the national championship. The team faced challenges with the loss of players to World War II for the next two seasons, but after the war ended, UGA rebounded. Overall, in the 1940s, UGA had a record of seventy-eight wins, twenty-six losses, and four ties; the team also played in six bowl games, with a record of 4-1-1. Georgia won the SEC championship in 1942, 1946, and 1948, as well as the 1942 national championship. The 1948 team went undefeated and was named national champion in one poll. Three players from that decade were enshrined in the College Football Hall of Fame; Frank Sinkwich in 1942 became the first player in the SEC to win the Heisman Trophy. In 2007, *Sports Illustrated* named UGA the team of the decade of the 1940s.[3]

Butts's success in the 1940s was limited a bit during World War II, when many football players enlisted or were drafted. Butts's reaction to the loss of his players to military service during the war was to call for college football players to be sworn into service but then allowed to remain in school until graduation. He argued that "football is more necessary today than it was during times of peace. . . . The game fits a lot of boys for any hardship they'll later have to undergo. If they can sign up . . . and get the added advantage of military training while in school, college football will be turning out thousands of first class leaders each year."[4] His suggestion was never adopted, and enough players were lost to military service that the SEC allowed freshmen (who before the war were ineligible to compete in varsity games) to play football for the duration of the war.[5] In 1943 and 1944, Butts fielded a team composed primarily of seventeen-year-old freshmen who were too young to enlist and players who were ineligible for the draft.[6] Those war-year teams still compiled winning records. Upon the return of the best players from war, the post–World War II UGA team was quite strong again—so strong that Butts was offered the position of head coach of the NFL Detroit Lions at an annual salary of $30,000 (more than ten times the average salary at the time) plus a car dealership in Detroit.[7] Butts chose to remain in Athens.

Butts himself was known among the press in the 1940s and 1950s as an affable storyteller and a coach who liked to minimize the talents of his teams. As such he was a popular dinner speaker; one sportswriter called him "the head man on the southern banquet circuit."[8] The *Washington Post* sports columnist Bob Considine wrote, "That roly-poly drawling little Butts is the best story teller the New York football writers lunch has heard since Jimmy Conzelman [the player-owner-coach in the NFL who was enshrined in the Pro Football Hall of Fame]." Considine devoted half of a column to Butts's stories, including one explaining why Butts was so famously and publicly pessimistic about the quality of his teams:

> When you open your mouth in front of sportswriters, you can't win. Not long ago one of them button-holed me and asked me what kind of team I was going to have this year [1941]. I said "Well it won't be much account. I lost a lot of men to the Army, and some of my boys are ineligible, and so on."
>
> "Aw! Quit bellyaching," the fellow told me. "We know you've got a lot of good stuff at Athens."
>
> So I figured I wouldn't kid with him any more. I said, "I guess you're right. I've got a fine looking team coming up. Ought to win a lot of games."
>
> "Listen, Butts, don't get so cocky. We've run more than one cocky coach out of this conference."[9]

In 1946 Butts similarly charmed columnist Shirley Povich with his story of watching his great player Charley Trippi play baseball; Trippi stole thirty bases in the war-shortened 1945 college baseball season. Butts recalled watching Trippi steal second, third, and home: "That was great stuff, but I was remembering that he had to play football for me in the fall. . . . I called the baseball coach in and told him to cut down on all that base running by Trippi or we'd be forced to get a new baseball coach."[10]

After Bear Bryant arrived to coach the University of Alabama in 1958, Butts would incorporate Bryant into his banquet-speaker routine. Speaking at the San Antonio Quarterback Club in 1961, Butts used a line he had likely used before when he told the crowd "the definition of an atheist in Alabama is a person who doesn't believe in Bear Bryant."[11] *Sports Illustrated* reporter Ray Cave highlighted the two men's commonalities in a 1960 article. Recounting that year's UGA–Alabama football game, the magazine called Bear Bryant the "pretender to the throne of pessimism. The king is Wally Butts." The two were further linked in their pessimism by the assertion, "Southerners say that when it starts to rain, Butts and Bryant think of building arks." The article claimed Butts once convinced a sports editor that his team was so bad that Furman University would beat them: UGA won that game 70–7. In the interview, conducted prior to the 1960 UGA-Alabama game (which Alabama won 21–6), Butts warned,

> "We're like a baseball team with only one pitcher." . . . He leaned back, infinite sadness in his kind eyes, and put a hand on his stomach. "Hurts," he said.
>
> [Likewise, Bryant said,] "We're in bad shape. . . . [But] I'm not crying," he protested, the hint of a smile in his eyes, "that's just the way the cooky [*sic*] crumbles."[12]

Cave's fondness for and amusement by both men was apparent in his description, proving that both coaches could charm a sportswriter.

For Wally Butts, the 1950s Georgia Bulldogs, with losing seasons in 1953, 1956, 1957, and 1958, were not nearly as successful as the team had been in the previous decade. Perhaps the brightest spot in the mid-1950s was the introduction of Uga, the English bulldog who became the team's mascot. In 1959, however, the team had a stunning turnaround from their tenth-place finish in the SEC the previous season. Led by quarterback Fran Tarkenton, who would eventually be enshrined in the College and Pro Football Halls of Fame, the team went 9-1 and won the SEC championship. The team then defeated the University of Missouri (14–0) in the Orange Bowl. This was the last team Coach Butts took to a bowl game. The following season in 1960, the team won six games, lost four, and Butts resigned as coach, but he remained at the university as athletic director. His coaching resignation came the day after he was named to the Helms Foundation College Football Hall of Fame, a private organization that supported amateur athletes and athletics.

The reasons for Butts's resignation were complicated. Butts told the press, "I've been under that pressure long enough. I think it would affect my health if I continue."[13] But in early December 1960 a group of alumni had asked him to step down as coach before he was fired, and he agreed to do so at the end of that school year. Butts's problem lay not just with losing in the years prior to the surprise 1959 season but also with another side of the funny, self-depreciating, storytelling coach, a side that seemed to have appeared relatively late in his career. Butts had allegedly spent too much time in the previous years in Atlanta, publicly drinking and frequenting clubs with his young mistress on his arm. The alumni believed his reputation made it impossible for him to recruit the athletes needed to compete in the SEC.[14] Butts had won four SEC championships at UGA, but in his final six years, his overall record was 29-34-1, not good enough to excuse his unbecoming behavior.

According to law professor James Kirby, the SEC observer at Butts's trial, Butts was not happy with stepping down as head coach, nor was he a great athletic director. Butts had never shown strong administrative or financial skill; as well, his personal behavior, which had contributed to the loss of his coaching job, also limited his security and status as athletic director. He was not thrilled, either, with his salary cut after losing his coaching position; he complained that other coaches who had stepped away from coaching yet remained athletic directors did not take pay cuts. Butts was disappointed as well that he did not have any input into the football program after his removal as coach. The new coach, Johnny Griffith, had been a player on the Bulldogs' championship team of 1946 and had served as one of Butts's assistant coaches. Butts had even loaned him money to move back to Athens after Griffith served a one-year stint as an assistant at Furman University. Butts expected that the young Griffith, who was just thirty-two years old when he was made head coach, would consult with him. In spite of their relationship, however, Griffith steered the program away from Butts and excluded him from strategy sessions and closed practices; university president O. C. Aderhold supported Griffith's choice and essentially banned Butts from the football facilities. The university further contributed to Butts's sense of isolation by refusing to pay all his submitted travel expenses.[15]

As athletic director, Butts spent more time focused on his own finances, and Kirby maintained that Butts was living far beyond his means and gambling on the stock market. College football coaches in the Butts era were paid far less than twenty-first-century coaches, and it was common for them to augment their incomes through investments. In 1959 Bobby Dodd, head football coach and athletic director at Georgia Tech, earned $18,000.[16] Butts likely earned close to this amount and had a history of investing in various stocks and businesses, many of which performed poorly.[17] Butts, along with Bryant, had invested heavily in Continental Enterprises, with the support of Louis Wolfson, a Georgia alum who would later be an owner of Triple Crown winner Affirmed and a financial advisor to Supreme Court Justice Abe Fortas—a relationship that cost Fortas the Chief Justice position and eventually forced him to resign from the Court altogether. Ultimately, Wolfson was indicted by the Securities and Exchange Commission and imprisoned for white-collar crimes.[18] Butts's investment in Continental Enterprises fell from $6.00 per share to $1.00 per share in 1960, which was indicative of his financial troubles. Butts also got loans from Frank Scoby, a Chicago beer distributor who wagered heavily on college football, a questionable association for the former head football coach.[19]

Butts's personal life was also falling apart. Throughout the 1960 football season, he appeared publicly, including at UGA football games, with his mistress. She flew on the team plane until players objected, and then she flew commercially to the games, on Butts's expense account. Butts even bought her a car and spent thousands of dollars on long-distance calls to her. Later, Butts's daughter wrote a letter to his lawyer explaining that Butts was very upset about growing older, implying that his behavior in the early 1960s after years of being a loyal family man and a disciplined coach was a kind of breakdown or late midlife crisis.[20] Butts's personal and financial problems were the perfect ingredients to give some credibility to the allegations that he had conspired to fix the UGA–Alabama football game. Because Butts was generally perceived as bitter and falling apart, betraying his employer and his team seemed conceivable in a way that it would not have a decade earlier.

THE BEAR BRYANT CONNECTION

Paul "Bear" Bryant was born September 11, 1913, in rural Moro Bottom, Arkansas, to a working-class family. A large young man, he played high school football and then, without graduating, accepted a scholarship to play at the University of Alabama. His first year in Tuscaloosa, he took classes at the local high school in order to earn his diploma and to prepare for college courses. When he finally enrolled at Alabama, he majored in physical education and played defensive end on Alabama's 1934 national-championship team. Before his senior year in 1935, he married Mary Harmon Black, and nine months later the first of their two children was born. Immediately after graduating from Alabama, Bryant became an assistant coach there for four years and then spent two years at Vanderbilt University as an assistant. With the entrance of the United States into World War II, Bryant enlisted in the navy, and after serving on a ship off North Africa, he eventually began coaching a football team at one of the navy's pre-flight schools in North Carolina.[21]

After the war ended, Bryant agreed to be the head coach at the University of Maryland, and his legendary career began. After a year at Maryland, he left to coach the University of Kentucky into national prominence, taking the team, in his eight seasons there, to four bowl games and one SEC championship (1950). He left after the exceedingly popular basketball coach Adolph Rupp signed a contract extension that the university president had told Bryant would not be forthcoming. Angry, Bryant landed at Texas A&M, where he became head coach and athletic director for $25,000 per year and one percent of the football gate. His first pre-season there, in 1954, he took his players to Junction, Texas, to train in extreme temperatures; most of the team quit in protest. After a dismal first season at A&M, the team won the 1956 Southwestern Conference championship, but the Aggies were not allowed to play in the Cotton Bowl because of NCAA sanctions for violations that had occurred in Bryant's second season. Bryant later admitted that violations had occurred, but that after the NCAA sanctions, he "always lived by the letter of the law, never won a game anything but the honest way."[22]

In 1958 Bear Bryant returned to Alabama as head football coach and athletic director. He already had a reputation as a tough coach who had skirted the NCAA rules about paying players, and he quickly earned a reputation as the coach of teams who played too rough, if not downright dirty. In November 1961 *Time* magazine called him the "most controversial coach," while adding, "He might be the best." The magazine noted his insatiable desire to win, his tendency to run up scores, and his "browbeating" of sportswriters. *Time* also called him a "relentless, brutal taskmaster."[23] An example of the supposed brutal play that Bryant was teaching occurred later that month during the Alabama–Georgia Tech game when an Alabama player blocked a Tech player so hard, the Tech player was knocked unconscious.

The incident started off innocuously enough. Just before receiving a punt, the Alabama punt returner signaled a fair catch. One of his blockers, Darwin Holt, had his back to the returner and did not see the signal, but the man he was blocking, Chick Graning, did. Graning relaxed his guard and Holt hit his forearm into Graning's cheek and jaw. Graning maintained that "it was a cheap shot," and Holt argued that he was playing through until he heard a whistle, which he said did not blow until after he had blocked Graning. After the incident, the Atlanta newspapers, as well as Graning's father, blamed both Holt and Bryant for the play and Graning's injuries. The following Monday the papers reported that Graning had broken his cheek, his teeth, and his nose, and had a concussion and possible skull fracture.[24] In October 1962 Furman Bisher, an Atlanta sportswriter, published an article in the *Saturday Evening Post*, "College Football is Going Berserk," and revisited the Graning-Holt incident. Bisher wrote that Bryant was a key example of coaches who taught players to play too rough and to hurt their opponents intentionally. Historian Andrew Doyle argued that Alabamans saw the article as an attack not just on their beloved coach but also on the integrity of their state. Some suggested Bryant should challenge Bisher to a duel or just horsewhip him.[25] Instead, Bryant filed a defamation suit against Bisher and the *Saturday Evening Post*, asking for $500,000 in damages.[26]

THE *SATURDAY EVENING POST*

While Butts's professional life was spiraling downward and Bryant was becoming a legend, the *Saturday Evening Post* was entering a new era. The magazine had a long and illustrious history; although it claimed to have been started by Benjamin Franklin, it instead evolved from one of Franklin's publications and was technically born in 1821. Its early success came in part because it published authors such as Edgar Allan Poe, James Fenimore Cooper, and Harriet Beecher Stowe. By the end of the Civil War, though, its success had faded, and in the late nineteenth century it was a sixteen-page sheet, filled with material edited down from other papers. It had a circulation in the 1890s of about two thousand people, and its advertising revenue averaged $300 per issue. In 1898 it was sold to Cyrus H. K. Curtis, owner and publisher of the successful *Ladies' Home Journal*, for $1,000. Curtis hired thirty-year-old George Horace Lorimer to be the editor, and Lorimer made major changes: he reduced the cover price to five cents an issue (lower than any of its competition), changed it from a newspaper to a magazine, and introduced color covers. It also published work of famous authors again, including Stephen Crane and Bret Harte. Every story came with illustrations. Circulation increased dramatically to five hundred thousand by 1903 and two million in 1913. Advertising revenues increased accordingly. Lorimer stayed with the magazine until his retirement in 1936. After a series of editors who stayed just briefly, Ben Hibbs became editor in 1942 and returned to the formula Lorimer had established: family-targeted fiction and illustrations, most notably by artist Norman Rockwell. The magazine remained highly profitable through Hibbs's retirement in 1961, but it was notably conservative, with its homespun illustrated covers and wholesome fiction.[27]

Clay Blair, who became the new editor of the *Post* in 1962, broke from the tradition of the magazine. He wanted to change its image and make it less nondescript, less Norman Rockwell, and more cutting edge. Clay said he wanted "important people speaking out . . . names that people really want to hear from." He announced that the purpose of the magazine henceforth would not only be "to inform but to crusade."[28] One result of that crusading journalism approach was the 1962 article accusing Bryant of encouraging unnecessary roughness. Another was the article accusing Butts and Bryant of fixing the football game.

THE PHONE CALL, THE STORY, AND THE TRIAL

These powerhouses, Butts, Bryant, and the *Post*, intersected in 1962. On Thursday, September 13, 1962, Butts was in Atlanta and phoned Bryant. George Burnett was an insurance salesman in Atlanta who was trying to place a long distance call himself in the same building at the same time as Butts's call to Bryant. Burnett, through a technological error called a cross-connect, overheard parts of the conversation between the two men. He later testified that when he heard the operator tell Butts that she had Bear Bryant on the line, his curiosity prevented him from hanging up as telephone etiquette dictated. When he heard what they were talking about, he began to take notes on the conversation. His notes included Butts's general comments on UGA football ("long count left half in motion") and about specific UGA players ("Woodard [the safety] commits fast" and "Reismuller [a tackle]: Greatest in history").[29] Burnett's notes were too detailed to have been fabricated. The question that would arise at the trial was whether the conversation was a simple, casual conversation about football, as both Butts and Bryant repeatedly maintained, that gave no information of value away, or if the conversation was an attempt by the coaches to fix the game.

Nine days after the phone conversation, on Saturday, September 22, 1962, the Bulldogs met the Crimson Tide in Birmingham, Alabama, for the annual rivalry football game. The Tide, the defending national champions, entered the game as a fourteen-point favorite. The team's brand-new starting quarterback was a sophomore named Joe Namath, a player who would eventually enter the Pro Football Hall of Fame. Alabama destroyed Georgia in the game; Namath was replaced by his backup in the third quarter, but the final score was 35–0. The 1962 'Bama team went 10-1, while that same season the UGA team went 3-4-3.[30]

At first George Burnett told no one about the Butts–Bryant phone conversation. Then, in January 1963, after being introduced by a mutual friend, he told Johnny Griffith, the UGA football coach, about it. At about the same time, but prior to when UGA's president learned about the conversation, Butts resigned from his post as athletic director, effective June 30, 1963; he did so in part because of deepening financial problems. Newspapers reported that Butts's impending resignation was also linked to his unhappiness at not being a coach and reiterated reports that he was being considered for other coaching positions.[31] Days later, UGA learned of the phone call, and Butts denied doing anything wrong, but after Burnett showed his notes to UGA officials, Butts changed his resignation date to the end of February. Burnett, though, felt his conversation with UGA leaders did not go well; one trustee specifically questioned him about a prior history of writing bad checks.[32] At this point Burnett told, and then eventually sold, his story to the *Saturday Evening Post*.

The *Post* found Burnett as the result of an investigation into Bryant's background in the attempt to prepare for and defend Bryant's libel trial over the 1962 article. Apparently, one of their investigators heard rumors that Burnett had overheard something, and arrangements were made for Burnett to meet Furman Bisher, the same Bisher who had written the first article about Bryant, in the office of Burnett's attorney.[33] After hearing the story, Bisher contacted the *Post*. Roger Kahn, the sports editor for the *Post*, decided that Bisher, given his history with Bryant, could not write the story, and so Kahn asked Frank Graham Jr. to do so.[34] Graham, a former baseball executive and the son of a sportswriter, began his own sports writing career after leaving the Dodgers. Kahn, a noted baseball writer himself, had joined the *Post* that year as an editor to make some money. He later wrote that he was told to "bring the *Post*'s sports coverage into the 20th century, to introduce depth and style." As Kahn described the evolution of the story, he was told about Burnett, and he suggested that the magazine give the story to the district attorney in exchange for an exclusive story after the investigation. He was told, however, that was the "old journalism" and that the magazine would investigate and report without the state's involvement.[35]

Graham reported that he met with Burnett, a lawyer, and a private investigator in a hotel in Atlanta. As Graham told the story, he was to offer Burnett $5,000 for the story if the lawyer thought it was true. The investigator surreptitiously taped the conversation and kept the microphone in his briefcase. Graham found Burnett fundamentally believable, even when the man explained about his bad checks (two, for a total of $45). Initially, Graham took only limited notes because he believed he could listen to the tapes, but early on in the conversation, the *Post* lawyer and the investigator left, taking the microphone with them. Within twenty-four hours of his return to New York, Graham completed what he considered a draft of the article and sent it to the *Post*. He expected to return to Atlanta to follow up, but the magazine told him that local reporters would be used to finish the investigation and the story.[36]

In March 1963, about six months after the UGA–Alabama football game, the *Saturday Evening Post* published, under Frank Graham Jr.'s byline, "The Story of a College Football Fix: How Wally Butts and Bear Bryant Rigged a Game Last Fall." Based on the conversation between Butts and Bryant that George Burnett had overheard, the story began with an editorial comment that Roger Kahn wrote: "Not since the Chicago White Sox threw the 1919 World Series has there been a sports story as shocking as this one."[37] Prior to the story's publication (in response to rumors that such a story was going to be published), Butts's attorney warned the magazine that the story was false, and after its publication he asked for a retraction. When Curtis declined to publish the retraction, Butts filed a lawsuit for libel.[38] Bryant did the same, separately, and each asked for $10 million in damages.

Contemporary reaction to the story tended to support the coaches. Dan Jenkins wrote for *Sports Illustrated* that everyone in the South was talking about the charge of fixing the game. In a story published immediately after the *Post* article was released, Jenkins cast suspicion on Burnett, writing that his "story was almost as queer as some of the bad checks he has passed." Although Jenkins noted that Burnett had passed a lie detector test, he also correctly noted that such evidence was inadmissible in court. Butts refused to take such a test, but Bryant passed his polygraph. The article concluded with questions about who was telling the truth and which lie detector test was most accurate, demanding further investigation to protect college football's reputation.[39] Columnist Red Smith acknowledged that the *Post*'s story was a concern to sports fans, but he did not consider it to be a "second Black Sox scandal," adding that no evidence of unusual or heavy betting on the game had been found. Like others, he questioned what information the athletic director could provide to a coach like Bryant who was well known for his detailed scouting reports.[40] Published letters to *Sports Illustrated* were uniformly supportive of Butts and Bryant. Several questioned Burnett's veracity,[41] and another written by football announcer Pat Summerall suggested that Burnett may have overheard the conversation and not understood its significance. Summerall wrote that the modern game was more "science than in the past" and that "a discussion of generalities might sound like inside and informative facts."[42] A *New York Times* article concluded that many Georgians saw no motive for Butts to tell tales to Bryant and no reason for Bryant to listen. The article also noted that the *Atlanta Journal* and the *Atlanta Constitution* had reported on the story but had not editorialized upon it.[43]

Prior to the trial but after the publication of the article, Butts's behavior was investigated by UGA and by the State of Georgia. His phone records revealed that he had spoken with known gamblers as well as to Bryant on several occasions.[44] A week or so later, the paper reported those calls had been to Butts's business partner Frank Scoby; Scoby had previously admitted to gambling on college football games, but he and Butts said that their phone conversations had been about business, and no evidence suggested that Butts or Bryant had gambled on the UGA–Alabama game.[45] *Sports Illustrated* would again support Butts when Georgia's attorney general claimed Butts had given Bryant "vital and important information that could have affected the outcome" of the game. The magazine disagreed completely with that assertion and demanded that if the attorney general had evidence of a crime, he should produce it.[46]

The *Butts v. Saturday Evening Post* trial was a circus. *Sports Illustrated* anticipated that this trial would be as emotional as the Scopes Monkey Trial in 1925.[47] In a parade of who's who of Southern football, everyone seems to have testified. UGA coach Johnny Griffith testified that he was certain that his teams' "secret plays" had been leaked to Alabama, but he admitted that Georgia probably would have lost the game anyway.[48] LeRoy Jordan, a star defensive player for Alabama, testified the team was surprised by several plays Georgia ran, implying they had not been warned about them. Charley Trippi, a former Georgia football star and the offensive backfield coach for the game, testified that the information on Burnett's sheet would not have hurt Georgia. Four Bulldogs testified that contrary to a quote in the article, they never told anyone the Alabama team "seemed to know every play we were going to run." When Wally Butts took the stand, he cried (Butts was known to be emotional in public), testified about how hurt he had been by the allegations, and denied telling Bryant anything useful or trying to collude to fix the game.[49] Bear Bryant used his testimony to give a football tutorial to the jury and to mock Burnett's notes on the conversation: "If I didn't know that, I oughta be bored for a hollow head."[50] Butts's defense attorney continued this homespun yet emotional approach when he concluded his closing arguments by telling the jury, "Someday, as must happen to each of us, Wallace Butts will pass on to where neither the *Post* nor anyone else can then bother him. Unless I miss my guess, they will put him in a red coffin with a black lid [red and black are Georgia's colors] with a football in his hands, and his epitaph will read 'Glory, glory to Old Georgia.'"[51]

The defense focused on painting Butts as a flawed man of questionable character. University of Georgia President O. C. Aderhold and three other members of the Georgia Athletic Board testified that Butts's character and reputation were poor. *Sports Illustrated* called it a "surprisingly weak defense."[52] Because the *Post* defense focused on character and less on proving the truth of the article, their lawyers chose not to put the author of the article, Frank Graham Jr., on the stand. Instead, his deposition was submitted as evidence by Butts's legal team in part because it underlined the flaws in the *Post*'s editorial process: Graham's deposition repeatedly acknowledged that the published article contained sentences that he had not written and research he had not done.[53] He added that when he concluded the article with "chances are Wally Butts will never help any football team again. . . . But careers will be ruined," he was thinking of both Butts and Bryant, and he suspected the damage that the article could do.[54]

In the end, the all-white, all-male jury in Atlanta ruled that Butts had been libeled and awarded him $60,000 in compensatory damages and $3 million in punitive damages. Wally Butts burst into tears again and later said, "I couldn't help it. It was six months rolling out of me. It's not the money. It's the vindication for all those folks that believed in me."[55] When the court clerk read the verdict, Clay Blair, the *Post*'s editor, turned to one of his lawyers and asked if she had actually said three million.[56]

Several scholars have examined the initial jury trial and offered their opinions on whether Butts and Bryant really tried to fix the game. James Kirby, a law professor who was the official SEC observer, argued in his 1986 book *Fumble* that Butts and Bryant did conspire to fix the game and that "the Bear Bryant–Wally Butts scandal put three of America's most revered institutions—big time college football, the law, and the press—to the test. All three fumbled."[57] Kirby believed that Butts talked to Bryant about the upcoming game out of spite toward UGA and the Bulldog football program and because he needed money, and that Bryant listened because he wanted to win. Kirby implied that some third party (presumably one of his gambling business partners) encouraged Butts to give Bryant information in exchange for either money or stock tips. Kirby argued that the jury was bamboozled during the trial because the lawyers for the *Post* were remarkably inept, because the judge should have removed himself as a UGA alum who had attended the game in question, and because Bear Bryant was "the single most awesome figure this writer has ever seen in a courtroom, including lawyers and judges."[58]

Allen Barra, a journalist and Bear Bryant's biographer, took issue with Kirby's conclusions that the Butts–Bryant conversation was an attempt to fix the game. He concluded that Kirby's assertion that a third-party financier was involved was unfounded because Barra could not determine how Bryant could have benefited from trying to fix the game. Alabama was an overwhelming favorite, Bryant pulled his quarterback early in the game, and he did not try to run up the score, yet he still covered the spread. Alabama simply was a much stronger team than Georgia in 1962. Barra argued that while Butts may have given Bryant information, none of it was likely unknown to the Alabama coach because most of it was opinion or available on any game tape. Further, Barra noted that Alabama did not change its game plan after the phone call, suggesting that Bryant got no new or useful information. Barra did not doubt that Butts could have been talking to Bryant to be vindictive, but he thought Bryant listened simply because he sympathized with a coach who was being run out of the profession and not out of an effort to fix the game.[59] The jury, in awarding damages for libel to Butts (Bryant's trial was separate), clearly agreed with Barra that Butts and Bryant did not fix the game.

THE APPEALS AND *NEW YORK TIMES CO. v. SULLIVAN*

It is not surprising that, given the size of the jury verdict, Curtis Publishing chose to appeal. Federal District Court Judge Lewis Morgan, who had presided over the jury trial, rendered his written decision on January 14, 1964. Curtis Publishing argued that the $3 million in punitive damages was excessive and that the original trial was flawed and therefore a retrial should be ordered. Morgan concluded that the article was "clearly defamatory and extremely so," and he added that the $60,000 for actual damages was reasonable.[60] Morgan did, however, believe that the punitive damages were excessive, and he reduced the award to $400,000. He ordered a new trial only if Butts refused to accept the reduced punitive-damages award.[61] Butts accepted the reduced award, but Curtis Publishing would get new life in light of a Supreme Court decision that followed the jury trial.

At Butts's trial, the jury was instructed essentially that the *Saturday Evening Post's* only defense was to prove that its story was true. On March 9, 1964, though, in *New York Times Co. v. Sullivan*, the U.S. Supreme Court changed the burden of proof on public officials suing for defamation in order to accommodate the press's freedom under the First Amendment. L. B. Sullivan, the Montgomery, Alabama, public safety commissioner, had sued the parent company of the *New York Times* because the paper had printed a full-page advertisement asking for financial support to defend Martin Luther King Jr. from a perjury charge, and the advertisement contained misstatements of fact. The ad was critical of how the police had handled recent student demonstrations demanding civil rights for black citizens. The jury awarded Sullivan $500,000 after finding the *Times* guilty of libel, and the Supreme Court overruled that verdict.[62] Justice William Brennan wrote in the majority opinion that the case needed to be considered "against the background of a profound national commitment to the principle that debate on public issues should be uninhibited, robust, and wide-open, and that it may well include vehement, caustic, and sometimes unpleasantly sharp attacks on government and public officials." Therefore, public officials who were plaintiffs could succeed in libel suits critical of their official conduct only if they established that "the statement was made with 'actual malice'—that is, with knowledge that it was false or with reckless disregard of whether it was false."[63] While this new standard made it much more difficult for public officials to recover damages from libel, the Court failed to define who a "public official" was. In essence, the standard was intended to promote speech about matters of public issues, in this instance the civil rights movement.

After the *New York Times Co. v. Sullivan* decision was published, Curtis's lawyers appealed the verdict against them, arguing that Butts was a public official because he was the athletic director of a state university. The *Post* asked for a retrial with new jury instructions requiring Butts to prove actual malice as a public official. Judge Morgan disagreed. Although Butts was employed as the University of Georgia football coach and athletic director, the Georgia Athletic Association, an incorporated organization separate from the university, supervised him and paid his salary. Judge Morgan noted that under state law, members of the Board of Regents of the University System of Georgia were public officials, but that teachers and instructors in the system were only employees and thus not public officials. He rejected Curtis's request to classify Butts, a football coach, as a public official, concluding that such a tangential position was beyond the scope of the *Sullivan* decision. Morgan added that even if Butts were a public official, ample evidence was presented at trial that Curtis had published the article with actual malice.[64] Curtis appealed again, and the 5th Circuit Court of Appeals affirmed the district court's ruling but did not address whether Butts was a public official.

The majority of the three-judge panel concluded that Curtis had failed to raise the public-official claim during the trial and had no right, therefore, to raise it afterward.[65] Curtis appealed again, and the U.S. Supreme Court addressed the issue and reached a conclusion—of sorts.

THE SUPREME COURT DECISION

The Supreme Court decided *Butts v. Curtis Publishing Company* jointly with *Associate Press v. Walker*.[66] In the latter case, Major General (ret.) Edwin A. Walker sued the Associated Press over a series of reports regarding his involvement in leading a crowd at the University of Mississippi in 1962 to protest the enrollment of James Meredith, the school's first African American student. The crowd attacked a group of federal marshals with rocks, bricks, and bottles. Walker, who had been in command of the federal troops enforcing the desegregation of the schools of Little Rock, Arkansas, in 1957, was charged with inciting insurrection and seditious conspiracy. At the time of the Ole Miss riot, Walker had retired from the military and was a private citizen. The newspaper reported, "Walker, who Sunday led a charge of students against federal marshals on the Ole Miss Campus" and "Walker assumed command of the crowd" (internal citations omitted).[67] The report also indicated that Walker had given an emotional plea to keep the crowd motivated, even as he warned that death was possible. But he alleged only that the statements of his leading the charge and being in command were libel.[68] The jury awarded him $500,000 in damages, an award affirmed on appeal when the court concluded that the charge and command statements in the story were presented as fact and not as opinion or fair comment. Ultimately, the Supreme Court joined the *Walker* decision with *Butts* to address the question of how libel law should be applied to people who are not public officials but are, in the Court's words, "public figures" who were "involved in issues in which the public has a justified and important interest."[69]

No single opinion garnered the necessary five votes to form a majority opinion. Instead, four different justices drafted four different opinions, and from those opinions a plurality decision was carved out, meaning that while no five justices agreed to any single opinion, a majority of justices agreed to certain ideas. Seven justices (John Marshall Harlan, Tom Clark, Potter Stewart, Abe Fortas, Earl Warren, William Brennan, and Byron White) agreed in three different opinions that Wally Butts was a public figure. Justice Harlan, joined by Clark, Stewart, and Fortas, concluded that Butts "was a well-known and respected figure in coaching . . . [who] maintained an interest in coaching and was negotiating for a position with a professional team at the time of publication."[70] Harlan recognized the historical and ideological tension between the First Amendment and the laws of defamation but noted that the Court had for some time limited defamatory speech. He concluded that public figures could win defamation suits if they could show "highly unreasonable conduct constituting an extreme departure from the standards of investigation." He added that Butts had met that burden.[71]

Chief Justice Warren, joined by Black and Brennan, wrote a concurrence, agreeing with the conclusion of the majority but offering different arguments. Warren supported the results, not the reasoning. Warren concurred that Butts was a public figure but expressed concern that Harlan created a new and separate standard from the *New York Times v. Sullivan* test of 1964. Warren preferred to apply the actual-malice standard of proving that defamatory statements were made with actual malice "with knowledge that it was false or with reckless disregard" of falsity to public figures as well as public officials.[72] He wrote, "Increasingly . . . the distinctions between governmental and private sectors are blurred," adding that people who are not public officials "are nevertheless intimately involved in the resolution of important public questions or, by reason of their fame, shape events in areas of concern to society at large."[73]

Four justices dissented at least in part. Justice Black issued a dissent in which Justice Douglas joined. The two shared the conviction that the First Amendment was absolute in its protection of the press. Black warned that the Court was entering a "quagmire" in which "no one, including this Court can know what is and what is not constitutionally . . . libelous."[74] Justice Brennan, joined by White, who had signed onto the Chief Justice's concurrence in part, wrote a dissent about Butts's case. Brennan and White agreed with Warren that the *Sullivan* standard applied, but they did not agree that the evidence proved Butts had met that standard. They wanted to see *Butts* retried with new jury instructions appropriate to the Court's decisions.[75]

When taken concept by concept, the Court's conclusions were varied. Seven justices concluded that public figures were different from public officials in that they were not necessarily employees of the government, but that as public figures these people were in the public spotlight in a different way than a typical citizen and thus should be held to a higher standard of proof in defamation cases. Five members of the Court in three opinions agreed that public figures should be held to the actual malice standard as described in *New York Times v. Sullivan* for public officials, although Douglas and Black endorsed *Sullivan* only as a lesser evil than Harlan's test, and they vastly preferred no restraint on the press at all.[76]

Part of the significance of this divided decision lies in the fact that it acknowledges the prominent role of sport in American society and the power of celebrity bestowed upon those who themselves are well-known leaders in sport. Essentially, the Supreme Court, fractured as it was, reached a kind of compromise regarding the competing tensions of reputation and free press with *Butts v. Curtis Publishing*. Public figures (who could be termed celebrities), which included prominent college football coaches, had a legal right to defend their reputations from false attacks in the press. The press did have some protection under the First Amendment. Unlike a private citizen who could prove simply that the statement was false and that his or her reputation was harmed, a celebrity had to meet a higher standard, had to prove that the press published the defamatory statement either with actual malice or, according to the Harlan opinion, with highly unreasonable conduct.

Worth noting is that Justice Byron White had once been a sporting celebrity himself. In the 1930s White earned nine varsity letters in football, baseball, and basketball while a student at the University of Colorado (CU). His impressive play in football was well-documented in the United Press syndicate, and he was the runner-up for the Heisman Trophy in 1937. He became a member of the College Football Hall of Fame. White, as a college athlete, was not particularly excited about being a celebrity. The CU basketball team was one of the teams invited to the first National Invitational Tournament at Madison Square Garden, and the press covered the event closely. White later said, "The New York newspapers put out quite a bit of publicity about the team and about me. I figured it the same way I always had—it was their job and they probably knew what they were doing, but I didn't like it, even so."[77] After graduating, White was the number-one draft pick for Art Rooney's Pittsburgh Pirates in the NFL, and Rooney offered White almost $16,000 as a guaranteed salary (twice what the next-highest-paid NFL player made). The press closely covered White as he debated whether to accept a Rhodes Scholarship at Oxford or to play in the NFL. He accepted the NFL job and deferred going to Oxford for a year. When he came back to the United States, White returned part-time to professional football while earning his law degree from Yale.[78] In the *Butts* decision, the only justice who really understood being a sporting celebrity agreed that Butts was a public figure.

LEGAL IMPLICATIONS

Soon after the Supreme Court handed down the *Butts* decision, legal scholars began their critique. Law professor Harry Kalven Jr. noted in 1967 that the case suggested that the Supreme Court believed the First Amendment limited tort protections of defamation. While interpreting the divided decision of the Court, he argued that "the appearance of victory for Harlan in *Butts* is a fluke, occasioned by Warren's vote to save the verdict for the plaintiff, [so] it is apparent that the Court stands 5 to 4 in favor of the Brennan–Warren standard and hence in favor of an across-the-board application of *New York Times*."[79] The divided nature of the decision meant that, as precedent, *Butts v. Curtis Publishing* was unreliable, and the Supreme Court would be forced to revisit the standard for libel and public figures in several cases in the upcoming years.

Subsequent battles would accept the *Sullivan* actual-malice test as the rule for determining defamation against a public figure, but they would focus instead on *defining* public figures. In 1971, in *Rosenbloom v. Metromedia, Inc.*, a magazine wholesaler sued a radio station after the station reported that the wholesaler had been arrested on obscenity charges. He claimed that the station's reports calling him a dealer of "smut" and "girlie books" was defamatory. The Supreme Court concluded that although the plaintiff was not a public figure, the matter being discussed (distribution of pornography) was a matter of public interest. Therefore, Justice Brennan, writing for a plurality, concluded that the actual malice standard of *Sullivan* applied.[80] In 1974, the *Rosenbloom* rule was overturned, and Justice Lewis Powell, writing for the five-judge majority, argued that a person could become a public figure by achieving pervasive fame or infamy and thus could always and perhaps forever be a public figure or, alternatively, a person could either voluntarily or involuntarily be drawn into a public matter and become a public figure for that controversy.[81]

Subsequently, the debate over who a public figure is has raged in the courts for more than forty years. Generally speaking, celebrity sport figures have conceded their status as public figures.[82] For those who have not, the courts have addressed the question in a case-by-case manner, often finding the individuals to be at least limited public figures after being thrust into or voluntarily entering a public controversy. The courts found the president/owner of the management company of professional jai alai to be a public figure after he sued ABC news for reporting that he fixed games. The court ruled the plaintiff was a limited public figure because gambling was commonly associated with that sport, and fixing games was a public controversy.[83] In 2004 an Ohio high school football coach who had a long history of telling the public that he required his players to pray before games and had spoken on various local religious channels was deemed a limited public figure because of these insertions into public controversies.[84] Even an American Kennel Club (AKC) dog judge was deemed a public figure. The AKC suspected she had lied in her application, and during the investigation, the AKC discussed the situation with another AKC judge who also published a column in a weekly magazine, *Dog News*. The columnist then reported on the investigation. The plaintiff sued and the court ruled that she was a limited public figure because the credibility of dog judges in the dog world concerned that community.[85]

Conversely, on a few occasions, courts have concluded that sport figures were not public figures. They have tended to protect children and to find them to be private figures. When a local newspaper published a photo of a Little League baseball team after the coach had been charged with molesting players, the players sued. The court said that although the controversy was public, the players on the team had not voluntarily thrust themselves into that controversy: they just appeared in the team photo.[86] In another case, a high school stand-out athlete was not deemed a public figure, despite the fact that that he had won awards, been recruited by a Division I college football program, and was the son of a professional athlete.[87] Each case was addressed on its own merits.

The legal link between Bear Bryant and the laws of publicity would not end with the *Butts* case. In 1984 the courts would again revisit the reporting of the incident in which the Alabama player, Darwin Holt, laid a hard hit on Chick Graning of Georgia Tech and knocked him out of the game. This was the hit that caused Bryant to sue the *Saturday Evening Post* the first time for defaming his character. In the 1980s, when Alabama and Georgia Tech renewed their football rivalry, an Atlanta newspaper ran a series on the history of the rivalry. The stories referred to Holt as an "animal" and a "caveman incarnate." Holt sued the Atlanta newspaper for violations of privacy when the Atlanta paper published a series on the particular incident, maintaining the articles cast him in a false light. The court concluded that Holt was a public figure and thus had to prove the articles were published with actual malice under the *Sullivan* standard. The court determined that he had failed to do so.[88]

PERSONAL AND SOCIETAL IMPLICATIONS

Wally Butts never coached again after the *Saturday Evening Post* article was published. In 1966, prior to the Supreme Court decision and prior to Curtis Publishing paying damages to Butts, the Internal Revenue Service charged him with owing $36,000 in back taxes and placed liens on his property. He had no money after the trial to pay them, and, with no football options, he entered a new career: selling insurance.[89] He collected almost $600,000 in damages and interest after the Supreme Court verdict, though, and his finances stabilized. He reportedly made millions from his insurance work.[90] On December 17, 1973, he died in Athens after a heart attack during his morning walk. He was 68. In his *Chicago Tribune* obituary, Bear Bryant was quoted, calling him "a great coach."[91] Furman Bisher, the Atlanta reporter who was frequently linked to Bryant attacks, called the late Butts the "Bona Fide Coach" and criticized that *Post* article (an article he had been involved in creating), calling the story "stretched beyond all bounds of imagination by a young sports editor just employed by the magazine attempting to break in with a big noise."[92] In 1997 Butts was posthumously inducted into the College Football Hall of Fame. An article in the *Sporting News* acknowledged that the way Butts had left football had been a factor in his delayed induction but that "he got a lot of support . . . especially from his former players."[93] In the ultimate signal of rehabilitation, in 1987 the University of Georgia named its Butts–Mehre athletic administration building after him and Henry Mehre (another former football coach).

Bear Bryant settled his two defamation lawsuits against the *Saturday Evening Post* five months after Butts won his jury trial and after the judge reduced the award to $460,000. Bryant, who had asked for damages of $10 million, settled for between $320,000 and $360,000.[94] In 1966 Bryant wrote in *Sports Illustrated* that he had asked for $10 million because the *Saturday Evening Post*, he said, "took ten years of my life. . . . If I had collected that much—which I didn't—it would not have paid for the suffering they put me through."[95] While reflecting on the lawsuits and his decisions to sue, he expressed some regret: "Well, you challenge somebody on one pack of lies and you wind up with a bigger pack of lies. It was a mistake. If I hadn't sued the *Post* on that one, I don't believe there'd ever have been the second story. They must have started working on that right after we filed the suit."[96]

Allen Barra, Bryant's biographer, argued that Bryant settled in part because of the stress and the fear that the *Post*'s investigations into him would reveal something that could put him in a bad light. Barra reported that the *Post* did, in fact, send reporters out to find as much negative information about Bryant as they could, even investigating his life in Kentucky in the 1940s. One of the reporters told Barra that he found nothing but rumors and respect for Bryant. Bryant's lawyers advised him to take the settlement Curtis Publishing offered, and he accepted because he admitted he had drunk and gambled more than he should have, and he did not want that information used in such a way as to hurt his family or the university. He also needed the money—at that time he, like Butts, had lost money in the stock market.[97]

After the lawsuits, Bryant had an incredibly successful business and coaching career. By 1980, he was reportedly a millionaire with investments in stock, land, and a variety of businesses. He was well paid for his endorsements and for his speaking engagements, more than augmenting the reported $54,000 a year he made as head football coach and athletic director.[98] When he retired at the end of the 1982 football season, after thirty-eight years as a head coach, he had won more football games than any other coach in history: 323. He won six national championships and had only one losing season. Bryant was fond of telling friends that he would die the week after he quit coaching; in actuality, he lasted twenty-one days. The day after being hospitalized for chest pains, he died in Tuscaloosa, Alabama, on January 26, 1983.

Although both Butts and Bryant survived the lawsuits and found measures of success with the remainder of their lives, the *Saturday Evening Post* was not so fortunate. Hit hard by the costs of fighting defamation lawsuits and with a declining circulation as well as dwindling advertising revenue, the magazine, the former flagship and cash cow of the Curtis Publishing empire, was shut down on January 10, 1969. It re-emerged, however, with the same title in 1971 and a new emphasis on health and medical breakthroughs. As of 2015, it was still in existence, published by a nonprofit organization, The Saturday Evening Post Society. The twenty-first-century version of the magazine still focused on health but also included fiction, humor, and social and political commentary, and the magazine still had color cover art.[99]

The Butts's defamation lawsuit had one social component that went undiscussed and unexplored at the time of the trial and yet still played a major role in the trial. The American South in the early 1960s was fraught with racial tension. After decades of Jim Crow laws, the South was reluctant to embrace racial integration, and many White Southerners were not comfortable with the civil rights movement. It was reflective of the era that when the Supreme Court heard the *Butts* case, the Court joined it with Walker's defamation lawsuit. Walker was angry over his portrayal in actions protesting the integration of the University of Mississippi.

Georgia and Alabama were both struggling with integration and the new era of social change in the 1960s. The University of Georgia admitted its first black student in 1961; the University of Alabama did so in 1963. The SEC itself was still all white during the Butts trial in 1963. The University of Kentucky teams were the first to integrate after the Butts trial: the first black basketball players were allowed on the team in 1966, the first black football players in 1967. Georgia football would remain all white until 1971, and Bear Bryant signed his first black player in 1970 and fielded the first black player in 1971. Integration did not come easily to either institution: throughout the 1950s UGA officials repeatedly threatened to close the university rather than enroll black students, although in 1953 the student paper was warned to stop writing pro-segregation editorials.[100] When two black students finally did enroll in January 1961, they were met with protests followed by a riot. They were briefly suspended for their own safety. In Alabama, black students were allowed to enroll only after being escorted by federalized National Guard troops past Governor George Wallace. Bear Bryant, according to historian Andrew Doyle, missed his moment to help integrate Alabama football sooner than he did. Bryant claimed in his autobiography that he wanted to recruit black players to Kentucky in the 1940s but that the university president had declined, yet at Alabama, Doyle reported, he made no such overt effort. Doyle said Bryant had a "policy of cautious moderation" that avoided political risks and harming Alabama football.[101] Bryant, at least, was at the helm when Alabama football did integrate.

Race was a subtext of the Butts trial as well. Given the segregation of the South and the fact that all the lawyers were UGA graduates, one can assume that all the principals—lawyers, judges, and witnesses—were white. Even the jury was all white and all male. Some jurors later admitted that they disliked Northern papers writing about Southern individuals in general. One juror specifically disliked the fact that the *Saturday Evening Post* had published articles supportive of racial integration and civil rights. Several jurors admitted to being segregationists but denied that the issues of civil rights and the *Post* were discussed in the jury room, although they admitted such matters might have come up in private conversations.[102]

CONCLUSION

This case marks the intersection of complicated ideas that are often at odds with or at least in tension with each other: celebrity, sport, freedom of the press, libel, and reputation. The very first time the United States Supreme Court defined a public figure beyond a public official, they used Wally Butts, an athletic director at a prominent college sports program and a former college football coach. Thus in 1967, for law, celebrity was fused with sport.

Celebrity, of course, is also why the *Saturday Evening Post* published the story in the first place. The magazine knew of the significance of college football in America, especially in the Southeast, and the magazine knew that Bear Bryant was one of the most prominent coaches in the game. The editors were much less likely to have published a story about any alleged cheating scandal that might have involved lesser sporting figures such as the football coaches of two minor regional universities. The magazine knew that the scandal was bigger (although perhaps not so big as the 1919 Black Sox scandal, as the editors maintained) because of the fame and celebrity of these two coaches, Bryant and Butts, and the prominence of football at these two schools, Alabama and UGA. The *Saturday Evening Post* knew that this story would sell copies of the magazine. Coaches Butts and Bryant, in contrast, successfully used the law of defamation to regain control of their reputations. They felt that they had restored their reputations and dignity, and the Court acknowledged that even though they were celebrities, football coaches had the right not to be defamed.

3

STOP THE PRESS: A BASEBALL LEGEND AND BIOGRAPHY

SPAHN v. JULIAN MESSNER, INC. (1967)

Warren Spahn was a remarkable baseball pitcher and a veteran of World War II. The two elements of his life intersected when Milton J. Shapiro, the author of a child-targeted biography (a juvenile biography, as it is called in the trade) about the great pitcher, included details about his war service that may have inaccurately credited Spahn with receiving the Bronze Star for his service.[1] Nothing in the biography made Spahn look bad; on the contrary, Spahn believed that the story made him look *too* good, and thus he successfully sued the publisher, Julian Messner Inc., to stop publication of the book and to recover damages for violations of his right of privacy under New York State law. The case is significant in part because it is one of the only instances wherein a celebrity has successfully enjoined publication of something that painted him or her in a positive yet false light. Further, the case clearly established the New York State courts' adoption of privacy law as a right that should be balanced against the press's rights under the First Amendment. The case is also important because it reflects the limitations of both the law and the celebrity in controlling one's image. The story about Spahn's Bronze Star would persist beyond his death.

THE UNDISPUTED WARREN SPAHN

Warren Spahn never wrote an autobiography, and, as of 2015, no definitive academic biography of the man had been published. Rather, brief biographies appear in various baseball histories, encyclopedias, and children's books, many with conflicting stories and statements. In some ways, Spahn's testimony at the publisher's trial has served as his autobiography—as it was in court, under oath, that he told much about his personal story. That said, some facts are undisputed. Not surprisingly, while his baseball facts and statistics are clear, his personal life and his personality are murkier and more conflicted.

The fifth of six children, Warren Edward Spahn was born April 23, 1921, in Buffalo, New York, and was named after President Warren G. Harding. His father, Edward, worked in wallpaper (some accounts describe him as a salesman and others as a hanger) and was a semi-pro baseball player with various local teams. Most stories of Spahn's life focused on his relationship with his father, perhaps because of the almost mythical father–son baseball link in the American imagination. Spahn's father was credited with teaching young Warren to pitch and play ball, although the degree of truth of this assertion was debated at Spahn's trial. Most biographies agreed that Spahn was a batboy for at least one of his father's teams. His mother, Mabel, was rarely discussed in his biographies and was only briefly mentioned in the book Spahn found so offensive.[2] Spahn played first base for much of his youth but became a strong pitcher in high school.

Spahn was offered a partial baseball scholarship to Cornell University, but instead, after graduating from high school in 1940, he signed a minor league contract with the Boston Braves. That first year he played in class D baseball, the lowest of the minor leagues, and won five of nine decisions. His season was cut short by an elbow injury, and he returned home to Buffalo to heal; during that time, his father was hospitalized, which would become a point of contention in the biography. In 1941 his elbow healed, and he was promoted to class B, where he led the league in wins and earned-run average. The following year he won seventeen of twenty-nine games in class A and was called up to finish the season with the parent club, the Major League Baseball (MLB) Boston Braves. He began his MLB career with Casey Stengel as his manager and started two games, appeared in two additional games, but earned no decisions.[3]

At the end of the 1942 season, Spahn entered the military. He was trained as an engineer and was initially stationed eighty miles outside Tulsa, Oklahoma. It was there that he met LoRene Southard, the woman he married after World War II.[4] Spahn spent three years in the army, notably serving in the Battle of the Bulge and at the Ludendorff Bridge as a combat engineer, where his unit received the Distinguished Unit Citation for repairing the bridge while under attack. He was ultimately promoted to second lieutenant by a battlefield commission, and at some point, he won a Purple Heart after being injured. His service years have never been clearly documented in any biography, and the details of his service as described in the Shapiro biography were hotly contested in Spahn's lawsuit against Julian Messner Inc. Indeed, what medals Spahn may or may not have been awarded remains unclear. Different stories and different biographies report different things.

After the war, Spahn returned stateside in 1946 and began pitching very effectively for the Boston Braves. In the decade after World War II, the south-paw won more games (183) than any other MLB pitcher during the same period. He won at least twenty games in six different seasons, led the league in strikeouts in four seasons, and twice led the league in earned-run average. As a result he became one of the highest-paid players in the league, earning $50,000 in 1956.[5] In 1948 Spahn and the other star of the pitching rotation, Johnny Sain, led the Braves to the World Series; between the two of them, they pitched seventy games in the regular season, sparking the phrase "Spahn and Sain and pray for rain."[6] Unfortunately for the Braves, they lost to Cleveland in the World Series. After the 1952 season the Braves left Boston and moved to Milwaukee, where Spahn remained a solid, durable pitching option for the club. In 1957 the Milwaukee Braves, who by this point had signed Hank Aaron, won the National League pennant and returned to the World Series. Spahn won the Cy Young Award that year, and the Braves beat the New York Yankees to win the series in seven games. Spahn pitched game 1 but lost and pitched again in game 4 to win. The 1958 World Series was a rematch: again Spahn pitched and won game 1 and also game 4, but he lost game 6 in the tenth inning. The Yankees won the World Series in seven games. Spahn was well established as one of the league's best pitchers.

Spahn stood about six feet tall and weighed around 175 pounds. He was noted for his large, hooked, hawk-like nose, which had been broken by a ball and never properly reset. His pitching technique made use of his long, lean body: he was famous for his extremely pronounced and high leg kick. His personality was described by *Sports Illustrated* in 1956 as easygoing and popular.[7] In 1957 *Sports Illustrated*, in a story about Spahn's roommate and fellow Braves pitcher Lew Burdette, described Spahn as "one of the game's biggest clowns," adding, "Vaudeville would never have died if Spahn and Burdette had been around with their routine of crooked caps, absurd faces, ridiculous pepper games and jockeying antics from the bench."[8] Aside from his jocularity in the clubhouse, Spahn was also known as a serious competitor who stayed fit year round and studied the game. After starting his career primarily as a fastball pitcher, he added a range of other pitches and was noted for his powers of concentration and memory of batters' strengths and weaknesses.[9]

Spahn's personal life seemed to be thriving as well. When he returned from war, he married LoRene. At the time, *Sport Magazine* reported that the Boston Braves became involved with the wedding plans because they, along with LoRene, were waiting in 1946 for Spahn to return from Europe. LoRene apparently was planning a June wedding in her hometown of Tulsa, while the Braves were planning to have Spahn pitching in Boston as quickly as possible. Giving up her personal plans, LoRene agreed to go to Boston to meet Spahn and get married. After one night there, frustrated with the Braves involvement in their lives and Spahn's focus on baseball, she left, telling Spahn that she would marry him in a ceremony in Tulsa in the fall. After a few weeks, she changed her mind, returned to Boston, and eloped with Spahn, foregoing the elaborate ceremony that the Braves allegedly had offered the young couple.[10] The couple's only child, Greg, was born in October 1948 during the World Series. In 1950 the Spahns confirmed their commitment to Oklahoma as their permanent home when they purchased a cattle ranch in southeastern Oklahoma. They lived there during the off-seasons, in Florida during spring training, and, during the baseball season, lived first in Boston and then Milwaukee when the Braves moved. By 1958 Spahn was doing well both personally and professionally, and because of his success, he became the subject of numerous articles and books.

MILTON SHAPIRO AND JULIAN MESSNER INC.

In 1958 the independent publishing house Julian Messner Inc. released a biography targeted for a youth audience about Spahn's life and career up to that point.[11] No doubt the project was at least partially inspired by the Braves' 1957 World Series win over the Yankees and Spahn's Cy Young Award. Milton J. Shapiro, the author, had already had some success with juvenile biographies about sport figures, having published books about Jackie Robinson and Sal Maglie the previous year.[12] Shapiro would ultimately publish more than twenty more sport books and a number of World War II books for juveniles, almost all with Julian Messner Inc. as the publisher. The publishing house itself was also quite successful. Julian Messner, after spending fifteen years with the established publishing house of Boni and Liveright, founded the company in 1933 with his wife Kathryn G. Messner.[13] In 1944 the two divorced but both remained with the publishing house. When Julian Messner died in 1948, Kathryn Messner became the president, yet the board of directors was concerned about a woman holding such an important position and created a vice-presidency in charge of the president. That position quickly disappeared as Kathryn proved her competence. Over the decades, she worked with and published a number of successful authors, including sportswriter John R. Tunis.[14] In 1956 she published *Peyton Place* by Grace Metalious, a book that quickly became a bestseller and ultimately sold more than ten million copies. A film version was released in 1957.[15] And thus 1958 would seem to be just another successful year for all parties involved.

Problems arose when Spahn became aware of Shapiro's book. At first glance, the book seemed innocuous enough: written for sports fans of junior-high age, the book used a common practice of creating or recreating dialogue between major figures in the book. The first trial court described the tone as being "gauged to project a supposed close association with the hero and the format can best be characterized as a series of vividly picturesque and detailed incidents profusely highlighted with dialogue."[16] The book was typical of juvenile biographies of this era: Spahn's life story was told in a fictionalized manner, complete with dialogue and descriptions of clothing, situations, and emotions. It was also typical of "gee-whiz" publishing—the protagonist of *The Warren Spahn Story* was a hero in every situation, from loving son to brave soldier to stand-out Major League pitcher. For example, Shapiro described how a young Spahn worried aloud to the doctor that a season-ending shoulder injury in the minor leagues made his father's illness worse, and in the book, the father recovered only after the shoulder did.[17] Shapiro fixated on Spahn's relationship with his father, claiming that his father taught him to play baseball and to pitch in afternoon sessions in the backyard. He wrote that the elder Spahn gave his young son a first-baseman's mitt for a birthday present and later counseled him to delay signing with the Braves until after he graduated from high school.[18]

As a soldier and husband, Spahn was described in the most glowing terms: Shapiro credited him with winning the Bronze Star for valor at the Battle of the Bulge.[19] He later emphasized Spahn's leadership in battle again, claiming that Spahn went from man to man "urging them on" during German bombing runs while his unit rebuilt the bridge over the Rhine at Remagen.[20] When the hero returned home from war, Shapiro wrote that he chose to surprise his fiancé and romantically showed up at her door: when she answered, he "swept [her] off her feet and carried her into the room . . . as he swung her around in his arms."[21] The fictional Spahn was flawless, and that laudatory portrayal rankled the real Warren Spahn so much that he filed a privacy lawsuit asking for an injunction to stop future publication of the book and for $175,000 cash damages because of the violation of his right of privacy.[22]

THE CIVIL TRIAL OF JULIAN MESSNER INC.

In his written decision after the trial, Judge Jacob Markowitz began by acknowledging that Spahn was a "baseball pitcher of wide renown and acclaim,"
establishing that Spahn was a public figure, a celebrity.[23] Although this would
be an important issue, Spahn needed to establish that this book "fictionalized" his life story, invaded his private life, and commercially exploited his
name and image. The publisher's lawyers argued simply that the book was
protected under the First Amendment of the U.S. Constitution.

New York was one the first states to legislate the right of privacy. In 1902
the New York Court of Appeals resoundingly rejected the idea of a right of
privacy, ruling against a woman who had sued a manufacturer that had used
her picture without her consent on their advertising circulars. The majority
feared that creating a right of privacy would open "a vast field of litigation."[24]
State legislators felt differently, and they promptly enacted Section 50 of Article 5 of the Civil Rights Law, which read: "A person, firm or corporation that
uses for advertising purposes, or for the purposes of trade, the name, portrait or picture of any living person without having first obtained the written
consent of such person . . . is guilty of a misdemeanor."[25] Spahn relied on this
New York law and the four-part right of privacy articulated by Dean William
Prosser in 1960. These included: the right to prevent widespread publicity
concerning personal information; the right to be free from intrusions into
one's solitude; the right to control the use of one's own name and image for
commercial enterprises; and the right to be free of publicity that casts one
in a false light—that is, publicity that tells the truth of sorts but presents it
in a way that has the same effect as a lie. Julian Messner Inc. argued that in
this case, Warren Spahn was, as a well-known professional baseball player,
outside the New York law's purview and that using the right of privacy to
protect Spahn in this case would unfairly and unconstitutionally infringe on
Julian Messner Inc.'s rights under the First Amendment.

Judge Markowitz looked to balance Spahn's rights with the publisher's
rights of free press. Although the decision in *New York Times Co. v. Sullivan*,
requiring actual malice of public officials, had been rendered by the Supreme
Court in 1960, Markowitz declined to apply it because Spahn was not a public
official. Markowitz did acknowledge that the First Amendment and the right
of privacy required a court to balance those sometimes-competing interests,
but he argued that the First Amendment did not immunize a publishing
house from all liability of an inaccurate and essentially fictionalized biography. He seemed, though, to give more weight to the defense's argument that

because Spahn was a public figure, he had no privacy rights. While the judge was unwilling to say that public figures had no privacy rights, he did agree that "the public figure's right of privacy is, however, far from absolute."[26] Judge Markowitz argued that it was up to the court to decide, based on the facts of each individual circumstance, where the line between the private and public parts of a public figure's life resided. In the case of the Spahn book, Markowitz noted that Shapiro had covered aspects of Spahn's public life (his career and statistics as a baseball player) and his private life (his thoughts about and relationships with his family and teammates). Markowitz concluded that Shapiro's research for the book was shoddy and that, because the book itself was riddled with factual errors and inaccurate implications, the book was not news but rather a fictionalized biography not protected by the First Amendment. He noted the factual errors in great detail, while acknowledging that (due to space constraints) he did not list them all.

In his decision, the judge noted that Spahn had established that many of the stories articulated in the book were false. Spahn categorically denied that he had ever worried that his injury (which was to his elbow and not his shoulder) in the minor leagues had exacerbated his father's illness, and thus he had never had such a conversation with the doctor as described in the book. The judge noted that Spahn's father had not taught him to pitch and had never given him a first baseman's mitt. Furthermore, Spahn insisted that he did not have extensive discussions with his father about when to sign with the Braves; in fact, it was his mother who signed the contracts for him because he was not yet of age.[27] Additionally, the judge wrote that far from surprising his fiancé with his return from World War II, she had met him at the train station. During the trial, Spahn's legal team provided a long list of factual errors and inaccurate implications within the book. And perhaps the factual error that frustrated the court most was that, according to Judge Markowitz, Warren Spahn had not won the Bronze Star, awarded to a military service person for heroic or meritorious achievement, for his service in the Battle of the Bulge.[28]

The judge noted that the basic error about the Bronze Star was reflected in the entire tenor of the description of Spahn's wartime experiences. Markowitz concluded that Spahn had proved that "the heroics attributed to him constituted a gross nonfactual and embarrassing distortion."[29] In the book, Shapiro described how Spahn was awarded the Purple Heart for a serious wound to his foot.[30] According to Shapiro, Spahn and his unit, the 9th Armored Division of the 276th Engineer Combat Battalion, were in Remagen, Germany, working "under shellfire and bombardment to repair the damaged span over the Rhine," when Spahn suffered the injury that "came close to ending it all for Warren."[31] Shapiro wrote that Spahn was treated by a medic in the field and then was "rolled . . . onto a stretcher."[32] Spahn established that he was never unable to walk and that he was treated only at the first-aid station,[33] suggesting that Spahn was not in any mortal danger from the wound, as Shapiro implied.

At trial, Shapiro admitted that he had never interviewed Spahn, his family, his friends, or anyone who knew him directly, nor did he obtain any information from Spahn's baseball team. Instead, Shapiro indicated that he relied on newspaper articles, magazine stories, and general books to develop the situations and that he "created dialogue based upon a secondary source."[34] The publishing-house lawyers argued that this was standard practice for juvenile biographies, but the judge did not find that to be a persuasive legal justification. On the contrary, Judge Markowitz concluded that the book "publiciz[ed] areas of Warren Spahn's personal and private life, albeit inaccurate and distorted, and consist[ed] of a host . . . of factual errors, distortions and fanciful passages. . . . [T]he offending characteristics of the book comprehend a nonfactual novelization of the plaintiff's alleged life story and an unauthorized intrusion into the private realms of the baseball pitcher's life—all to Spahn's humiliation and mental anguish."[35] Going even further, Judge Markowitz began to separate Spahn's life as celebrity from his life as a person. Markowitz concluded that by describing Spahn's intimate private relationships with his wife and family, Shapiro had moved beyond the boundaries of Spahn's public life and that which was fair to comment upon. As a result, he ruled in favor of Spahn, concluding that Shapiro and Julian Messner Inc. had "used Spahn's name and pictures to enhance the marketability and financial success of the subject book" and that Section 50 of the New York law and all four of Prosser's privacy torts had been violated. At that point (May 28, 1964) about sixteen thousand copies of the book had sold for $3.25 each, so Judge Markowitz ordered Julian Messner to pay Spahn $10,000 in damages and to stop further publication of *The Warren Spahn Story*.

THE APPEALS

It is not surprising that, given that Julian Messner Inc. had disposable cash because of the success of *Peyton Place* and because a large portion of its list contained biographies—specifically juvenile biographies (many by Milton J. Shapiro)—the publishing house appealed the decision. Warren Spahn also appealed, asking for greater compensatory damages. Because neither Shapiro nor anyone from Julian Messner Inc. contested Spahn's assertion that the dialogue was fabricated and that the facts were inaccurate, the important part of the lawsuit, and the reason perhaps that the publishing house spent the time and money on multiple appeals, was the question as to what degree of privacy a public figure is afforded in published biographies.

The Supreme Court of New York, Appellate Division, heard the appeal, and Judge Charles D. Breitel wrote for the unanimous four-person court, which included Judges Benjamin J. Rabin, James B. M. McNally, and Harold A. Stevens. Judge Breitel concluded that only one significant issue was at hand: the question of whether the publication of the book was exempt from the New York law about utilizing someone's name or image for advertising or trade purposes. He concluded that the book was not exempt, even though Spahn was a public figure.

The appellate court rejected Spahn's request for more money for two simple reasons: the book was laudatory, and Spahn was a baseball hero who had "long permitted widespread exploitation" of his performance on the diamond. The court would later note that while these were the very reasons Julian Messner Inc. argued that the book itself was privileged under the First Amendment, these reasons were only relevant to the assessment of damages.[36]

Next, the appellate court addressed Julian Messner Inc.'s argument that in order to find an audience, juvenile biography needed to be fictionalized with created dialogue, adjusted chronologies, and imagined events. The court acknowledged that this might be true, but concluded that even public figures had the right to control a fictionalized image from which someone else was profiting. The court rejected the defense's argument that getting public figures to consent to publication would be too expensive, noting all the publisher had to do to avoid obtaining a living public figure's consent was to limit itself to factual biographies. The court concluded, "Nor will the children who read suffer unduly if the biographies purveyed for their reading are restricted to the duller factual ones or only to the livelier ones for which the subjects, if living, have given their written consents."[37] The court also rejected Julian Messner Inc.'s argument that because the fictionalization was laudatory, Spahn's privacy was not invaded. Judge Breitel called that argument "immaterial" and noted that "laudatory treatment may make one appear more ridiculous," adding that determining what was laudatory might be difficult.[38] The appellate court confirmed the verdict as well as the damages Judge Markowitz had imposed.

Undeterred, Julian Messner Inc. appealed to the highest state court in New York in 1966.[39] Judge Kenneth Keating began the unanimous decision with an acknowledgment that Warren Spahn was one of the "great left-handed pitchers" in baseball and that baseball was one of the most popular pastimes in America. He added, "Professional privacy is thus the very antithesis of the player's need and goal."[40] Despite this signal that the court was a bit suspect of protecting a public figure's privacy, the court affirmed the lower court's decision, noting that while Spahn's baseball career was public information, his "personality" could not be fictionalized and then published and promoted as a biography. Julian Messner Inc. again argued that the *New York Times Co. v. Sullivan* decision should raise the bar, that Spahn should have to prove actual malice and intentional falsity or reckless disregard for the truth, but Judge Keating found no public interest to be served in protecting publications of "fictitious" biographies and refused to apply the standard to a public figure who was not a public official.[41]

In 1967 Julian Messner Inc. received a short reprieve. Nationally, the state of privacy law and how to balance the interests of the press with those of the public figure were in flux. That year, the U.S. Supreme Court ruled that in privacy cases, just as in defamation cases, public figures were required to prove actual malice under the *New York Times Co. v. Sullivan* decision; they were to prove that the information was published with knowledge of the inaccuracy or in reckless disregard of the truth.[42] Relying on this new decision, Julian Messner Inc. appealed this case to the U.S. Supreme Court, which ordered the decision vacated (set aside) and the matter remanded back to the state court to reconsider in light of their new decision.[43] The New York court presumed that the U.S. Supreme Court had found fault with the fact that at every level of the New York system, the New York courts had explicitly declined to apply the *Sullivan* actual-malice standard to Spahn's case. Therefore, the New York high court took the opportunity, first, to establish that the state laws on image and the rights of privacy were constitutional and, second, to consider Spahn's specific case in light of the new burden of proof itself. Thus Shapiro's research and literary techniques were closely examined.

Rather than arguing that he was accurate in his facts, Shapiro and Julian Messner Inc.'s attorneys argued that facts were not as important as telling a good story in juvenile biographies, and that the literary techniques in his "instant biography" were "customary" in the genre. In a brief submitted to the court, the defense quoted an expert critic, teacher, and author who said dialogue was "'created, and based on probable facts and possible dialogue, which the biographer . . . through the vast amount of research . . . can assume might have happened.' . . . Basically a juvenile biography 'has to be a lively story to catch the youngster away from television.'"[44] The court did not consider this explanation of the genre to be an adequate defense.

In the fourth published decision regarding this matter, the majority of the highest court in New York State again considered whether Spahn's privacy rights were violated, and for the fourth time the court concluded that they were. The court noted that the defense never argued that the book was not published with reckless disregard for the falsity of its contents, rather that the author and publisher simply justified it as a matter of literary technique and economic expedience.

The court noted specifically the story of the Bronze Star: Shapiro published that Spahn had received the award, and Spahn categorically stated that he never had. The defense offered evidence that Shapiro had actually researched the issue and that the Department of the Army said they had no record of Spahn winning the award; instead, the army told Shapiro that their records were incomplete and that if Spahn claimed he had won the award, there was no reason not to believe him. Shapiro, therefore, gave the fictionalized Spahn the Bronze Star even though he admitted Warren Spahn never claimed to have won it.[45] The court took this example as further proof that the book was published with reckless disregard for its inaccuracies and reinstated the original judgment.

In his dissent, Judge Francis Bergan argued that if the U.S. Supreme Court had agreed that Spahn had met the actual-malice standard, the Court would not have vacated the judgment. He added that the case should be sent back to the trial court for a matter of review. He argued that if a person chose to be a public figure, New York law should not protect that person from "fictionalization not shown to hurt him and not . . . designed to hurt him." Judge Bergan noted that the court should consider "calculated falsehood" rather than simple falsity because all fiction by definition is false. Julian Messner Inc. clearly preferred Judge Bergan's dissent, and appealed this decision as well, but the U.S. Supreme Court dismissed the case without comment.[46]

IMPACT OF THE CASE

The extensive legal battle between Julian Messner Inc. and Warren Spahn helped to shape the law of privacy in the United States and showed how deeply invested the parties were in the matter. Legally, the case established that live public figures have a right to control their images and a right to their privacy when the description extends into their private lives. These public figures cannot be "fictionalized" without their permission, regardless of literary techniques, if that fictionalization is presented as biography. While Spahn was alive, an author might have been able to publish a story of a fictional baseball character named Warren Spahn who lived in the nineteenth century. Similarly, factual biographies were protected as were pure fictionalization using a character's name—for example, an author might have been able to publish a story about a spaceman named Warren Spahn who traveled the galaxy fighting crime.[47] Legal scholar Jonathan Kahn has argued that the implication of *Spahn* is that if a person's name is incidental, appropriation is not an issue, but if the name is central to the work and, in fact, calls attention to the work, appropriation is an issue.[48]

Part of the challenge of Spahn's battle was a question of truth and of sources. Judge Markowitz at the trial-court level clearly believed that Spahn was in control of his memory and had an appropriate interpretation of the past. Although no mention is made in the published decisions, legal scholar Isidore Silver stated in a law review article published in 1966 (prior to the fourth published *Spahn* decision) that the defense introduced evidence that Spahn himself was the source of several of the stories. The Julian Messner Inc. attorneys offered as evidence some of the newspaper articles that Shapiro had relied on that were co-authored by Spahn himself. When confronted with this evidence, Spahn argued that the implication that he was the source of the information was not true, and that he had not seen those portions of the articles prior to their publication.[49] Silver argued that "even if [a book] is written in a racy and informal style which entertains as well as informs, it would still be entitled to some sort of constitutional protection."[50] Silver argued also that using secondary sources like newspapers and magazines was a legitimate form of research, worrying that "'truth is elusive, especially when the biographer attempts to assess character, which is the heart of the average biography." Silver maintained that the *Spahn* case was wrongly decided.[51] Silver raised the significant specter of the courts determining what was acceptable research and of the courts' determining past truths or true history.

In 1989 legal scholar Diane Leenheer Zimmerman agreed with Silver, arguing that because of the uncertain nature of truth and the precarious balance between the public's legitimate interest in public figures' lives and the right of defamation, the false-light branch of the privacy tort should be pruned.[52] Both scholars argued that defamation would still protect egregious violations of privacy that false light only partly protected. In the twenty-first century, *Spahn* has not been overturned in the state of New York; however, New York has subsequently adopted Zimmerman's proposal and does not recognize the false-light tort of privacy.[53]

The decision stopped publication of fictional biographies of living public figures without their consent. Even further, scholars have argued that the *Spahn* decision forced authors and directors of unauthorized biographies and docudramas to be certain of the relative accuracy of their portrayals and to avoid wholesale creation of scenes and relationships even if they are not negative in their portrayal.[54] When Spahn was alive, other authors did write juvenile biographies based on his public baseball career. For example, Al Silverman's book *Warren Spahn: Immortal Southpaw* was published in 1961 without apparent protest from Spahn. The book, also written in a laudatory, gee-whiz style, focused on Spahn's baseball career and public details of his life, offering no imagined dialogue.[55]

The independent publishing house of Julian Messner Inc. did not survive even as long as the appeals of the lawsuit. Kathryn G. Messner, the publisher at the time of *The Warren Spahn Story*'s publication in 1958, died in 1964 before the legal battle ended. In December 1964, Pocket Books acquired Julian Messner Inc. Leon Shimpkin, the president of Pocket Books, specifically wanted Julian Messner Inc.'s backlist of children's books—including *The Warren Spahn Story*—so the continuation of the lawsuit appeals, despite the change in ownership, was not surprising.[56] Julian Messner Inc. remained somewhat autonomous and continued publishing under its own label, first with Pocket Books and then with Simon and Schuster throughout the mid-1990s.

Interestingly, Pocket Books, as the successor to Julian Messner Inc., did survive a 1967 attempt by three other MLB players to follow Spahn's game plan. Don Drysdale (a pitcher for the Los Angeles Dodgers), Hank Aaron (Spahn's teammate with the Braves), and Eddie Mathews (with the Houston Astros), each filed separate lawsuits against the publisher, claiming that the juvenile biographies the company published were inaccurate and violated the same New York state laws that Spahn had claimed. All three players used Spahn's lawyer, and each asked for an injunction to stop publication. Milton J. Shapiro, author of *The Warren Spahn Story*, wrote the books about Drysdale and Aaron, and Al Hirshberg, who had published a book on Spahn with a different press, wrote the book about Mathews.[57] The lawsuits were filed after the U.S. Supreme Court ordered a rehearing of the Spahn case but before that rehearing occurred. In August 1967 the lawsuits were dismissed because the players' lawyer failed to file a formal complaint.[58] No public explanation as to why the lawyer failed to continue with the cases exists.

While Julian Messner Inc. and Milton J. Shapiro's investment in the proceedings might be self-evident (fictionalized biographies made them money), Spahn's persistence in the case is more complicated, and what it reveals about his personality is subtle. His amazing career as a Major Leaguer is undisputed: he was elected to the Baseball Hall of Fame the first year he was eligible. He was arguably the greatest left-handed pitcher of all time, and his impressive list of wins (363 in MLB, the most by a left-handed pitcher) might have been longer had his career not been delayed by his stint in the army during World War II. His baseball prowess made his status as a public figure undeniable.

Spahn's perseverance is also reflected in both his baseball career and this case: in baseball he pitched nineteen seasons with the Braves, yet when the team sent him to the Mets at age forty-three, he did not retire. He tried to pitch the next season with two other teams. Even after Major League Baseball executives clearly believed he was finished as a pitcher, Spahn refused to quit. He reportedly liked to say, "I did not retire. . . . Baseball retired me," and after leaving MLB, he pitched in Mexico, where he was also a pitching coach.[59] Nor did he quit when the defendants kept appealing this lawsuit.

Spahn's persistence is also explained in a conversation he had with legal scholar Ray Yasser when the two discussed the case years later at a baseball-card signing. Yasser wrote:

> My recollection is that the gist of Spahn's account was that it was simply wrong to just make up stories about someone. Spahn thought that the falsity hurt him in a variety of ways. Insofar as the false portrayal of his relationship with his father was concerned, Spahn thought it sent a false message to youngsters that sports prowess turned on a positive relationship between a father and a son. Insofar as the depiction of his military experience was concerned, Spahn was embarrassed by the way the author glorified Spahn's experience. Spahn also was concerned that some people would think he planted the account to make himself look heroic. Spahn was upset that entirely invented dialogue could be foisted upon readers, and sold as true accounts. Spahn went on at some length about how it was not about money—that, in fact, the case cost him significantly—but it was about vindicating what he thought to be an important principle—that truth matters.[60]

Ironically, years later, defining the "truth" of Spahn's life is challenging, if not impossible.

THE MYSTERIES OF WARREN SPAHN

Warren Spahn died on November 24, 2003, in Broken Arrow, Oklahoma, yet his life remains shrouded in myth. In spite or perhaps because of all the published mini-biographies and media stories, tales of Spahn's life abound and yet also conflict. The stories surrounding his first demotion from the Major Leagues and his time with manager Casey Stengel reflect that conflict. Shapiro's biography claimed that Stengel saw beyond Spahn's 5.63 ERA in several games at the end of the 1942 season and that Stengel told a sportswriter that someday Spahn would be the best left-handed pitcher in baseball.[61] While that source is obviously suspect, the myth was repeated.[62] Other versions of the story claim that Spahn refused Stengel's orders to throw a beanball at Pee Wee Reese and was demoted from the Braves at the beginning of one season with the announcement from Stengel that "you'll never win in the major leagues."[63] Spahn himself is quoted as saying, "I'm probably the only guy who worked for Casey Stengel before and after he was a genius," which suggests that the Shapiro story was a myth.[64] Similar gaps exist about Spahn's entry into the army. Some authors claim he enlisted in during World War II,[65] others that he was drafted.[66] Given that he entered the army in 1942 at age 21, almost a full year after the attack on Pearl Harbor and after his first few games playing in the Major Leagues, it seems more likely that he was drafted.

The most convoluted of the myths surrounding Spahn's life is the story of the Bronze Star. The first reference I found asserting that Spahn had won the award was in Milton Shapiro's 1958 biography.[67] Although eventually the publication of the book was suspended, at least ten thousand copies were already in existence, and even in 2015, copies could be purchased online for $28. The distribution of the book was widespread enough that the myth became almost institutionalized as more and more people included Shapiro's assertion in their own work. And yet Shapiro's book has little detail about the circumstances in which Spahn allegedly won the Bronze Star. There is but one paragraph describing the 1944 Battle of the Bulge and giving an overview of the challenges that Spahn's division faced.[68] The book has a detailed description of how Spahn was injured (which resulted in his being awarded a Purple Heart), an honor he clearly did win, so the dearth of information about the Bronze Star is surprising. Or it would be surprising if the story were true. In the first published legal decision, Judge Markowitz accepted Spahn's lawyers' assertion that Spahn had not won the Bronze Star, and that was part of his reasoning for ruling in Spahn's favor. Given this legal documentation of Spahn's assertion that he did not win a Bronze Star, one must assume that

Spahn did not win a Bronze Star during the war for his bravery at the Battle of the Bulge.

Nevertheless, the story persisted in so many places that, as a researcher, I began to doubt what I initially believed. That doubt increased when I read Ray Yasser's article, which included a footnote wherein Greg Spahn, Warren's son, asserted that his father had won two Bronze Stars and that they were at the Ivan Allen Jr. Braves Museum and Hall of Fame at Turner Field in Atlanta, Georgia.[69] I called the museum to confirm the presence of the Bronze Stars and to prove once and for all to myself that somehow Judge Markowitz had gotten it wrong and that Shapiro was right (no matter what Spahn's lawyers had asserted). It took several days for the museum director to return my phone call, and in the interim a colleague and her brother agreed to go to the museum to get a photo. There was no Bronze Star in the Warren Spahn exhibit, so my colleague's brother asked the staff about it. The staff insisted the museum had no Bronze Star belonging to Warren Spahn.[70]

That would have been the end of it except that the next day, the museum's director left me a phone message telling me that Warren Spahn's Bronze Star was in the museum's archives. My colleague in Atlanta pursued the matter directly. She was able to reach the director via phone and the director agreed to look for the Bronze Star in the archives and perhaps pull it for a photograph. Within days, though, the director contacted my colleague via email and told her that she had been mistaken: the museum did not have Warren Spahn's Bronze Star, but rather they had briefly had possession of another person's Bronze Star, which had been returned.[71]

The myth of the Bronze Star is further complicated by the fact that the military did not keep detailed records of who won the medal during World War II. Military representatives told the Julian Messner Inc. lawyers that if Spahn said he had won the award, he probably had.[72] The Bronze Star, created during World War II, can be awarded "to any person who, while serving in any capacity in or with the Army of the United States after 6 December 1941, distinguished himself or herself by heroic or meritorious achievement or service, not involving participation in aerial flight, in connection with military operations against an armed enemy."[73] The situation is even more convoluted because Bronze Stars could be awarded retroactively:

> Award may be made . . . to each member of the Armed Forces of the United States who, after 6 December 1941, has been cited in orders or awarded a certificate for exemplary conduct in ground combat against an armed enemy between 7 December 1941 and 2 September 1945, inclusive, or whose meritori-

ous achievement has been otherwise confirmed by documents executed prior to 1 July 1947. For this purpose, an award of the Combat Infantryman Badge or Combat Medical Badge is considered as a citation in orders.[74]

Spahn's unit did apparently receive the Distinguished Unit Citation for repairing the Ludendorff Bridge while under attack. The army did make some soldiers (in a Pacific campaign in which Spahn was not a part) eligible for a Bronze Star if they had been awarded a Distinguished Unit Citation.[75] Thus it seems possible that Spahn was awarded a Bronze Star later, but it appears unlikely that he was aware of or willing to admit such a retroactive award.

CONCLUSION

On the face of it, this case seems relatively minor, but its implications rippled through the world of law, publishing, and baseball history. The very existence of the lawsuit seems almost trivial. Yet from a legal perspective this lawsuit was important in establishing that public figures did have a right of privacy in New York and that laudatory overstatement could be a violation of the false-light prong. Pragmatically, the false-light prong in New York did not last much beyond this case, but the right of privacy on the whole remains. In the publishing world, the style of juvenile biographies moved away from the stylized recreation of emotion and dialogue done without the subject's approval. For baseball historians, the facts of the case seem to have been lost, as even the Web site of the Society for American Baseball Research (SABR) in 2015 credited Spahn with winning a Bronze Star.[76]

Who gets angry enough to spend years, money, and energy trying to stop publication of a book that paints a portrait of someone too good to be true? Warren Spahn might be the only one. This was the lawsuit filed by a man who wanted to set the record straight about his life, who wanted to make sure that his accomplishments were not unjustly compared to those who died in World War II, those Spahn felt were real heroes. He wanted to control his image, what he believed was his real identity.

Spahn may have won his lawsuit and may have given future subjects of biographies greater legal protections to ensure the "truth" of their lives, but the myths that Milton J. Shapiro created have endured far beyond Warren Spahn's death. Despite his amazing baseball career and his service in World War II, which should have been heroic enough, when Spahn died, many of his obituaries reported that he had won the Bronze Star.[77]

4

SUPER BOWL ICON OR MARKETING TOOL?

MONTANA v. SAN JOSE MERCURY NEWS (1995)

Joe Montana was an outstanding quarterback. Countless sports articles, blogs, and football junkies have debated whether he was the best quarterback ever to play in the National Football League (NFL).[1] After leading the San Francisco 49ers to victory in each of the team's four Super Bowl appearances (1982, 1985, 1989, and 1990) and being named the Most Valuable Player in all but the 1989 game, Montana was also a valuable commodity. His endorsements during that time spanned a range of products, including razors,[2] video games,[3] and underwear.[4] Montana's image had value, not just for him and the companies whose products he endorsed, but his image was also valuable to the media because he was newsworthy. It is not surprising that after each Super Bowl victory, a local newspaper (but one with a growing national reputation), the *San Jose Mercury News*, published action photographs that included the winning quarterback. Without question, these photographs were protected as newsworthy under the freedom of press clause of the First Amendment of the United States Constitution. After the fourth Super Bowl victory, the *Mercury News* published and sold posters of the photos of Montana from the Super Bowls. Montana felt that the use of his photographs in these posters was a violation of his right of publicity—that the newspaper had used his image without his permission and profited from it. Montana sued and the result was a victory for the press that complicated the legal debate about what was newsworthy and what was merely marketing.

JUST JOE

Joe Montana was born in 1956 in New Eagle, Pennsylvania. This small town is located near Pittsburgh, in a region noted for its mines, mills, and quarterbacks—George Blanda (Youngwood), Johnny Unitas (Pittsburgh), and Joe Namath (Beaver Falls), as well as Montana's contemporary, Dan Marino (Pittsburgh), were all born in the area.[5] Montana was the only child of Theresa and Joe Montana Sr.; his parents worked at the Civic Finance Company. Montana's almost mythologized youth included stories about how his father lied on the entry forms so that Joe Jr. could play peewee football at age eight instead of the league-minimum age nine and how his father would not let Joe Jr. quit football at age eleven to join the Boy Scouts with his friends because he had made a commitment to the team. Montana credited his father with teaching him to "deal with any obstacle and fight through it" in part by tripping him during pick-up basketball games.[6] Montana's description of his childhood in his 1986 autobiography described parents who supported his athletic goals without question and perhaps lived out their dreams through him. His father, who had played baseball as a sailor in the navy and loved sports, was so devoted to his son's sporting pursuits that he rented a gym so that the younger Montana and his friends could play organized basketball before entering high school.[7]

At least partly because of his father's love of the school, Montana enrolled at Notre Dame in 1974 and played college football there. One of seven quarterbacks entering the school as first-year players, Montana played on the scout team and rarely saw game time in the freshmen games (at that time freshmen were ineligible for the varsity squad). Prior to Montana's sophomore year, Dan Devine replaced Ara Parseghian as head coach, and Montana tended to be substituted into games after other quarterbacks' injuries or failures. On several occasions he led the Irish to fourth-quarter victories, but he never solidified his hold on the position of starting quarterback until his senior season. Although Notre Dame won the national championship in 1977, Montana's most famous collegiate victory was the January 1, 1979, Cotton Bowl in Dallas, when he passed for a touchdown to tie the game as the clock expired. The extra point meant the Irish beat the University of Houston, 35–34. Despite the team's overall success and Montana's legendary games, Montana later described his years at Notre Dame as being "filled with doubt and frustration," which he credited with ultimately preparing him for the challenges of the professional game.[8]

Bill Walsh, the coach and general manager of the San Francisco 49ers, drafted Montana in the third round of the 1979 draft as the team's quarterback of the future. He was the eighty-second pick of the draft, and years later speculation about why he was drafted so low centered on the scouting reports that he lacked a strong arm and had problems working with the Notre

Dame coach. Walsh recalled that when Montana worked out for him before the draft, Walsh particularly liked his "quick, nimble, Joe Namath–type feet." Montana signed his first pro contract for a reported $50,000/$70,000/$85,000 scale over three years, with a $50,000 signing bonus.[9]

Just as in high school and college, Montana did not walk into the starting position. During his first two years, Montana played only in relatively safe moments inside the opponents' 50-yard line with comparatively little pressure on him, while Steve DeBerg started. Montana credited his being eased into the league, as well as Walsh's system, with helping him to develop more confidence.[10] Just prior to the 1981 season, the 49ers traded DeBerg, and Montana became the team's quarterback. Happily for Montana and 49ers' fans, the team won the Super Bowl that season by defeating the Cincinnati Bengals in January 1982.[11]

After the victory, Montana was given a $1.7 million four-year contract and was offered many new endorsements as the ill-fated 1982 season began. He did so many commercials that some blamed the 49ers' poor performance during the 1982 strike-shortened season on his absences. Montana, in fact, had opposed the strike, something some of his teammates blamed on his large contract, but when the team supported the players' union and walked out after week two, Montana joined them. He would later say that the strike so divided the team that they were never again unified enough to win consistently.[12] Bill Walsh disagreed and blamed the team's complacency, drug use, and other distractions. He considered Montana the primary example of the distracted player, fixated on his many commitments and his travel. Walsh and the local paper agreed that Montana's extensive commitments affected his conditioning and his performance. This would be the beginning of a rocky relationship between the coach and the quarterback.[13] Montana, for his part, argued that the appearances and commercial work only affected his off days and insisted that he never missed practice.[14]

The team won the Super Bowl again at the end of the 1984 season, beating Dan Marino and the Miami Dolphins. Montana was rewarded with a new, six-year contract worth $6.3 million.[15] The 1985 season, though, started badly for the 49ers after they lost four of their first seven games. Bill Walsh again blamed distractions, telling the press that he believed Montana was more focused on the impending birth of his first child than he was on football. After the baby was born, Walsh and the press stopped blaming Montana for the team's play, although the team did not make it past the first round of the playoffs.[16]

Two weeks into the 1986 season, Montana underwent back surgery, and many people, including his coach, suspected his career was over. He returned to the field in fifty-five days and played eight weeks after surgery. Unfortunately for the team and Montana, the New York Giants handily won their playoff game with the 49ers, knocking Montana unconscious and out of the game. Before the 1987 season, as insurance because of Montana's back as well as his cumulative injuries, Bill Walsh acquired Steve Young, the quarterback for the Tampa Bay Buccaneers who had once been a highly paid player in the failed United States Football League. Adding Young was a logical move, given Montana's history, but it ended up changing Montana's relationship with Walsh and the 49ers.

The 1987 season was also interrupted by a player's strike. After a one-week bye to allow teams to find replacement players, the season resumed. Following the first replacement-player game, rumors leaked that several of the 49ers' starters, including Montana, would cross the picket line and play in the next game. Walsh, concerned that the return of key players would disrupt locker-room harmony when the strike ended, encouraged the players to wait one more week. They did so, but when the strike ended several weeks later, the team had some internal issues. Any difference in the team members' opinions regarding the strike was not reflected in their play. Although still winning games, an injured Montana was replaced by Young, who performed well in several games. Montana started the NFC divisional playoff game against the Minnesota Vikings, but he played so poorly that Steve Young replaced him during the third quarter. The 49ers lost the game, and a quarterback controversy began.

Prior to the 1988 season, rumors that Montana was on the trading block flew around the league. Walsh furiously told the press that Montana was not being traded, but Walsh's biographer David Harris wrote that Walsh had considered it, given Montana's health history and Young's potential. The rumors made Montana worried for his job, and as a result he tried to conceal an injury during the first game of the season. Despite his efforts, the coaches noticed and replaced him with Young, who again played well. Consequently, Young started game 2, but after a poor first half, Montana was substituted in for him. The two took turns starting various games during the first eleven games of the season. Beginning in week 12, however, Montana took over and played well for the rest of the season, leading the team to a third Super Bowl victory.[17] Walsh retired at the end of that season, and George Seifert, the defensive coordinator, was named the new head coach. The 1989 49ers won fourteen of their sixteen games that season, capturing the team's fourth Super Bowl victory and giving Montana and the team back-to-back Super Bowl victories.

The Super Bowl victories further established Montana as a celebrity, and he bemoaned the loss of privacy in his 1986 autobiography, writing, "I have this fantasy about privacy. . . . [W]hy not football without fanfare? . . . No interviews, no people to meet, nobody trying to pick my brain."[18] While acknowledging that he appreciated the financial opportunities linked to his celebrity status, he bemoaned the inability to eat a meal in public without being interrupted to sign autographs. Montana, a self-described "quiet," "regular guy," was not comfortable with the tension between fame and endorsements as well as the loss of privacy, both of which resulted from celebrity.[19] Worth noting is the fact that Montana had lost much of his privacy even before winning the Super Bowls. During the 1981 playoff run, the 49ers hired a bodyguard for him after Montana received death threats. The bodyguard, Jim Warren, stayed with Montana for the remainder of his 49ers career.[20]

Montana seemed to have a particularly prickly relationship with the press. In a 1990 *Sports Illustrated* article, Paul Zimmerman wrote that Montana was regarded as a "lesser god" in his hometown of Monongahela, Pennsylvania. Apparently, Montana and his old high school football coach, Chuck Abramski, were not on the best of terms, and just before the Super Bowl that year, an article in the *Baltimore Sun* quoted the coach as saying, among other less-than-flattering things, "If I was in a war, I wouldn't want Joe on my side . . . his dad would have to carry his gun for him." Montana later said that Abramski was angry because he had never gotten an autograph and that he still resented Montana's absence from Abramski's summer weight program in high school; Montana had been playing American Legion baseball and summer basketball instead. In 1990 Zimmerman went with Montana back to Monongahela to hear Montana speak at a dinner; Zimmerman observed, "There was an edge to Montana's return." He reported on a *Pittsburgh Post-Gazette* article that had run the previous week, which said Montana was not popular in the area because he no longer visited, and the locals felt betrayed when he and his parents moved permanently to California. Zimmerman blamed the feelings and the stories on Montana's desire for privacy. Montana had visited the area to see relatives but had not appeared publicly because he wanted to spend time only with family and bemoaned the attention he received when he dined out.[21]

In his autobiography, Montana seemed antagonistic toward the press. He accused reporters of taking his quotes out of context and of deliberately timing negative stories about the 49ers to maximize damage to the team. Further, his personal life was the subject of gossip and rumor. Montana had been married twice (once to his high-school sweetheart, Kim Moses, while a student at Notre Dame, and then to flight attendant Cass Castillo from 1981 to 1984). He met his third wife, Jennifer Wallace, during a commercial shoot and married her in early 1985. The combination of Montana's success on the field and his third marriage was grist for the gossip mills that followed the dashing quarterback. Stories about Montana speeding through the Bay Area in his red Ferrari abounded, even though the car was garaged in Los Angeles, and those stories resurfaced when he was in Atlanta playing the Falcons. Montana himself was rumored to be addicted to cocaine. His wife Jennifer told a story of watching the local news and seeing a photo of Montana with the word "drugs" underneath it and feeling frustrated at being unable to do anything to protect him.[22] His coach, Bill Walsh, considered the rumors to be "absolutely ridiculous" but because of the persistent innuendos, which he said "always surfaced after Joe had had an average game," the team violated its own policy of not commenting on drug use or reports of drug use among the team. At the press conference, Montana denied using drugs and challenged the reporters to present him with any evidence of his alleged use.[23] The event seemed to have no effect, as the next day a reporter with the *San Jose Mercury News* called Montana's agent to confirm rumors that Montana had checked into a drug rehabilitation center. He had not, but Montana was irate enough to call the reporter "obtuse and shallow" in his autobiography.[24]

Montana was caught between multiple desires. On the one hand, he bemoaned his lack of privacy and the desire of his fans to have greater and greater access to him. He distrusted the press, who he felt had unfairly and inaccurately represented him in its reporting. On the other hand, Montana sold his name and his face in the form of endorsements. He benefited financially from his celebrity. Being a celebrity usually means loss of privacy and the ability to profit from one's image, but it also means a greater loss of control over that image and reputation because of the public's desire for an intimate relationship with whom they imagine the celebrity to be. Montana wanted to choose when he was left alone, he wanted to control his public reputation, and he wanted to profit from his name and image. This is a difficult balancing act, and one way to try to achieve balance is to control your name and visual representation and make sure no one else profits without giving you a cut.

SAN JOSE MERCURY NEWS BACKGROUND

San Jose was California's first state capital in 1850 and as such it needed newspapers. The next year, two partisan papers, the *California State Journal* and the *Daily Argus*, began publishing with the opening of the second state legislative session. Neither paper would be around for the next session, but then neither would the state legislature return to San Jose after March 1851.[25]

The departure of the state legislature made the town a quieter place, and the *Visitor Weekly*, which began publishing in June 1851, became the local newspaper. It had multiple publishers over time and multiple name changes. In 1852 it was renamed the *Santa Clara Register*; the following year the name changed again to the *San Jose Telegraph and Santa Clara Register*. Throughout the name changes, the paper was a weekly publication until 1859, when it was (for just three months) a semi-weekly. In 1860 the publishers changed again, and the new publisher renamed the paper the *San Jose Mercury*, a name that would last longer than all the others. The *Mercury* faced extensive journalistic competition through the years but survived, sometimes as a daily and sometimes as a weekly paper, to the present day.[26]

The *Daily City Item*, founded in 1883 by Hugh A. DeLacey, was one of the *Mercury*'s competitors; two years later, when Charles O. Williams became the co-publisher, the name was changed to *San Jose Evening News*.[27] J. O. Hayes, the *Mercury*'s publisher, acquired the *Evening News* in 1942.[28] The two papers were published separately, one as a morning paper and one as an evening paper, until 1983, when the papers were merged into the *San Jose Mercury News* with only one paper published daily.[29] Ridder Publications had acquired both papers in 1952, and Joseph B. Ridder published the papers, along with many others in the family holding, for twenty-five years. The combined circulation during that time grew from roughly 173,000 to 811,000.[30] Ridder Publications merged with Knight Newspapers in 1974 to form one of the largest newspaper publishers in America. In part because of its location in the heart of a technology center, the Knight conglomerate chose to use the *San Jose Mercury News* to explore how to utilize the quickly growing internet in journalism. In 1993 the *San Jose Mercury Center*, an online version of the paper with many add-ons, was launched quite successfully and may have been the first full-content newspaper available entirely online. In the mid-1990s the paper had four hundred people in the newsroom, annual revenue of roughly $300 million, a bureau in Hanoi, a Sunday magazine, and foreign-language editions in Spanish and Vietnamese.[31]

THE LAWSUIT

Montana's legal issues with the *San Jose Mercury News* began in 1990 after the 49ers won their fourth Super Bowl, when the newspaper published a

"Souvenir Section" in its Sunday paper on February 4. The section, titled "Trophy Hunters," carried an artist's rendition of Montana on the first page, while on subsequent pages the paper reprinted photographs from earlier Super Bowls. The first was a photo of Montana and three other players celebrating on the field after beating the Cincinnati Bengals in Super Bowl XXIII in 1989; the second was a photo of Montana celebrating a touchdown pass against the Denver Broncos during Super Bowl XXIV in 1990. Each of the pages was reprinted in poster form within two weeks of the original publication and was available for sale to the general public for $5. About one-third of the posters sold, and the remainder were given away at charity events.[32]

Montana filed his lawsuit two years after the distribution of the posters and argued that the *Mercury News* had appropriated his name, photograph, and likeness. Montana based his lawsuit on the common-law right of publicity and the California state statute banning appropriation. To prove his case that the paper violated his common-law right of publicity, Montana needed to meet the elements of appropriation: that the *Mercury News* used his identity; that it did so to its advantage; that Montana never consented to the use of his identity; and that Montana was injured by the publication.[33] He also needed to prove the elements of § 3344 of the California Civil Code.

The California legislature first enacted California Civil Code § 3344 in 1971. The state, home to Hollywood and an untold number of celebrities, wanted to protect the economic interests of public figures by banning the use of the name, likeness, voice, or image of the public figure unless the living public figure gave consent to the use (the next subsection of the law gave protection to dead celebrities). As with all privacy and publicity laws, the courts have had to balance the economic interests of the celebrities with the rights of the press under the First Amendment, and as a result the rights of celebrities have sometimes been curtailed in favor of the rights of the press.[34]

The *Mercury News* promptly countered with a motion for summary judgment to dismiss the case prior to trial on the grounds that the poster was protected under the First Amendment and under subsection (d) of the statute, which attempted to account for the balance by acknowledging that no prior consent would be necessary for the "use of a name, . . . photograph, or likeness in connection with any news, public affairs, or sports broadcast or account, or any political campaign."[35] The trial court granted the motion for summary judgment, awarding the newspaper $20,000 in attorney's fees.[36] Montana appealed that decision, arguing that the trial court was wrong to dismiss his lawsuit.[37]

THE APPEAL

The three-person appellate court rejected Montana's appeal and affirmed the trial court's dismissal of the case on essentially two grounds. Presiding Judge Christopher Cottle wrote the majority opinion in which Judges William M. Wunderlich and Nathan D. Mihara concurred. First, the court focused on the exceptions to both the common law and the statute, the publication of matters of "public interest, which rests on the right of the public to know and the freedom of the press to tell it."[38] Further, the civil statutes specifically stated that no prior consent was required for any use of name or image in connection with "any news, public affairs, or sports broadcast."[39] Thus the California Court of Appeals ventured into the grey area of what is newsworthy and what constitutes profiting from someone else's image. Montana never argued that the *Mercury News* was wrong to use his photograph in the paper following the Super Bowl victories; he argued that the reproduction of those images as posters for resale was problematic. The appellate court disagreed and stated that his name and likeness were used in the posters "for *precisely* the same reason they appeared in the original newspaper front pages: because Montana was a major player in a contemporaneous newsworthy sports event."[40] The court noted that an earlier right of publicity claim against a documentary filmmaker by a surfer who appeared in his video was rejected because the courts concluded that the documentary about surfing was a matter of public interest and thus protected under the First Amendment.[41] This court believed that professional football was of the same, if not more, public interest in the Bay Area than surfing. Essentially, the court argued that the photographs remained newsworthy.

FOLLOWING JOE NAMATH

The other reason the court rejected Montana's appeal was that the *Mercury News* had a right to advertise itself by reprinting its work. In this section of the decision the California Court of Appeals relied on the precedence of another football player who lost his lawsuit against a popular publication: Jets quarterback Joe Namath sued *Sports Illustrated* in 1973 after the magazine used his photos from the 1969 Super Bowl in advertisements; he asked for $2.25 million in damages.[42] He argued that when *Sports Illustrated* ran advertisements in *Cosmopolitan Magazine* (a publication targeted at a female audience) with the caption "The Man You Love Loves Joe Namath" and in *Life* with the caption "How to Get Close to Joe Namath" in conjunction with his photos, the magazine violated his right of publicity. He maintained the prominent

placement of his name in conjunction with his image implied an endorsement which he had not granted and for which he was not compensated.[43]

Montana and Namath had much in common beside their profession and
success. Like Montana, Namath was a Super Bowl–winning quarterback who
would eventually be elected to the Pro Football Hall of Fame. Like Montana,
Namath had not complained about the original publication of the photo in
the magazine because Namath recognized that, as a star football player, he
was newsworthy to a sports magazine. Further, Namath, like Montana, had
benefited financially from his celebrity. He endorsed a wide array of products
and appeared in films and television shows: he had even shaved his Fu Man-
chu mustache with a Schick razor in a production studio in an advertisement
for which he was paid $10,000.[44]

And like Montana, Namath also had a sometimes-rocky relationship with
the press. In 1968, Namath became part owner of a club in New York called
Bachelors III, which became a popular hangout for many in the city, including
celebrities such as Bing Crosby as well as gamblers and members of organized
crime. By 1969 the club was being investigated by the New York district attorney's office, the New York police department, and the Federal Bureau of
Investigation because of its suspected ties to the mob and gamblers. When
NFL Commissioner Pete Rozelle learned of the investigation and the presence of questionable associates at the club Namath owned and frequented,
Rozelle told Namath to sell his part of the club or be suspended indefinitely
from the league. In a press conference, Namath announced his retirement,
arguing that he had done nothing wrong, had not gambled on football, and
that he could not stop associating with gamblers because his father was one.[45]

The press had helped build Namath's celebrity by reporting on his football
success and by describing Namath's drinking and various flirtations with a
wide range of women. Now the press focused on the Bachelors III scandal and
Namath's retirement at age twenty-six and looked for other scandals. *Sports
Illustrated* reported that Namath had hosted high-stakes crap games in his
penthouse apartment. Namath, who had rarely been in the city at the times
he was supposedly hosting the games, called it a "an out-and-out smear job."
He added, "The press doesn't care how much it hurts people like me, so long
as there's a good headline."[46] In the end, Namath agreed to sell his part of the
New York Bachelors III but retained the right to franchise the club elsewhere,
provided Rozelle had the right to reject investors. Namath returned to the
Jets, but his relationship with *Sports Illustrated* was not repaired.

Namath's biographer, Mark Kriegel, noted that the court papers in the
lawsuit against *Sports Illustrated* and its parent company Time Inc. "left little

doubt that Namath's fury over the Bachelors III coverage, now four years past, had hardly subsided."[47] Kriegel quoted those papers as saying: "From June, 1969 to the present, the defendants have conducted through the magazine SPORTS ILLUSTRATED, a malicious campaign to malign, disgrace and impugn the plaintiff's integrity and honesty." In his own affidavit, Namath said, "It is well known among people in the sports, entertainment and publishing industries that I have been grossly mistreated over the years by *Sports Illustrated* magazine. The magazine has always attempted to project me in the worst possible light."[48]

Although the court papers and the affidavit's assertions of a concerted attempt to denigrate Namath's character help to explain why he might have pursued the lawsuit, both were legally irrelevant to his argument that the magazine had violated his right of publicity. Intriguingly, Namath's biographer questioned why Namath was so angry with the magazine, because Kriegel had found the craps game article to be the only negative portrayal of the player. Kriegel did note that Namath, like Montana decades later, was well aware of the value of his image and worked hard to protect it from those who would violate what would ultimately evolve into the right of publicity. In addition to the ill-fated *Sports Illustrated* lawsuit, in 1974 Namath sued Topps Chewing Gum for using his photo on a card and in a puzzle. Eventually, the NFL Players Association and the NFL's treasurer were added in various countersuits, and the lawsuits were all apparently settled and dismissed in 1976.[49]

In January 1978 Judge Harold Baer dismissed Namath's complaint against *Sports Illustrated*. Baer concluded that the use of Namath's photo in the advertisements caused him no property loss, and he seemed skeptical that Namath, a celebrity with many endorsements, had suffered any violation of his privacy. The judge further noted that New York state law allowed reproductions of names and photographs if their use was limited to "establishing the news content and the quality of the media."[50]

On appeal, the majority of judges affirmed Judge Baer's decision. Judge Louis J. Capozolli wrote the decision; Judges Myles J. Lane and Emilio Nunez concurred. Capozolli agreed with Baer and concluded that there was no inference of endorsement in the use of the photos and that the image and name simply illustrated the magazine's quality. Judge Theodore R. Kupferman, with Judge Francis T. Murphy concurring, wrote the dissent. Kupferman argued that Namath's status as a celebrity was less important than Judge Baer had found it to be. Kupferman maintained that the proper question to examine was whether *Sports Illustrated* was "trading on the name of the personality" to increase sales and to generate a profit.[51] No doubt to Namath's dismay, the majority ruled against him, and his appeal to the highest court in New York was rejected.[52]

Montana's attempts to distinguish his California case from Namath's New York case failed. At the hearing on the summary judgment motion, the *Mercury News* offered what the court characterized as "undisputed evidence" that its motive in selling the poster was simply to describe the quality of work in the paper. The paper even submitted evidence that the $5 price point for the poster was selected as the minimum needed to cover the production costs of the posters, although in a footnote the court explained that selling the posters was irrelevant to the protection—First Amendment protections are not limited to nonprofit organizations. The court noted specifically that the posters were exact reproductions of the drawing and photos that had originally appeared in the newspaper and that they did not state or imply that Montana endorsed the paper.[53] Montana lost on every count, and to add insult to injury, he was ordered to pay the newspaper's attorneys' fees.

MONTANA AS MARKETER

The basis of the right of publicity is the assumption that a person should be able to control and profit from his or her image and identity. As a successful high-profile professional football player, Joe Montana did an outstanding job of creating a quintessential American, masculine, sporting-hero image and in marketing himself to the American consumer, even when plagued by drug-use rumors. At various points during his football career he endorsed not just Schick razors and Nuprin pain relievers but also athletic shoes by L.A. Gear as well as a bank—Continental Savings of American in San Francisco, where his mother worked as an account executive.[54] He was generally and effectively marketed, as media scholar Leah Vande Berg described, as a "strong, rugged, seductively heterosexual yet clean-cut family man."[55]

Part of the Montana mystic was his aura of "coolness." Nicknamed Joe Cool, in part because of his penchant for bringing his team back from defeat to victory in the fourth quarter, Montana had a reputation as being cool and collected under the pressure of the game. He was said to never sweat, at least metaphorically. To describe Montana's quickness even off the field during the game, one columnist told a story about a prank that Montana's bodyguard played on him in the middle of the game:

> Once, as a prank during a 49ers rout, Warren used a field phone behind the bench to call Joe's wife, Jennifer. Warren then handed the phone to Joe, who thought it was an assistant coach.

"What the hell do you want?" Joe said.

"Honey, it's me," Jennifer said.

"I told you never to call me at work," Joe said without missing a beat. "And I'll bring home the milk and cookies."[56]

The prank, and the reporting thereof, reaffirmed Montana's reputation for self-collection and coolness under pressure. This too would lend itself to his marketing prowess: not only was Montana a seductive yet humble family man, he was also not prone to nerves or pressure in the way that mere mortals are.

Montana's marketing power rested largely on the media representations of the man and his athletic ability. While his expertise on the field was remarkable (he is enshrined in the Pro Football Hall of Fame for a reason), he was also positively portrayed in the media. Not only did the media cover his football exploits, it also created a persona, an image of a man mastering a series of challenges and always competing to the best of his ability while remaining just an ordinary guy. In 1990, *Sports Illustrated* ran a story describing his overcoming being benched, being ignored until the third round of the professional draft, and being disabled by a back injury. After each description of Montana's triumph over adversity, the story reiterated, "He was the best."[57] Even the *San Jose Mercury News* published laudatory stories about the man, despite Montana's claim that the paper had undermined his integrity. In 1985 the paper asserted that he might be the greatest NFL quarterback ever, and the article emphasized his humility and love of family.[58] In 1989 the *News* called him a "legend," comparing him to Elvis Presley in terms of star power and success after the 49ers' third Super Bowl victory.[59] Despite the frenzy in the mid-1980s over Montana's rumored cocaine use, in 1990 the paper was indignant when reporting that he was asked to "defend himself against an allegation that didn't name him in the first place" with regard to rumors that the NFL had covered up cocaine use by several quarterbacks over the previous decade.[60]

Montana's marketing is an example of what scholar David Tan called the "Trinity of Celebrity," which requires the celebrity individual, the producer (including the media and the marketers), and the fans. Tan further argued that the three linked together practically cry for celebrity endorsements of products:

> People don't concentrate their emotional energy on products in the way fans abandon themselves to the heroes of their games. But great products that were necessary to great athletic figures, [Nike founder Phil] Knight reasoned, could create customers, who were like fans. "Nobody roots for a product,"

Knight would say; the products needed to be tethered to something more compelling and profound.[61]

Montana's success on the field led to the media's reporting on his exploits, which gave him celebrity status leading to endorsements from a wide range of merchandisers in the hopes that his fans would buy products he hawked.

Given Montana's ambivalence about his celebrity status and his appreciation of his endorsement value, the lawsuit against the *San Jose Mercury News* was not out of character. In fact, Montana was prone to lawsuits. In 1991 he sued a New York company for using his image on a poster without his permission.[62] In 1993 he and his wife filed a lawsuit alleging violation of privacy, intentional infliction of emotional distress, and a loss of property value after their neighbors cut down a number of trees that Montana claimed were on his property. He originally asked for $1.5 million in damages, but many of the claims were dismissed, and the judge ordered the parties to settle.[63] In 1997 Montana sued Sega for breach of contract after the video game manufacturer severed ties with him without explanation.[64] These lawsuits reiterate the value he placed on his privacy and his endorsements, despite the potential paradox of trying to be a private celebrity.

LEGAL IMPLICATIONS AND DEBATE

The California Court of Appeals decision that the Super Bowl photos of Montana remained newsworthy and that the newspaper had a right to give examples of its work in its own marketing is reasonable in light of the Joe Namath case. Although the Montana case may have been decided consistently with the *Namath* decision, the editor of the *Entertainment Law Reporter* noted that Montana's lawsuit raised valid legal questions: "In the eyes of many, posters are closer to toys or other products than they are to newspapers, magazines and books. Since the right of publicity clearly gives people the right to prevent or be compensated for the use of their names and likeness on toys and products, this case could have resulted in another victory for Montana."[65] *Sports Illustrated* had used Namath's photo in an obvious advertisement for the magazine: the *San Jose Mercury News* had put Montana's photo on a separate poster.

The *Montana* decision also failed to distinguish between marketing and newsworthiness. Legal scholar Darren F. Farrington argued that the decision was simply wrong because the First Amendment does not protect the media when the media is simply marketing merchandise.[66] Farrington's point was valid: posters of athletes' performances require the athletes' permission to use their likenesses, but the *Montana* decision allows a newspaper to print and distribute a poster of an athlete without his or her permission. At no point did the California Court of Appeals explain its distinction, and the door remains open to any newspaper publishing, selling, and profiting from an action poster of an athlete so long as the paper utilizes one of its own photos. Lawyers J. Mack Webner and Leigh Anne Lindquist called the decision "egregious," adding that "such an undertaking by anyone else would be a clear infringement of Montana's Right of Publicity and, to make an exception for news media, mocks the publicity right."[67]

Legal scholar Stephen R. Barnett argued that the California court was limited by the wording of the California statute, which defined the tort as using the name or likeness of a person for the purposes of "advertising or selling." He acknowledged that the "line is not easy to draw" when it comes to determining what is newsworthy and what is for advertising and selling. He pointed to an earlier Georgia Supreme Court decision that a plastic bust being sold of Dr. Martin Luther King Jr. was commercial and not newsworthy.[68]

Law professor F. Jay Dougherty argued that the courts' decision in *Montana*, as in other cases, manipulated the facts and avoided the real question of how art (and how art is defined) is protected by the First Amendment. He contended that in the *Montana* case, the California courts seemed to say that art (posters) were newsworthy if they were designed to sell newspapers. In general, Dougherty reasoned that courts have decided that artwork is either newsworthy or merchandise, while failing to define art or explain what kind of art is protected under the First Amendment.[69] Dougherty's concern about the distinction between what is art and what is a product would be relevant as the right of publicity evolved.

LIFE AFTER THE LAWSUIT

Joe Montana's career, endorsement deals, and life continued with great success after he lost the lawsuit. Interestingly, after the trial court dismissed Montana's case, but before the appeal was decided, Montana tried again to sue the *Mercury News* over the use of the photographs as posters in 1993, using a different legal theory. This time he filed a breach of contract suit, alleging that the press is given a pass to games but that the passes do not allow for "secondary or non-editorial use of any picture." The lawsuit argued that the pass thus created a contractual relationship between the *Mercury*

News and the NFL and that Montana was a third-party beneficiary of the contract.[70] The case disappeared from public record, so presumably it was dismissed or dropped.

Montana's professional life changed dramatically in the course of the right of publicity lawsuit. In 1993, a year after he sued the *San Jose Mercury News* but before the appellate court's final verdict, Joe Montana was traded to the Kansas City Chiefs. Injuries and poor play had led 49ers coach George Seifert to bench Montana in favor of a younger, healthier, and talented Steve Young. A great player, Young would be inducted into the Pro Football Hall of Fame in 2005. Montana's departure from the Bay Area, though, caused great consternation at the time among the area's football fans. Mark Purdy, a columnist for the *Mercury News* who also wrote for the *Sporting News*, claimed that the city went through a "nervous breakdown." He wrote, "Newspapers put out special sections. Sports talk shows became therapy sessions as the 49ers' fans fell into the Super Bowl of funks. 'I don't think anyone or anything in San Francisco history has had the cultural impact of Joe Montana,' one caller opined."[71] Montana spent two seasons in Kansas City and led the team to the playoffs each year.

In the end, when he retired in April 1995, Montana had played sixteen NFL seasons for two different teams and finished with 40,551 passing yards, 273 touchdown passes, three Super Bowl MVP awards, two regular-season MVPs, and millions of dollars from football and endorsements. He was enshrined in the Pro Football Hall of Fame in 2000. When Montana retired in early 1995, he moved home to his large house in Napa Valley, California, with his wife, Jennifer, and their four children. His parents had moved to California to be closer to their only child and their grandchildren. He planned to do some broadcasting and to start a winery. He enjoyed flying and golf.[72]

Through 2015 Montana remained a successful endorser for a variety of products. He makes appearances as a motivational speaker and in 2005 coauthored a book on leadership.[73] In 2012, Montana endorsed "Joint Juice," a glucosamine and chondroitin supplement. The ad showed Montana running, biking, hang gliding, and fencing, among other physical activities, presumably emphasizing the power of the supplement and Montana's own athleticism despite his age.[74] He also appeared in a national advertising campaign for Skechers Shape-Ups (a walking shoe with a curved sole that rocks as the wearer walks).[75] In 2009 he created a signature guacamole recipe as part of his role as a spokesman for the Hass Avocado Board.[76] He was also the face of a development project involving offices and a hotel near the new San Francisco football stadium.[77] His retirement from football and his decision not to work as a sports commentator on a regular basis has had limited effect on his marketability. His family continues to do well: his two daughters graduated from Notre Dame, and his two sons played quarterback at a variety of colleges.[78] With their children out of the house, Montana and his wife moved to a condo in San Francisco. But Montana still has seemed ambivalent about his loss of privacy as a celebrity. When he was present at a city hall meeting to listen to a discussion about a real estate development he was involved in, he said nothing until an eighty-two-year-old fan asked to shake his hand. He hugged her and later took her into a more private hall for a photo, but he did not speak to the press about the incident.[79] Although Montana liked the idea of riding public transit and argued that people get used to seeing him and then he is left alone, a reporter asked if he was still bothered by his fame. Montana's response was telling:

> Some people have no respect whether you are with your family or not. That's the hardest part. I was shopping in a grocery store in Seattle looking for stuff for Nicholas [his youngest son]. This guy kept following me with his cell phone video on. The lady comes up and says, "Can I have a picture?" I said, "I don't do pictures anymore." If you're out to dinner, one is never enough. The same person will shoot 10 while you're eating. I sign autographs. It's getting a little bit easier because I'm getting older, and a lot of the younger people are like, "Who's that?" You will be walking through an airport, and you get, "Aren't you Joe Namath?"[80]

The inevitable comparisons to Namath aside, in 2015 Montana remained focused on his family, protecting his privacy, and marketing his image.

The *San Jose Mercury News* also survived, but it would change. At about the time Montana lost his lawsuit, the paper achieved even greater national prominence for the "Dark Alliance" stories written by Gary Webb. Webb, a Pulitzer Prize–winning journalist, had conducted an extensive investigation and published three stories in the *Mercury News* in 1996. In the series, Webb alleged that a San Francisco–based drug ring with ties to a CIA-sponsored Nicaraguan contra group sold cocaine to a dealer in South Central Los Angeles. The money acquired from the drug sales then circled back and was used to help fund the efforts to destabilize the Sandinista government. A number of newspapers ran stories arguing that Webb's theory was wrong, and in 1997 the *Mercury News* backed away from the story as flawed, and Webb resigned. Although the next year a CIA report specifically denied any connection between the U.S. government and the drug dealers Webb had named, it admitted to funding contras despite their connections to drug dealers.[81] Even though the foundation of the story seems to have been accurate, Webb's inaccurate details undermined both his and the newspaper's credibility.

The "Dark Alliance" series was in some ways the apotheosis of the *San Jose Mercury News*. In the 1990s the newspaper transitioned from being a local paper to a powerful, national force with a staff of more than four hundred people and multiple foreign-language editions. That success did not survive the tech bubble in 1998 and the decline in classified ad revenue and other losses in the early 2000s.[82]

The *San Jose Mercury News* was a longtime holding of Knight Ridder Publishing, and Knight Ridder was sold to the McClatchey Company in 2006. This was simply the first in a series of mergers, making the *Mercury News* an even smaller and smaller piece of larger and larger corporations. With the backing of the Hearst Corporation, MediaNews Group acquired the newspaper. Despite the fact that the two companies owned every major newspaper in the Bay Area, the merger was approved.[83] In December 2013, 21st Century Media (another large news conglomerate) consolidated with MediaNews Group and announced that all companies would operate under the Digital First Media name, reaching an estimated 67 million Americans across the country. The *San Jose Mercury News* operated as part of the Bay Area News Group, a subdivision of the larger Digital First Media empire.[84] Like many print newspapers, the *Mercury News* faced layoffs in the twenty-first century because of the change in medium and the consolidation of newspapers, seeing the number of full-time journalists cut from four hundred to two hundred between 2000 and 2007.[85] As a cost-cutting move with the smaller staff and because of the appreciation of the land, the newspaper's thirty-four-acre campus was sold in 2013, and the paper's offices moved to the downtown area in San Jose in 2014.[86]

CONCLUSION

Joe Montana's lawsuit against the *San Jose Mercury News* tied together several recurrent figures in publicity cases. Joe Namath not only filed the lawsuit that the California court relied on in part to reject Montana's claim, but he also quarterbacked Bear Bryant's Alabama football team in 1962 that beat the University of Georgia. That game, of course, was the game the *Saturday Evening Post* claimed Bryant and Wally Butts of UGA had fixed. That story in turn led to Butts's lawsuit against the magazine's owner and the U.S. Supreme Court's ruling that to win defamation cases, public figures like Butts needed to prove the false information was published with knowledge of the falsity of the story or with reckless disregard for the truth.

Additionally, Judge Charles D. Breitel of the New York state court system was the author of the majority decision in Warren Spahn's appeal to the Supreme Court of New York, Appellate Division, in 1965. Breitel's decision concluded that Warren Spahn, despite his celebrity status, had a right to privacy and that the publisher of his juvenile biography had violated Spahn's right with its fictionalized dialogue and imagined relationships. Judge Breitel was indirectly involved in Montana's case because he was the one of the judges on the New York Court of Appeals who unanimously affirmed the ruling against Joe Namath in 1976.[87] The two decisions are not philosophically incompatible. Spahn's case was about the right to privacy under the false-light tort, whereas Joe Namath was suing under the right of appropriation. Although both athletes were suing under the right of privacy, they approached their cases under different prongs with different results.

Montana v. San Jose Mercury News, at first glance, was not a hugely important case in terms of the right of publicity. After the decision was announced, few law review articles focused on the case, instead placing it in a broader context of the right of publicity and usually tying it closely to the *Namath v. Sports Illustrated* case from twenty years earlier. Yet the case was legally significant enough that it is mentioned in almost every sports law textbook and many First Amendment casebooks because it broadened the protection for the press and the power of the First Amendment when the right of publicity was growing in power. The second half of the twentieth century saw a large increase in media, both in terms of the number of outlets and in their competition and quest for profits. The *Montana* and *Namath* cases reaffirmed the rights of the press to advertise itself without, as the critics note, distinguishing between the marketing of the press and the actual function of the press. That said, without the profit, the press in a capitalistic America could cease to exist.[88]

The *Montana* case is problematic. The court concluded that the newspaper could re-use its photographs of Montana in promoting itself, but the facts of the *Montana* case differ significantly from *Namath*. The *San Jose Mercury News* created a poster, something people were intended to buy and display, whereas *Sports Illustrated* created an advertisement that appeared in another magazine. While consumers could certainly purchase that other magazine, cut out, and display the ad with Namath's image, that was not the intent of *Sports Illustrated*. Although the court concluded that the newspaper intended the poster simply to advertise the quality of its product, I am less persuaded. Posters have generally been deemed to be merchandise, and the people in them have been protected from unauthorized use by a range of laws (including publicity, privacy, trademark, copyright, and contract law).[89] The *Montana* verdict limits the right of publicity and expands the newsworthy exception seemingly without limit of time or arguably of purpose. The questions of what is art, what is newsworthy, what is merchandise, and what the First Amendment protects remained unclear after this case and would be addressed in subsequent lawsuits.

5

OWNING A FACE: PUBLICITY AND ADVERTISING

NEWCOMBE v. COORS BREWING (1998)

Donald (Don) Newcombe played in the Negro baseball leagues until the Brooklyn Dodgers signed him as one of the first three African Americans in the National League. He had a stellar career; he was the first Major League Baseball (MLB) player to win the Most Valuable Player award, the Cy Young Award, and the Rookie of the Year award. He was also a four-time all-star, batted over .300 in four different seasons, and had the most wins in the National League in four other seasons. His MLB career was cut short in 1960, however, in part because of his continuing battle with alcohol. Ultimately, Newcombe acknowledged his problem, and as a recovering alcoholic, he served as a spokesman for the National Institute on Drug and Alcohol Abuse under Presidents Nixon, Ford, and Reagan. As an anti-alcohol advocate, Newcombe was shocked when he discovered an advertisement for Killian's Irish Red Beer (a brand produced by Coors Brewing Company) that featured a drawing of an old-time baseball game in which the pitcher was a recognizable version of Newcombe. Newcombe promptly sued Coors for a violation of his right of publicity and lost in the federal district court. He then appealed to the Ninth Circuit of the U.S. Court of Appeals.[1]

Newcombe argued that the Ninth Circuit should follow the lead of the dissenting judge in *O'Brien v. Pabst Sales Co.* (1938), who said that football players should be able to control the commercial use of their names and images. Newcombe also believed the Second Circuit's conclusion in *Haelan Laboratories, Inc. v. Topps Chewing Gum, Inc.* (1958) that found a property interest in a baseball player's image through the New York state privacy laws should apply to him. The Ninth Circuit agreed with Newcombe and in 1998 ruled that the test for a violation of publicity rights (also known as the appropriation of privacy) was in four parts. First, Newcombe needed to prove that Coors used his identity. Second, he needed to establish that the appropriation of his name or likeness was to Coors's advantage commercially. Third, he needed to prove that he did not consent to the use of his image, and fourth, that he was injured by Coors's actions. After acknowledging that there was no question that Coors had profited from his image and that he had not consented to the company's use of it, the court concluded that the identifiability of the picture was the key issue and that a reasonable jury could conclude that the image belonged to Newcombe.[2]

DON NEWCOMBE, THE PERSON AND PLAYER

Don Newcombe was born in Madison, New Jersey, on June 14, 1926, the second of four boys. His father was a chauffeur and drove for the same family for nearly thirty years, including throughout the Great Depression. Newcombe began playing baseball in junior high school, but when his family followed his father's employer to Elizabeth, New Jersey, Newcombe's new high school did not have a baseball team. So after failing biology, Newcombe dropped out of school. He repaired and drove trucks until he enlisted in the navy at age sixteen. He later said he was discharged by "Special Order" and assumed it was because he had enlisted underage without his parents' consent. He claimed to have enjoyed the navy, so after his discharge, he enlisted in the army. But instead of reporting to boot camp, he got a job driving a truck; the job took him out of town, so he skipped boot camp. When the army contacted his father to find out why he had not reported for duty, his father reported his son's true age and withheld parental consent from the underage enlistment.[3]

When Newcombe was about seventeen years old, someone in a poolroom where he hung out suggested that he should try out for baseball. Standing six feet four inches tall and weighing 220 pounds, he tried out for and signed with the Newark Eagles of the Negro National League for the 1944 and 1945 seasons. Effa Manley, the team's owner, found his size impressive. In his career with the Eagles, he pitched and hit well and in his second season made the Negro National League All-Star team. According to Newcombe, though, he thought that he had gone as far as he could with the Eagles after two seasons.[4] Plus, he had another option.

Newcombe's ties to Branch Rickey, the Brooklyn Dodger's team president and general manager who signed Jackie Robinson, began in December 1945 when Rickey signed Newcombe to play for a proposed Negro League team, the Brooklyn Brown Dodgers. After Jackie Robinson signed a contract with the Montreal Royals, a white team in the Dodgers' farm system, Newcombe met with Rickey again in early 1946. His original contract was torn up, and he signed a new one to play in the Major League Baseball (MLB) minor league system.[5] His Newark teammate, catcher, and future Baseball Hall of Fame member Roy Campanella signed with the Dodgers organization soon after, although the signings were not initially publicized. Together, the two played in the class B league in Nashua, New Hampshire. The original plans to send them to the class A Danville Dodgers ended when the team and the league expressed concern about African American players.[6] Instead, the two were sent to a brand-new class B team in overwhelmingly white Nashua, New Hampshire, where the team's birth had been carefully orchestrated to maximize local fan support and loyalty. On April 4, 1946, the Dodgers announced that Campanella and Newcombe had been assigned to Nashua, and the local newspaper commented that their placement would "test New England fandom's democratic attitude towards the racial question."[7] When the two arrived several weeks later, they were pleased to discover that they were well treated at the local inn and restaurant: "Twasn't any name calling," Newcombe recalled.[8] The two became particularly popular (Campanella was quoted as saying they were "treated like long-lost sons") after showing their excellent baseball skills.[9] In his first season with the team in 1946, Newcombe won fourteen of the eighteen games he started, with a 2.21 earned run average and batting .311.[10]

Newcombe spent three years in the minor leagues. After a second season in Nashua, Newcombe was promoted in 1948 to the International League, where he played for Montreal.[11] After beginning the 1949 season with Montreal again, he was promoted to the Brooklyn Dodgers in May 1949.[12] In his first MLB season, Newcombe was named to the All-Star team, and he (along with Roy Sievers of the St. Louis Browns) won the Rookie of the Year award.[13] Newcombe's Dodgers also won the National League pennant before losing to the New York Yankees in the World Series that year; Newcombe started and lost games 1 and 3.

Newcombe hired a publicist who acted as his agent after his first season with the Dodgers. Irving Rudd garnered Newcombe endorsements for hair tonics, hats, and insurance companies, totaling about $10,000—quite a lot for an African American athlete at the time. He also arranged for Newcombe to referee a series of wrestling matches, but Branch Rickey asked him to stop after the first bout because he did not like seeing the Dodgers image demeaned.[14] Newcombe responded that he was just a fan who enjoyed watching the matches on television, but he stopped officiating them.[15]

Although Newcombe apparently did not face overt racial discrimination in his first season in Nashua, the same was not true during his MLB career. In 1949, Newcombe's first season with the Dodgers, the African American players on the team were not allowed to stay at the racially segregated Chase Hotel (now renamed the Chase Park Plaza Hotel) in St. Louis, Missouri. The black players were forced to stay at a "black" hotel without air conditioning, a serious problem because of the summer heat. Sam Lacy, a black sportswriter, reported in April 1950 about the challenges of Jim Crow laws for the black Dodgers players at spring training in Florida: "Once we leave Dodgertown . . . we are on our own," he wrote. For example, after several players obtained a rental car, the rental company demanded the car's immediate return after learning that the African American players had ridden in it. Lacy noted the irony of three excellent players—Jackie Robinson, Roy Campanella, and Don Newcombe—being treated far worse than players who would be waived at the end of spring training.[16]

In the winter of 1951, after the regular season ended, Newcombe, who was married (he had married his wife Freddie in 1946) but had no children, was drafted into the army. Prior to his induction, he had multiple physicals to determine his fitness to serve, and the press was abuzz with the story that he had previously served briefly in the military and been discharged sometime in 1943 (when he would have been sixteen years old).[17] This time he spent two years in the Medical Corps in a special demonstration unit.[18] His return to the Dodgers was rocky; two years away from the league had taken its toll, and in 1954 he won only nine games and lost eight, with an ERA of 4.55.[19]

The next few seasons were better for Newcombe professionally: he won twenty games in 1955, and the Dodgers won the World Series. He then won twenty-seven games in 1956 as well as the Cy Young Award and the MVP. Newcombe began also to stand up against the racism he was experiencing, particularly after serving in the integrated army. In 1955 the Chase Hotel in St. Louis still would not allow the African American players to stay there with the rest of the Dodgers. Newcombe and Jackie Robinson went to discuss the matter with the hotel's manager, and when they asked why they could not stay, the manager explained it was about the pool: he did not want African Americans in his pool. Robinson told the manager he could not swim, and Newcombe promised not to, so the players were allowed to stay at the hotel after that.[20] Furthermore, Newcombe, a large black man on the pitcher's mound with a hard white ball was in a unique position to protect his teammates. In a game against the Phillies, for example, Robinson complained to Newcombe about opposing players calling him derogatory names from the dugout. After hearing this, Newcombe threw the next ball at the head of Del Ennis who, instead of charging the mound, went into the dugout and told his teammates to keep quiet.[21] Newcombe admitted that he was the enforcer for the team, and he threw at opposing batters to stop the racial abuse toward his black teammates.[22]

Despite Newcombe's strong performance and his growth as an activist, the Dodgers lost to the Yankees in the World Series, and Newcombe again failed to win a World Series game. Although he was pitching well prior to the series, his behavior during and after the series was erratic. After giving up a grand slam to Yogi Berra of the Yankees in a losing effort in game 2, Newcombe punched a parking lot attendant who allegedly called him a "bum with no guts." The subsequent $25,000 lawsuit against Newcombe was dismissed when Judge Matthew Fagin concluded that "a man who is a celebrity, whether in baseball, football, the theater, or anything else, has a right to get to his car and not be slandered."[23]

But Newcombe's problems off the field were just beginning. Newcombe disappeared briefly after that 1956 series. His wife told reporters that he had stopped by his home after losing game 7 and told her he would be out all night. She said Newcombe was frustrated not only with losing but also with the struggle of adopting their eighteen-month-old son, Gregory Joel. The couple had successfully finalized the adoption of eight-month-old daughter Evit Yolanda, but there were problems with adopting Gregory. Newcombe was supposed to leave for a tour of Japan with the Dodgers later in the week and did not want to go for a number of reasons, including the adoption difficulties. The team was not happy that Newcombe did not want to go and was further upset that Newcombe left the ballpark before game 7 ended.[24]

Newcombe pitched better for the Dodgers in the following seasons, but in 1958 the Dodgers traded Newcombe to the Cincinnati Reds. Arthur Daley, a columnist for the *New York Times*, explained that the Dodgers had "finally given up" on Newcombe and called him an "oversized problem child." Newcombe, Daley said, "is a huge man and most of his 240 pounds seems to consist of complexes, fears, neuroses, traumas, and what-not."[25] Daley pointed to Newcombe's fear of flying (he consulted a hypnotist trying to overcome it) and the loss of Roy Campanella, his former catcher and roommate who was paralyzed in an automobile accident in January 1958, as part of his problems with the Dodgers.[26] Prior to being traded, Newcombe had argued with the Dodgers' manager, been fined for breaking curfew, and fought with the parking attendant after a game.[27] David Condon, a columnist for the *Chicago Daily Tribune*, agreed that Newcombe was a problem. He wrote that Newcombe was "a man of strange behavior," noted that "he has been a chronic complainer of injury," and concluded that he "never reached the brilliant potential that was so . . . so . . . close."[28]

Newcombe's problems continued both on and off the field. Except for the 1959 season, he never again won more than half of the games he pitched. In 1958 he and a brother were charged with assault and battery after a bar fight in Newcombe's New Jersey tavern. Another Newcombe brother was charged with possessing a revolver with intent to use it unlawfully.[29] The charges were later dropped.[30] Newcombe's marriage to his wife Freddie ended in 1959, and he married Billie, his second wife, in 1960.[31] During the 1960 season, the Reds traded Newcombe to the Cleveland Indians for cash. In 1961 Newcombe was out of MLB and playing in the Pacific Coast League, but he was released at the end of the season. Arthur Daley of the *New York Times* reported Newcombe's retirement in 1962 with a sense of disappointment. After reminding readers of Newcombe's success as a regular-season pitcher for the Dodgers and his failures (he never won a single World Series game), he noted also Newcombe's "rebellion," describing his "fits of sullenness." Daley concluded that Newcombe had the "physical equipment to be one of the great pitchers. . . . This huge and tormented man kept falling short of expectations."[32] Newcombe attempted a comeback in Japan but stayed for only one season.

The Dodgers' franchise moved from Brooklyn to Los Angeles in 1958, and Newcombe had played only a few games with the team in Los Angeles before being traded to Cincinnati, but his home remained in the New York/ New Jersey area. In 1963 after retiring from the game, Newcombe announced that he was selling his two bars and a liquor store in Newark and moving to Los Angeles because a builder had refused to sell him a house in what was a white neighborhood in Montclair. Newcombe said, "I don't want to bring up my son in such an atmosphere. . . . I had heard about things like this happening to other people, but I somehow never thought it would happen to me."[33] Newcombe apparently did not sell all of his liquor businesses because in 1967 he filed for bankruptcy and reported that because of the failure of one of his package stores in New Jersey, he was insolvent. At that time he was reportedly a public relations consultant in Los Angeles.[34]

Despite the subtext of Newcombe as a problem player, a pitcher who could not win a World Series game, and all the reports of his bad behavior and financial problems, none of the articles in the 1950s and 1960s alluded to what was likely a major cause of Newcombe's on- and off-field issues. He had been drinking heavily throughout his career and, in fact, throughout his life.

Newcombe's behavior off the field was always considered a little wild throughout his time in the game, but just as the reporters minimized or ignored his drinking, so, too, did his teammates. Newark Eagles and MLB player Monte Irvin believed Newcombe needed a strong manager to control him and said Newcombe got "a little boisterous, but he only drank beer."[35] Something affected his play and likely his behavior, and in retrospect it was surely the alcohol.

Only in 1966 did he admit he was an alcoholic and was able to stop drinking. His violence and rages at home had led his wife Billie to announce she and their three children were leaving, and he swore on the head of four-year-old Don Jr. that he would never touch alcohol again or bet on horses. Drinking and gambling had taken a financial toll on Newcombe: he sold his 1955 World Series ring and lost at least one business to bankruptcy and back taxes. He also thought alcohol had shortened his baseball career because he drank instead of trained: his weight reflected this, increasing from 220 pounds as a rookie to 250 pounds his final season. He admitted that he weighed 300 pounds after retiring. He said he drank more in the 1950s to combat his fear of flying; owning taverns encouraged him to drink even more.[36] Newcombe told reporters in the 1970s that he finally stopped drinking in 1966 at age forty; he'd been drinking since he was eight. He recalled that his parents drank heavily and that his first wife was an alcoholic as well. He said that as a young man with the Dodgers he would drink a six-pack of beer in the dugout after the game, another couple of beers after his shower, and a six-pack on the way home. He and his father or his wife would drink for the rest of the evening. He claimed that early in his career he did not drink if he was going to pitch the next day, but after the losing in the 1955 World Series, he toured Japan with the Dodgers under protest and under the influence. He admitted he was drunk every day of the thirty-day tour.[37] As he aged, Newcombe said, it was harder to recover: "That's why I retired at 34. It became too much of a hassle. I'd rather drink than play."[38]

Newcombe's sobriety came with respect and opportunity. Long an entrepreneur, he continued throughout his life to found businesses, including an annuity amortization company.[39] After overcoming the bankruptcy of 1967, Newcombe rejoined the Dodgers family in 1970 as director of community relations. Part of his job was to distribute free tickets to games that were unlikely to sell out and to encourage different segments of the Los Angeles community to come to games.[40] Newcombe also tried to help others avoid problems with alcohol: he spoke to schoolchildren, organized an MLB-sponsored alcoholism group, and persuaded Commissioner Bowie Kuhn to include alcohol in the league's drug awareness program.[41] He served as a spokesperson for the National Institute on Drug and Alcohol Abuse and other governmental organizations and worked tirelessly to help those who had problems with alcohol.[42] Understandably, Newcombe was not at all thrilled when he saw what he believed to be a picture of himself in a beer ad.

COORS AND KILLIAN'S RED

Coors Brewery was founded in Golden, Colorado, in 1873 by Adolph Coors, a German immigrant who had been trained as a brewer in his native land and had worked in a brewery in Illinois before resettling in Colorado. After a brief foray into the world of malted milk and porcelain during Prohibition, Coors continued its strong production.[43] By the mid-1950s the company produced over a million barrels of beer each year, and within twenty years that number had increased to seven million barrels annually. The Coors family retained control of the privately owned company until 1975, when the company went public, but the family remained active in the business. Coors was a western beer and only began distribution east of the Mississippi River in 1981.[44]

In 1981 Coors expanded its beer selections with the introduction of Killian's Irish Red beer. Killian's was produced as a super-premium beer (priced at an imported-beer rate) under a license from the George Killian Lett family in County Wexford, Ireland. The Lett family had brewed that recipe through the 1950s in Ireland. Coors initially marketed Killian's in West Coast markets and did no advertising prior to 1986. In 1988 Coors began marketing Killian's nationally.[45] In 1994 Killian's was Coors's fastest-growing brand, beating out craft brews such as Sierra Nevada and Samuel Adams.[46]

The Coors company had a problem of perception in the 1960s and 1970s. Many in the large Coors family, which for decades were the sole proprietors of the company, had a long history of conservatism, both politically and socially. In 1964 Bill Coors had told the employees to tell their representatives to vote against the Civil Rights Act, warning that the law would require him to fire them and hire black employees. Additionally, the company administered polygraph tests to new employees before their hiring was official; one of the questions was about sexual orientation. In 1966 a local activist analyzed the hiring patterns at Coors and noticed that only nine of the 4,500 employees had Hispanic surnames. He organized a Hispanic boycott of the company and its products. By 1974 the boycott had spread across the entire western part of the country and included people of all colors, as well as union leaders. In 1975, despite the boycott, the company was doing relatively well, although the family had been charged $15 million for inheritance taxes. To pay those taxes, the company went public. The company's reputation fared a bit better when Peter Coors began working with customers. This was one of the first times the family had someone with an MBA involved in consumer relations, indicating that the family finally recognized the importance of a trained professional working with the consumers rather than simply relying on the family's best guesses.[47]

The boycott against Coors continued through 1978, as did the family's conservative reputation. In 1978 the company removed the questions about sexual orientation from the polygraph test of new employees and became the first major U.S. brewery to prohibit discrimination based on sexual orientation. The *Advocate*, a gay magazine, called for an end of the gay community's boycott of Coors. The company also hired several high-profile Hispanic employees to undermine the commitment of Hispanics to the boycott. The Coors workers voted to end union affiliation. Despite a CBS *60 Minutes* episode that portrayed the company as a victim, Coors sales did not jump. In March 1984 Bill Coors was invited to speak to a meeting of minority business owners in Denver. He spoke off the cuff about a trip to Africa and the value of American capitalism. He suggested that black Americans had benefited from being removed from Africa generations earlier because they could do well in the United States. Further, he added blacks in African countries like Zimbabwe were not leading their own economies as effectively as when white people had led the country. He suggested that it was a matter of education. Although the audience seemed to assume Bill's intentions were good, the story that appeared in the local newspaper the next day was not so forgiving. The *Rocky Mountain News* ran the headline "Coors Calls Blacks 'Intellectual' Inferiors." To avoid prolonging the boycott even further, the company offered affirmative action for black employees and beer distributors, but that move did not appreciably increase sales among African American beer drinkers. In 1993 the Coors family turned over leadership of the company to someone outside the Coors family for the first time in the brewery's history. The new leadership promptly cut the workforce dramatically.[48] By 1994, the company was not in great shape.

THE OFFENDING AD

In the February 14, 1994, swimsuit edition of *Sports Illustrated* a one-page ad ran for Killian's Red beer (an Adolph Coors Brewing Company product). In the ad was a drawing that featured an African American baseball pitcher in mid-windup. Newcombe believed that he was the subject in the drawing because the image seemed to portray his unique, unusually expanded windup stance. The number on the jersey was thirty-nine, however, which was Roy Campanella's number. Newcombe wore number thirty-six.[49]

The ad itself is an interesting attempt to play on words of color. The left half of the ad contains the image of the pitcher; his face is obscured by his shoulder and the brim of his blue-and-red cap. An infielder crouches behind him in the same uniform, but the name on the front of the jersey is blurry and unreadable. The uniforms are clearly from the middle of the twentieth century and not the mid-1990s. On the right side of the page, underneath a superimposed photo of a pint of beer with the George Killian's Irish Red logo obscuring part of the text, the text reads:

> Most of all, it's always been a game about color. Where the grass is green and the ball is white and the men in blue yell at guys nicknamed Whitey and Red (who wear hometown white pinstripes and away city greys). And in the stands, blue and white collared fans wave multi-colored pennants, eating red-hots and drinking Red cold. Killian's Irish Red has the face of [unreadable under photo] Irishman Casey, wi[unreadable] town of Mudville [unreadable] mightily struck out [unreadable] Killian's Red as fro[unreadable] opening day when pour[unreadable]ed badged vendors fr[unreadable] cherry bat shaped bottl[unreadable] brown paper cups (the crisp amber lager softly spilling over with a wave of red). Yeah, it's always been a game about color . . . and I think about this as I sip a cold Killian's Red—watching my team whitewash their rivals. Killian's Red[.] Ask for it by color.[50]

Although the ad attempted to tap into a nostalgic memory of the game, the overt references to a "game about color" with a drawing from the era when baseball dissolved the color line was perhaps in questionable taste. Newcombe told the press that he found the headline and reference to color to be "racially derogatory." Coors said that the tag line about color was not problematic but simply playing off of the "color" theme of the red-tinged beer as it had in a number of ads.

The discomfiting text, though, was not Newcombe's primary concern. He argued that the drawing was recognizably his image—it was similar to a photo of Newcombe in the 1949 World Series, in fact. The company that created the ad, Foote, Cone and Belding, stated that the ad was "entirely proper."[51] Coors said that the drawing was "original art work that did not represent any identifiable person."[52] Later, a spokesman said that no one recognized Newcombe "until he called a press conference."[53] Newcombe seemed angrier over what he thought his image was selling than the fact that it had been used without his permission. He said, "I'm mad because I think about what alcohol did to me and my baseball career."[54] Newcombe has repeated throughout the years since he stopped drinking that he believed his alcoholism and its effect on his playing kept him from being a Baseball Hall of Fame–caliber player, and as of 2015 he was not a member. Coors acknowledged the work that Newcombe did to prevent alcohol abuse, called it "important," and added that the company "would not want to do anything that undermines the impact of his message in any way."[55] Newcombe sued Coors, the advertising agency, and Time Inc. (the publisher of *Sports Illustrated*), asking for $100 million in damages.

NEWCOMBE'S LEGAL SAGA

Newcombe's legal case was significant because it built on a series of other lawsuits by athletes who tried to control their images as they had appeared in advertisements. These court decisions worked generally in a kind of progression, expanding on the rights of athletes.

O'BRIEN v. PABST SALES CO.

Don Newcombe was not the first teetotaling athlete to discover that his image had been placed on a beer advertisement. Davey O'Brien was a physically small quarterback (5'7" and 151 pounds) who was a huge star for Texas Christian University's football team in the late 1930s. As a senior in 1938, he led TCU to a national championship and won the Heisman Trophy; not surprisingly, he was also named to a number of All-American teams. O'Brien's collegiate career represented such a benchmark that all current college players named "Quarterback of the Year" receive the Davey O'Brien Award. O'Brien was so popular while at TCU that the school's director of publicity reported that he had received more than eight hundred requests for O'Brien's photo during the 1938 season. After the season ended, TCU received a request for a photo of O'Brien (in uniform, throwing a football) from a publisher who said he wanted to use it on a football schedule. The letter did not indicate that the publisher was connected to Pabst Brewing Company, but the publicity director testified that his office never asked questions about the use of their athletes' pictures. He was quick to add that he never knowingly sent out photographs for endorsements without the athlete's permission.[56]

Once Pabst had the photograph, the company used the image in its annual calendar of football schedules. Centered at the top of the calendar was the phrase "Pabst Blue Ribbon"; below that was "Football Calendar, 1939." O'Brien's photo was to the left; to the right of the image was a picture of a glass with the Pabst Brewery name and logo as well as a beer bottle with the words "Pabst Blue Ribbon." Below that was the intercollegiate football schedule for the year.[57]

When O'Brien discovered that he was in the calendar, he filed a lawsuit against Pabst for an invasion of his privacy (the tort of publicity or appropriation had not yet been articulated). He argued that because he did not drink and was a member of the Allied Youth of America, which encouraged young people to avoid alcohol, he was "embarrassed and humiliated" at being associated with beer.[58] He noted that he had previously refused a variety of paid endorsements for various alcoholic products because of his moral convictions. Pabst countered with three defenses. First, it said that O'Brien was not a private person but a public figure whose photo as an All-American had been heavily circulated in a variety of publications and that the calendar was completely truthful—O'Brien was an All-American and the schedule was accurate. Second, the company argued that O'Brien had authorized TCU to take and circulate his photograph and that Pabst had compensated TCU for the photograph. Third, Pabst noted that its use of the photograph had not injured O'Brien in any way.

O'Brien lost at the district court level and appealed to the 5th Circuit Court of Appeals. Judge Joseph C. Hutcheson, who drafted the majority opinion, called O'Brien "a modern David" and Pabst Brewery "a modern Goliath,"[59] but he apparently failed to recall the ending of that tale, as the majority agreed with the district court and concluded all three of Pabst's defenses were valid. The court believed that one more publication of O'Brien's photo did not harm him, and nothing in the calendar implied that he was a beer drinker. Further, Hutcheson quoted the district court judge approvingly: "The business of making and selling beer is a legitimate and eminently respectable business and people of all walks and views in life, without injury to or reflection upon themselves, drink it, and that any association of O'Brien's picture with a glass of beer could not possibly disgrace or reflect upon or cause him damage."[60] It is worth noting that this case was decided just eight years after Prohibition in the United States was repealed, and the court's enthusiastic endorsement of alcoholic consumption may have reflected that era. Regardless of its possible cultural motivation, the court simply ignored O'Brien's moral opposition to alcohol and instead focused on the fact that he had been frequently photographed. The court noted that O'Brien was not suing for the implied endorsement of the beer because he, as a nondrinker, would never have endorsed it. Therefore, the majority concluded that O'Brien was unable to meet the burden of proving as a public figure that the use of his picture damaged him in anyway.[61]

Judge Edwin R. Holmes dissented from the majority opinion and articulated a foundation for a Texas common-law right of publicity in which a person could control his or her image. Holmes believed that the "right of privacy is distinct from the right to use one's name or picture for purposes of commercial advertisement. The latter is a property right that belongs to everyone; it may have much or little, or only nominal, value; but it is a personal right, which may not be violated with impunity."[62] He argued that O'Brien had been injured because he had a property interest in his image and his power of endorsement. The proof of this assertion was the fact that O'Brien had previously turned down a $400 endorsement offer from a New York beer company, indicating that both O'Brien and the brewery recognized the commercial value of his image. Judge Holmes argued that associating O'Brien's photo with a beer company implied an endorsement for which he should have been compensated. Holmes added that the majority decision allowed any company to use any image of any famous person in advertisements without compensating the person behind the image. [63]

Perhaps the most interesting part of the decision was the majority's response to the Holmes dissent. They argued that TCU had given its permission to Pabst to use O'Brien's image and that O'Brien had sought and received attention, adding that O'Brien had not complained about the use of his image in advertising generally but only about the fact that it was used in a beer advertisement that he found personally insulting.[64] This position suggests several things that would have long-term implications—primarily, that the college and not the athlete owned an athlete's image and could distribute it as the college wished.

What rights of publicity, privacy, and property college athletes have would be the subject of a class-action lawsuit some seventy years after O'Brien's case, when former University of California Los Angeles basketball player Ed O'Bannon sued the National Collegiate Athletic Association (NCAA) in 2009. In August 2014 a federal judge ruled that the NCAA could not prohibit athletes from profiting from their images and concluded that the NCAA could set a cap of not less than $5,000 per year per athlete. Confusingly, the judge later in the decision added, "Schools may offer lower amounts of deferred compensation if they choose but may not unlawfully conspire with each another in setting these amounts."[65] On appeal Judge Jay S. Bybee wrote for the majority of a three-person panel of the United States Court of Appeals for the Ninth Circuit, both affirming and reversing the district court. He determined that the lower court was correct in ruling that the NCAA was subject to antitrust law but that the lower court's remedy was problematic. Bybee concluded that the NCAA could not prohibit providing the full cost of attendance to its athletes.[66] The other implication of the *O'Brien* case, although it was less clearly articulated, was that anyone who enjoyed publicity could not control an image or prevent someone else from profiting from it. Obviously this argument is counter to the entire tort of appropriation that would develop in the 1960s.

O'Brien survived the loss and played in the National Football League for one season before becoming a Federal Bureau of Investigation (FBI) agent and then an FBI instructor for the remainder of his career. After retiring from the FBI, he became a land and oil developer; he died of cancer in 1977 at age sixty.[67]

Newcombe's case differed from O'Brien's in several important ways: first, he was filing a lawsuit fifty years later, and the rights protecting a celebrity's image had evolved; second, he was not a college athlete: no college could give permission to a third party to use his picture. Newcombe also benefited from later court cases involving athletes and the courts' changing attitudes toward public figures and their rights to control their image.

HAELAN LABORATORIES, INC. v. TOPPS CHEWING GUM, INC.

Judge Holmes's dissenting position in *O'Brien* would be vindicated in the Second Circuit Court of Appeals a few years later. In *Haelan Laboratories, Inc. v. Topps Chewing Gum, Inc.* (1953) Judge Jerome Frank, writing for the majority, found a property interest in one's image through the New York state privacy laws and the Second Circuit became one of the first courts to articulate a "right of publicity." Haelan Labs sold chewing gum and also enclosed a baseball card in the pack. The company had a contract with a player for the exclusive use of the player's image on a baseball card. Topps also sold gum and baseball cards, and it signed an agreement with the same player to put his photograph on its baseball card. When Haelan Labs sued for interfering with its contract, Topps argued that professional baseball players did not have property interests or rights of publicity in their image because they were photographed frequently, which meant that the professional athlete could not sign an exclusive contract regarding his image (because he did not control his own image as a ballplayer). Judge Frank disagreed. He wrote that people have a right to the publicity value of a photograph because

> it is common knowledge that many prominent persons (especially actors and ball-players), far from having their feelings bruised through public exposure of their likenesses, would feel sorely deprived if they no longer received money

for authorizing advertisements, popularizing their countenances, displayed in newspapers, magazines, busses, trains and subways. This right of publicity would usually yield them no money unless it could be made the subject of an exclusive grant which barred any other advertiser from using their pictures.[68]

Frank's decision acknowledged the endorsement value that celebrity athletes had and the power an exclusive contract could wield.

KIMBROUGH v. COCA-COLA

In another example of the shifting position of the American courts, John Kimbrough successfully stopped Coca-Cola from using his picture in advertising supplements in 1975. Kimbrough had been a star running back for the Texas A&M University football team in the late 1930s, finishing second to Michigan's Tom Harmon in the 1940 Heisman Trophy balloting. He and Davey O'Brien likely competed against each other in Southwest Conference games in 1938 when Kimbrough was a sophomore and O'Brien a senior. In the 1970s Coca-Cola told Kimbrough he had been selected by A&M as its most outstanding former player. He was asked to sit for a portrait and was told that he would receive the original, the school would get a copy, and the new Texas Sports Hall of Fame would get another copy. He was also told that reproductions might be used to promote college football. After Kimbrough's daughter saw her father's portrait in a Coke ad in the program of a Southern Methodist University–Wake Forest football game, he sued for appropriation. In 1975 a Texas appellate court rejected Coke's argument that, as a public figure, Kimbrough had no right to control his image. The court concluded that essentially under the right of publicity, he had exactly that right. Coke had argued that under *O'Brien v. Pabst*, Kimbrough had no right to his image, but the Texas appellate court disagreed, distinguishing Kimbrough's case from O'Brien's on the grounds that O'Brien's complaint was about the injury of using his name in a *beer* advertisement whereas Kimbrough was upset about the unauthorized use of his name and image in advertisement generally.[69]

Kimbrough had long been in the public eye before this lawsuit. After his All-American days at A&M, he, like many sports stars of the era, flirted with Hollywood, where he stared in two films in 1942 (*Sundown Jim* and *Lone Star Ranger*). He subsequently served as an army air corps pilot until 1946, when he was released from his military service. He spent several years playing professional football but left the sport in 1949 to return to Texas, where he owned and worked a ranch with his wife; he served in the Texas state legislature from 1953 to 1955. He died in 2006 at age eighty-seven.[70] His lawsuit moved the right of publicity forward in Texas.

HIRSCH v. S. C. JOHNSON & SON, INC.

In 1979 another case involved an athlete and the right of publicity. Elroy "Crazylegs" Hirsch was a freshman star running back at the University of Wisconsin in 1942. He was able to play only because the NCAA during World War II had waived an existing rule prohibiting freshmen from competing on varsity teams. After the fourth game of the season (during which, skimming precariously along the sideline, he ran for a sixty-two-yard touchdown), Francis Powers, reporter from the *Chicago Daily News*, nicknamed him Crazylegs. Powers apparently wrote that Hirsch looked like a "demented duck" whose "crazy legs were gyrating in six different directions all at the same time."[71]

Hirsch completed his athletic career at the University of Michigan because he was stationed in Ann Arbor with the marines. His athletic prowess at Michigan was noteworthy because he was the only athlete to letter in four major sports (football, basketball, baseball, and track) in the same year. Hirsch played professional football for eleven years and was inducted into the Pro Football Hall of Fame in 1968. His nickname is included in his enshrinement. For much of his professional career, he played in Los Angeles; in his spare time he starred in a number of movies, often as himself, as he did in *Crazylegs* (1953). After retiring from playing football he worked in the front office of the Los Angeles Rams until 1969, when he returned to the University of Wisconsin as athletic director. Throughout that time, Hirsch accepted endorsement deals and used the name Crazylegs. He seemed careful to protect his reputation; he turned down ads for cigarettes and withdrew from a beer commercial after returning to Wisconsin.[72]

Thus, when Hirsch discovered that his nickname had been used for a new moisturizing shaving gel for women by S. C. Johnson, he sued. S. C. Johnson argued that Wisconsin did not have a common-law right of privacy and that the name Crazylegs did not necessarily refer to Hirsch. The Wisconsin Supreme Court addressed these issues in 1979 after a lower court granted S. C. Johnson's motion to dismiss the case. After an extensive discussion regarding the literature about the right of privacy and the right of publicity, which included a reference to *Haelan Labs v. Topps Chewing Gum*, Justice Nathan Heffernan concluded that Wisconsin did have a common-law right of publicity (which Heffernan equated with the appropriation prong of the right of privacy) and that whether or not the use of the word Crazylegs was associated with Hirsch was a question for a jury.[73] Subsequent to that decision, the case disappeared from public record, suggesting the parties reached some sort of settlement.

After the lawsuit, Hirsh's life continued much as it had before the lawsuit. He spent eighteen years as the athletic director of the University of Wisconsin, retiring in 1987 and becoming a radio commentator for the Badger football games. That same year he was criticized for appearing in a beer advertisement to raise money to build an indoor practice facility at the university. Throughout the remainder of his life, he served as the honorary chair and race starter for the Crazylegs Classic, a run to benefit the University of Wisconsin Athletic Department. Hirsh died in 2004 at age eighty.[74]

NEWCOMBE v. COORS

Newcombe's case was one in a line of other cases examining what rights athletes had in controlling their image. Newcombe's lawsuit pushed the boundaries of *Kimbrough v. Coca-Cola* because, unlike the Coke ad, the Killian Red ad did not overtly identify Newcombe. Initially, Newcombe looked as if he would have as much success as Davey O'Brien had. In December 1994, U.S. District Court Judge Stephen Wilson dismissed most of Newcombe's complaints. He said that "no average reader would be aware that the pitcher allegedly depicted in the advertisement is opposed to the consumption of alcohol,"[75] and then he dismissed the claims for appropriation, invasion of privacy, defamation, and intentional infliction of emotional distress. It is interesting to note that the artist who did the drawing, Michael Cassidy of Southern California, admitted in a deposition that he had, in fact, based his drawing on the photo of Newcombe pitching in the 1949 World Series, just as Newcombe had suggested from the beginning. The judge, however, believed that the origin of the drawing was irrelevant if the average person did not recognize or think less of Newcombe. Newcombe's attorney said that everyone who knew Newcombe recognized him in the drawing and that Newcombe felt "humiliated and angry that it could be perceived that he is endorsing an alcoholic beverage. . . . It gives the impression that he might have sold out." Further, Newcombe submitted depositions of a number of retired baseball players from the era who recognized him, but the judge dismissed this evidence because they were "not members of the consuming public."[76]

Newcombe appealed the district court's dismissal of his case and won the right to go to trial. The Ninth Circuit Court of Appeals used California law to examine Newcombe's appeal. Relying on prior case law,[77] Chief Judge Proctor J. Hug noted that to win his claim that Coors had violated his right of privacy, Newcombe needed to establish that his likeness had been used, that the use of the image was to Coors's advantage, that Newcombe had not consented to the use, and that he had suffered some injury from its use.[78]

Hug then addressed each component in order. He concluded that a drawing was parallel to a photograph and that because the California statue regarding privacy required that the photograph be "readily identifiable" in order for the plaintiff to prevail, so too must Newcombe.[79] Judge Hug believed the drawing in the ad to be "virtual identical" to the 1949 photo of Newcombe, "as though the black and white newspaper photo had been traced and colored in."[80] Further, the judge rejected Coors's claim that the drawing was generic because it just showed the pitcher's stance, in part because the art director of the advertising company had previously rejected the work of the same artist showing another pitcher with the distinctive stance of pitcher Juan Marichal as being too identifiable. Judge Hug clearly believed the drawing was recognizably Don Newcombe. With regard to the question of how the use benefited the defendants, Hug agreed with the lower court that Time Inc. did not benefit and was rightfully dismissed from the lawsuit. Coors and the advertising firm of Foote, Cone, and Belding did, conversely, benefit. Judge Hug concluded that Newcombe had not consented to the use of his image and that he was injured because there was no compensation; the court overruled the dismissal of the privacy violation complaint against Coors and the advertising firm.[81] The Ninth Circuit also rejected the notion that Coors was not trying to use Newcombe's image to sell beer. Judge Hug wrote that "it would not be unreasonable for a jury to conclude that there was a direct connection" between Newcombe and the product being advertised.[82]

The Ninth Circuit rejected Newcombe's theory that the defendants had defamed him. The court concluded that the former ball player had presented no evidence that the average person would think his endorsement of alcohol defamatory. Only if the average person knew of Newcombe's position as a recovering alcoholic might that person think less of Newcombe.[83]

The Ninth Circuit reversed much of the lower court's decision and ordered the matter set for trial, but no such trial seems to have occurred. As with many such decisions, the case disappeared from the legal record, public documents, and even the Denver-area newspapers. Presumably, Coors and the advertising company reached some sort of settlement with Newcombe, given the strong language of Judge Hug regarding Newcombe's recognizability.

IMPLICATIONS OF THE CASE

Newcombe's victory was the culmination of a series of lawsuits attempting to create or protect athletes' rights of privacy under the appropriation prong, or as it was dubbed in *Haelan Labs*, the right of publicity. The rights of the athletes, though, had to be balanced with the right of free speech. Generally, the cases described above were about commercial speech—the use of an athlete's image or name used without permission to sell a product. The flip side is that athletes' names and images are often in the press as part of the news. The athletes in these cases gained their fame largely because the press reported their sports performances. The courts continue to struggle to distinguish between what is protected "communicative" speech and less-protected "commercial speech."[84]

For Coors Brewery, the lawsuit was likely an annoyance but seemed to have limited effect on the company. The Killian's brand was expanded to include a brown ale and a honey ale in the mid-1990s, but neither was terribly successful, and the company refocused its efforts on marketing the red beer with a commercial spot called "Red Is Not a Color."[85] By 2006 the Killian's brand had declined by fifty percent over the previous five years,[86] and in 2015 the brand had been renamed George Killian's Irish Red but was still marketed by Coors. Coors Brewery itself only expanded. The company bought Bass Brewers in the United Kingdom in 2002, and three years later, Coors merged with Molson Brewery of Canada to form Molson Coors.[87] Molson Coors, the third-largest American brewery, merged with Miller, the second-largest American brewery, in 2008.[88] The merger was an attempt to compete more effectively with Anheuser-Busch, the largest brewery in America. MillerCoors was, in 2014, the second-largest American brewery, controlling roughly 30 percent of the U.S. beer market.[89]

For Don Newcombe, this case was important enough to pursue, but he did not discuss it publicly after the trial, perhaps because of a settlement agreement. In 2014, at age eighty-eight, Newcombe was still affiliated with the Dodgers as a special assistant to the chairman. Jason Verlander joined Newcombe in 2011 as one of the only two players to win Rookie of the Year, MVP, and the Cy Young Award. The following January, Newcombe introduced Verlander at the Baseball Writers' Award dinner, where Verlander received the Cy Young and the MVP. MLB still lauds Newcombe's work in the community and with individuals with substance-abuse problems.[90] Newcombe seems to have kept the oath he swore on his son's head to never drink again and has been diligent in helping other people, especially baseball players, deal with their own alcoholism. His very public battle required that he fight against Coors's use of his image.

6

ART VERSUS IMAGE: THE FIRST AMENDMENT VERSUS THE RIGHT OF PUBLICITY

ETW v. JIREH PUBLISHING (2000)

In 1997 Tiger Woods made golfing history when he won the prestigious Masters tournament for the first time. He not only won the tournament in his first attempt as a professional, but the twenty-one-year-old multiracial golfer won by twelve strokes, a Masters record. The conservative Augusta (Georgia) National Golf Club, which sponsors the tournament, had not allowed nonwhite players to compete in the tournament until 1975 and had only accepted its first nonwhite member in 1990, just seven years before Woods's remarkable victory. The club, with an estimated three hundred members, remained elite and conservative and excluded women from membership until 2012, when it admitted as members former Secretary of State Condoleezza Rice and South Carolina business executive Darla Moore.

Woods's victory, not surprisingly, inspired artistic tributes. The Franklin Mint created, advertised, and sold advance copies of the Tiger Woods Eyewitness Commemorative Medal, which had Woods's image on it. The victory also inspired Rick Rush, an artist specializing in sports memorabilia, to create an image of Woods driving the ball while flanked by his caddie and his opponent's caddie. Floating in the sky above the scene were the faces of Jack Nicklaus, Arnold Palmer, and other legendary golfers. The serigraph image was then reproduced as a lithograph, and more than five thousand copies were offered for sale. Woods promptly sued both the Franklin Mint and Rick Rush, trying to stop production under his legal right of publicity, a derivation of the right of privacy. The artists relied on the First Amendment freedom-of-speech clause as a defense. The courts ruled that prints were art but that coins were not.

BUILDING TIGER'S IMAGE

The story of Woods's youth has been well documented in many books and book chapters.[1] In fact, one challenge in writing about Woods is that so much has already been published. Much of this material was issued prior to 2009, when problems in his marriage became public and his public image took a negative turn. But before 2009, Woods and his team were remarkably good at mediating his image in the press. Some of the positive publicity Woods received was because he was a likeable young man, and many journalists were rooting for his success. Another aspect seems to have been the fear of crossing "Team Tiger." For example, Tim Rosaforte, a *Sports Illustrated* writer, devoted the preface of *Tiger Woods: The Makings of a Champion* to explaining how he, as a journalist, had followed Woods and gained his trust. Rosaforte allegedly lost that trust when he wrote that Earl Woods had predicted his son would win fourteen major championships, which would be a record. Earl had also apparently said other things about Tiger—as well as others—that were not reported. Allegedly, Tiger was unhappy with Rosaforte for publishing information that young Tiger felt was off the record. Rosaforte defended himself, both to Tiger and readers, writing, "I thought I was going out of my way to protect *his* interests, that if any other writer was in that tent they would have printed *everything*, and Earl *really* would have looked bad."[2] Should Rosaforte have reported everything? Maybe, maybe not, but the point is that he chose to protect the Woods family rather than reporting everything he heard. Even with that decision, he felt that he had been disavowed by Team Tiger for at least that moment. Reporting or offering negative opinions about the young golfer appeared to place the reporter at risk of alienation.

Woods's multiracial background also seems to have contributed to the mythology surrounding him in the press. In an analysis of the early and extensive coverage of Woods between January 1996 and June 1997 (the first eighteen months of his professional career), communication scholar Judy Polumbaum and sociologist Stephen G. Weiting noted that media coverage relied on superlative language and helped to create or retell the mythology of Woods that his father had provided or perhaps sold. Much of that myth was about his athletic excellence (which Woods would fulfill over time), but the myth was also about Woods's potential and his possibility for being golf's, and perhaps America's, messiah. Woods was represented as the hope for a better, multicultural America. Presciently, the scholars wrote in reference to some early gaffes the young professional made: "Somehow Woods always recovers. Somehow he's always forgiven."[3] Communication scholar Andrew C. Billings noted in his analysis of the early media coverage of Woods that tradition-ally there had been an extensive history of commentators using racialized language about nonwhite athletes. Black quarterbacks in football were often described as athletic, while their white counterparts were described as cere-bral and hard working. Billings found that in television coverage of Woods, "black" stereotypes were used much more often when he was losing. At that point, commentators discussed his physical attributes and his athletic abil-ity, but if he was in contention, they commented on his concentration and work ethic.[4] No matter the motivation, young Woods received an amazing amount of good press.

WOODS'S YOUTH

Eldrick (Tiger) Woods was born December 30, 1975, in Cypress, California, to Earl and Kultida Woods. His father was a retired U.S. Army lieutenant colonel, and his mother was a native of Thailand. His father gave him the same nickname he had given to a Vietnamese soldier and friend with whom he had been close during the Vietnam War. Woods began swinging a golf club almost as soon as he learned to stand; at age two he appeared on the *Mike Douglas Show*, where he putted with Bob Hope. The next year he shot a 48 on a nine-hole course. He appeared in *Golf Digest* two years later and won the first of six Optimist International Junior Tournament titles when he was eight years old. Prior to turning pro when he was twenty, Woods had won six United States Golf Association National Championships, three junior championships, three amateur championships, and the NCAA col-legiate championship.[5] By the numbers, he was one of the most successful amateurs in modern golf history.

Most sources insist that while Woods's parents were supportive of his golfing ambitions, they did not pressure him to play. Stories abound of their attempts to encourage Woods to try other sports or to go out with friends, but Woods made golf his priority. That said, the family spent thousands of dollars for travel and coaches and countless hours on Woods's golf. Woods's father was his first coach and his first psychologist, working subtly to build Woods's concentration by trying to distract him during his swing. Woods's mother served as Woods's chauffer and support crew until Earl retired from work and could travel with their son; Kultida encouraged Woods to crush his opponents but to be a good sport both during and after the match. Both parents believed, and publicly stated, that their son would be both a remark-able golfer and an important person beyond the world of golf.

Golf in the United States has generally been the preserve of wealthy whites. The equipment and greens fees are expensive, and many private courses were, and still are, restricted to members; furthermore, many of those restrictions have excluded people of color, and all have means restrictions. Woods's mother is of Thai, Chinese, and Caucasian descent. His father's heritage included African American, Native American, Chinese, and Caucasian. Woods's multiracial and middle-class background was significant because he was not the typical golfing protégé. Woods's father, as retired military, had access to military courses and consequently so did his son. Woods's family was also willing to borrow money to pay for his coaches and fees. Fairly quickly, Woods's fame and success gave him access to almost any course he wanted, but his golfing success likely was accelerated by the access to more reasonably priced military courses.[6]

As famous as Woods was as a child, he took another step forward in high school, when he continued to win both amateur titles and began to appear in professional events. At age sixteen he played in the PGA event Nissan Los Angeles Open, where he failed to make the cut, but he shot only five over par during the course of the two days he played. Given his age and the fact that this was his first PGA event, his performance was a harbinger of the future. Although he would not make the cut in any of the PGA events as a high school student, his presence indicted that the sponsors and tournament organizers recognized his potential as a golfer and, more important, as a selling point. As a golfer, Woods's experiences with the older players improved his game and showed him the challenges of being a touring pro.[7]

After high school Woods announced he would attend Stanford University on a golf scholarship and major in accounting. According to one biography, Stanford did not have an undergraduate accounting major, but Woods apparently reported that "the dean, the athletic director and the business director said, 'We'll work with you. We'll create you a major.'"[8] Stanford at the time offered the option of an individually designed major for any student interested in creating one.[9] Beyond academics, Woods's golfing career continued to develop while he was in college. He won the USGA Amateur title two more times, the NCAA title once, and a number of other tournaments. He also tied for forty-first place at the 1995 Masters, his first appearance at a major championship, and he was the only amateur to make the cut. As a college student, he carried a full academic load, lived in the regular dormitories, and had to abide by NCAA regulations. While the academic load was challenging, the NCAA regulations in many ways proved more frustrating.

Prior to entering Stanford, Woods and his parents repeatedly said that he would complete his college degree. Phil Mickelson, another successful young amateur, had completed his degree at Arizona State University before turning pro in 1992. Woods, it seemed, planned to model his collegiate career after Mickelson's. While Woods had, in some ways, a more successful amateur career than Mickelson had, Woods had more problems maintaining his eligibility with the NCAA and the USGA. At one point the NCAA denied Woods the opportunity of accepting an honorary membership at a golf club, although it later reversed itself. Subsequently, while he was still enrolled at Stanford, Woods went to dinner with golfing legend Arnold Palmer. Palmer, despite Woods's offer, picked up the check—a possible NCAA violation. After Stanford declared Woods ineligible over the incident, the NCAA investigated and determined that because Woods had known Palmer since before college, Palmer could pay for dinner. One version of the story claimed Woods wrote a check to Palmer to pay his share of dinner and that Stanford athletics asked for the canceled check to auction at a fundraising dinner.[10] In addition, Woods had issues with the NCAA regarding his choice of golf balls (not the Stanford-issued ones) and where he could conduct golf clinics. When Earl wrote his first book, *Training a Tiger*, the NCAA informed him via Stanford that Tiger could not appear on the cover or make promotional appearances; he could only write the book's forward and appear in instructional photos on the interior.[11] The combination of Woods's success, the challenges of balancing his life as a full-time student as well as college athlete and top-ranked amateur, and the frustration with the NCAA and USGA limitations on him all likely contributed to Woods's decision to turn pro in 1996 at age twenty. The inordinate amount of money awaiting him may also have been a factor.

SELLING TIGER

Early in Woods's career the sport management giant IMG recognized his potential as a revenue source and hired his father, Earl, to scout junior golf circuits for future IMG clients. Hiring a parent to recruit the child as an athlete has long been a practice in college sports, and Earl's hiring may have been along those lines. Regardless, when Woods announced in 1996, immediately after winning his third consecutive U.S. Amateur title, that he was turning professional, IMG was his management company. IMG was prepared. Before Woods stepped to the podium on August 27, 1996, to face the press about his decision to turn pro, he had already signed a deal with Nike for $40 million for five years, including a $7.5 million signing bonus. He agreed to play with Titlist balls and other equipment for roughly $3 million annually.[12] At the press conference, he began with, "Well, I guess it's hello world." Within two days that line was the cornerstone of a Nike advertisement in which the text overlaid the ad. Written as if spoken by Woods, the text reads in part, "Hello world. There are still golf courses in the United States that I cannot play because of the color of my skin. I'm told I'm not ready for you. Are you ready for me?"[13] Fortunately for both Woods's wallet and for the companies sponsoring him, Woods was quickly a success in his rookie season on the PGA. Despite beginning the Tour late in the season, he finished twenty-fourth on the money list, earning $790,594.[14]

Although a remarkably successful golfer, most of Woods's wealth early in his career came through endorsements. In 1997, the year he won the Masters in record fashion, Woods earned almost $2.5 million playing golf, the leading money winner on the PGA Tour.[15] That money paled compared with his endorsement dollars. In addition to his $43 million deals with Nike and Titlist, after winning the Masters, Woods signed a deal with American Express for an estimated $13 to $30 million.[16] The idea behind companies hiring individuals to endorse their products is that the buyer feels an affinity toward the brand because of the endorser and will then buy the product.[17] Woods's youth, his success, his story, and his being different from other golfers in terms of race and background made marketers think he would be an ideal endorser. They were right. Prior to signing Tiger Woods, Nike did not manufacture any golf equipment beyond shoes, but in 1998 the company established a golf division. Two years later, Woods began using Nike golf balls. Marketing scholars estimate that because of Woods's use and endorsement, Nike was able to charge an extra 2.5 percent per ball, and the company made an extra $103 million on the sales of almost ten million balls.[18]

Woods, Woods's name, and Woods's image represented big money for both Woods and IMG, and anyone else who could to stake a claim. When the Woods family learned that journalist Tim Rosaforte was writing his biography, Tiger was less helpful than Rosaforte would have liked, although Earl did speak with him. Rosaforte noted that "Tiger obviously didn't like the fact that somebody was going to cash in on his fame. The International Management Group [IMG] didn't like it because they weren't getting their 20 percent."[19] When others learned of his plan to write the biography, Rosaforte wrote, "I quickly found out that Team Tiger and IMG were not going to help me in any way. . . . I need [Tiger], and someday even with the $40 million from his Nike contract in the bank, he may come to learn that he needs me, and the rest of the media too."[20] Rosaforte published his book in 1997 when Woods was twenty-two years old, but his words about protecting Woods's cash flow reflected Woods and IMG's strategy. His words about Woods one day needing the media were prophetic, given the later circumstances of the breakup of his marriage and the media's coverage of that event.

Woods has reason to want to protect his image; he may be one of the most popular subjects of sporting biographies in history. He has been the subject of countless books, mass media articles, and academic articles. Titles of works published prior to 2009 ranged from the overstated *The First Coming: Tiger Woods, Master or Martyr?*[21] to the overblown: *The Chosen One: Tiger Woods and the Dilemma of Greatness.*[22] Many writers, from journalists to academics, seemed determined to profit from Woods. Woods seemed equally determined to protect his own assets.

In part to market and in part to protect his image, Woods and his team formed the ETW Corporation. Early in Woods's professional career, the company filed multiple applications with the U.S. Patent and Trademark Office for the mark of "Tiger Woods" for a number of different products such as art prints, calendars, photos, pens, and posters.[23] In 1996 and 1997, ETW sued six companies that it claimed had violated Woods's right of publicity.[24] Two of those companies were the Franklin Mint and Jireh Publishing Corporation, both of which attempted to profit from Woods's record-setting Master's win in 1997.

Woods's first major victory was historic. Not only did Woods win by a record twelve strokes (a record low score), but he was also the youngest man to win the tournament as well as the first man of African or Asian descent to do so. The event was the highest-rated golf event in history. Scalpers demanded $10,000 for a pass, and used passes sold for $50 after the tournament was over. Columnist Rick Reilly wrote at the time, "If you were there the week everything changed in golf, you just had to reach out and touch a piece of history." Reilly was impressed by everything Woods had accomplished but particularly noted the racial significance: Clifford Roberts, the founder of the tournament, had once said, "As long as I'm alive, golfers will be white, and caddies will be black"; Reilly noted that with Woods's victory "the golfer was black and the caddie was white." Reilly reported that Woods acknowledged the historic moment too. After his victory, Woods hugged Lee Elder, who in 1975 was the first black man to play the Masters, and thanked him for making his victory possible.[25] It was an inspirational event, even for artists.

FRANKLIN MINT

The Franklin Mint, located in suburban Philadelphia, was founded in 1964 by Joseph Segal (who later created QVC, one of the first home-shopping television networks). The company created and sold collectibles such as figurines and coins, although by 1996 coins and ingots were about one percent of its product line. At one point the company had licensing agreements with such diverse clients as the Vatican, Graceland, Coca-Cola, and 20th Century Fox. In 1996 the Franklin Mint sold items to some seventy million households per week and had an annual revenue of $600 million in U.S. sales alone. It employed roughly forty-five hundred people in twenty different countries.[26]

In 1997 Woods (or the ETW Corporation) discovered that the Franklin Mint had begun selling the "Tiger Woods Eyewitness Commemorative Medal." The Eyewitness series had documented significant world events, such as the signing of peace treaties and presidential inaugurations, for the previous twenty-five years without incident.[27] The Franklin Mint marketed the Woods medal for about $37.50 (plus shipping and handling) and pre-sold between two thousand and twenty-five hundred medals.[28] Woods, who had neither been contacted by the Franklin Mint for his permission nor given a piece of the profits, promptly filed for a preliminary injunction to stop production of the medal. He won.[29] The ETW Corporation relied on laws such as copyright, trademarking, and the right of publicity in their lawsuits against companies and individuals who tried to use Woods's image without permission. Woods's father, Earl, was the first president of ETW, and the incorporation address matched that of the International Management Group (IMG) in Cleveland, Woods's agency.[30] The power of Woods's machine eventually led to a settlement of an undisclosed cash payment and a permanent injunction from ever using his name or likeness.[31]

Prior to the settlement, the lawyers for the Franklin Mint argued that the company promoted communications and thus the medals were protected under the freedom-of-speech clause of the First Amendment. Federal District Court Judge Kim Wardlaw disagreed, stating that "the defendant's medal appears to be an attempt to capitalize on the plaintiff's fame. There is little if any protected speech. This is a commercial object."[32] This statement refers to the fact that the First Amendment has never been held to be absolute—one cannot yell fire in a crowded room without repercussions—but, rather, different kinds of speech receive different levels of protection. Political speech has been the most protected. Artistic speech has often been deemed to be political and therefore also has received greater protection. Purely commercial speech, speech for selling or profit, has received the least protection and can be restricted by law. For example, television stations were prohibited by law for years from accepting advertising for hard alcohol. Because the Franklin Mint argued that it was engaged in communication rather than art, the judge could easily say that the company was engaged in commercial speech and afford it less protection. This would not be a legal mistake that the next artist would make.

ETW CORP. v. JIREH PUBLISHING, INC.

Like the Franklin Mint, Rick Rush was also inspired by Woods's epic Masters victory. A sports-memorabilia artist from Tuscaloosa, Alabama, who had been painting famous athletes and athletic moments for more than twenty years, Rush painted a numbered and signed series of 250 serigraphs called "The Masters of Augusta," which sold for $700 each. Additionally, five thousand smaller lithograph versions of the painting were produced and sold for $15 each.

Rush combined his love of sports and his art. He was himself a high school athlete; on his Web site, his biography states "an early claim to fame was leading his [high school football] team to victory over Foley, led by future Super Bowl XI winner Ken Stabler."[33] He was a graduate of the University of Alabama (the subject of many of his images), and after a stint of working for magazines, in 1975, he made art his primary career. Rush's preferred methodology is serigraph printing. In this medium, each color is laid on the canvas one at a time, given time to dry, and then the next layer is added. It is an evolution of silk screening that relies on patient and painstaking artistry. A serigraph print is the final product. According to Rush's Web site, many of his serigraph prints are also available as lithographs. Lithographs are not quite as time consuming to create as serigraphs, but they are still more complicated and detailed than a simple copy of the original serigraph.

Rush's artwork has documented victories and great performances in almost every major American sport. Athletes from Michael Jordan and Magic Johnson to John Elway and Mary Lou Retton are recognizable in Rush's art. On Rush's Web site, each painting has text below it explaining the significance of the athletes and the event. The athletes are named in the text as well as often having their name visible on a jersey in the image itself.

After Woods won the 1997 Masters tournament, Rush created a detailed serigraph commemorating the historic moment. He called it "The Masters of Augusta." In the image, Woods is represented in three poses: in the center in full swing, he is in his trademark red shirt (he wears always wears red on Sundays of tournaments); to the right is an image of Woods wearing white and crouching with his hands as blinkers lining up a putt; and to the left, in red again, he is crouched, placing the ball for a putt. In the background on one side is his caddie, Fluff Cowen, and on the other side stands the caddie for his playing partner. In the near background is the Augusta Clubhouse, an iconic Southern-mansion-style white building, and in the far background, acting as the sky (in shades of grey and blue), are former Masters champions in various stages of swinging clubs in front of the Masters leaderboard. The legends floating in the sky above Woods include Arnold Palmer, Sam Sneed, Ben Hogan, Walter Hagen, Bobby Jones, and Jack Nicklaus.[34] An insert accompanies the print, which specifically identifies Woods, notes that the image shows "his awesome swing."[35]

Unlike many of Woods's famous predecessors (including the others in the offending print) who had been subjects in Rush's work, Woods filed a lawsuit charging the Jireh Publishing Corporation (owned by Rush and his brother) with violating Woods's trademark and right of publicity. It was the first time in twenty-seven years that the company had been sued for trademark infringement.[36] Early on during the trial, the situation looked bleak for the much-less-powerful Jireh. ETW had the power of IMG and IMG's legal cadre; Jireh had a solo practitioner representing it. Prior to the trial, Federal District Court Judge Patricia A. Gaughan ordered Jireh to provide the names of the 879 distributors and customers who had purchased the prints. Woods's attorneys announced they planned to depose all of those 879 and that they would amend their complaints to request that Jireh pay Woods's legal fees. Because of those additional depositions, the legal fees would be exponentially larger, and if Jireh lost, paying those legal fees would likely bankrupt the company. At that point, some scholars wondered if Jireh would be forced to settle the case.[37] Jireh chose to move forward and risk losing.

The case generated intense interest. Amicus briefs (briefs filed by parties not directly involved in the case but with a deep interest in the proceedings) were filed on both sides. Those supporting Woods tended to be those with an image worth protecting, including the estates of Frank Sinatra, Elvis Presley, Jimi Hendrix, Gene Autry, and golfer Bobby Jones. Live celebrities, including those in the sporting and entertainment fields, filed briefs as well; the players' associations of professional football and baseball and the Screen Actors Guild contributed. It is no surprise that Jireh supporters were those who might themselves be at risk of future lawsuits if Woods won. They also were firm supporters of the First Amendment. The list included the *New York Times*, Time Incorporated, the Newspaper Association of America, the Society of Professional Journalists, and seventy-three law professors.[38]

At the district-court level, Judge Gaughan dismissed Woods's claims that his right of publicity and his trademark rights had been violated, concluding that Rush had a right under the First Amendment to create art. Woods's team had asserted six claims: three different federal (and one state) trademark violations, deceptive trade practices, and a violation of Woods's right of publicity. Both sides had moved for summary judgment, to end the case before a full trial. The judge concluded that despite Woods's trademark of the phrase "Tiger Woods," Rush had not violated the trademark because Woods had failed to prove that he had trademarked absolutely every image, every pose, or every photograph of himself. Trademark law is dependent on a clear, consistent representation of the trademarked image (such as the Nike swoosh) and Woods could not do that with his entire body and range of life. Woods's team argued that Woods's image had been trademarked for the purpose of posters, but the judge noted that the six posters offered into evidence all had different poses. She suggested that "if anything, the posters show that plaintiff does not use a consistent image of Tiger Woods as a trademark" because of the different poses.[39]

Further, Judge Gaughan was unwilling to allow Woods exclusively to control the use of his name. She noted that doing so would eliminate all fair use of his name and any reference to him without his permission (and make this chapter perhaps legally actionable). Judge Gaughan found a Second Circuit case to be relevant to her decision. Babe Ruth's daughters had trademarked his name for "paper articles, namely, playing cards, writing paper and envelopes." The defendant in that case had published a calendar with photos of Babe Ruth. Although the daughters had argued that their trademark restricted the use of their father's name and image, the Second Circuit disagreed.[40] Judge Gaughan found this case to be applicable to Woods's case and rejected all his trademark claims.

Woods's claims that his right of publicity had been violated failed because Rush, unlike the Franklin Mint, argued that his work was art and not commercial speech and thus protected under the First Amendment. The judge noted that there needed to be a balance between the publicity rights of a public figure and the First Amendment rights of an artist. Woods's attorneys had not focused their brief on the right of publicity, preferring to argue the trademark complaints; Rush's attorneys, however, insisted that Rush's work was artistic and not commercial speech. The judge acknowledged that art had been broadly defined to include music, books, and movies. Woods's attorneys argued that the serigraphs and lithographs were analogous to posters and sport memorabilia, but the judge was unwilling to deny posters art status, and she was even more leery of saying that the prints of Rush's work were not art. She noted that Rush's art was not "mere copying of an idea but

. . . a unique expression of an idea."[41] She concluded that Rush's images were art and thus protected by the First Amendment. In general, defining what is art is not simple and tends to be done by the courts (and the individual) on a case-by-case basis.[42]

Reaction to the judge's decision in this case was not popular among celebrities and their camps, who naturally sided with Woods. "The judge's opinion threatens the very existence of the right of publicity, because nearly every commercial product, be it a figurine, trading card, replica jersey or poster, has design elements that could be characterized as artistic," argued an attorney for the NFL Player's Association.[43] Woods's appellate lawyer argued to the press that artists had the right to create art under the First Amendment but not to sell or profit from it. Although initially he implied that it was acceptable under the First Amendment to create a painting and hang it on a wall without profiting from it, he later argued that an artist should ask permission of a subject prior to creating the art. If the subject said no, then the artists should not do the work. [44]

ETW appealed the judge's decision, and Jireh Publishing retained the legal and financial support from those other groups who supported a strong First Amendment. In a joint amicus brief, three media sources argued that the right of publicity should be understood to limit the fraudulent use of the celebrity's image implying commercial endorsement and not ever to apply to any artistic expression (with artistic expression broadly defined). The brief read:

> The point ETW seems blind to is that the use of Mr. Woods's name or likeness in the context of artistic expression does not imply his endorsement of the art. Art is not a product for these purposes. The fact that visual art by its nature generally involves tangible media does not convert artistic expression into a product. The medium is incidental. Where speech is the thing being sold, the speech is protected. Mr. Woods's extraordinary accomplishments give rise to many benefits and a few burdens. One of the burdens, we submit, is having to see himself depicted in words and pictures by people who have things to say about him.[45]

To the delight of the scholars and the press, the Sixth Circuit Appellate Court upheld the district court's ruling in favor of Jireh Publishing. In 2003, Judge James L. Graham, joined by Judge Eugene Siler in a 2–1 decision, dismissed Woods's trademark claim: "ETW asks us, in effect, to constitute Woods himself as a walking, talking trademark" and "this is an untenable claim."[46] The majority noted that Woods's name did not appear in the title of the work or anywhere in the print; it appeared only in the supportive, descriptive materials. Although the court stated that a celebrity's name could be used in the title so long as there was "artistic relevance," in this case the use of Woods's name was "purely descriptive."[47] The majority noted that nothing in the text implied that Woods was the artist or was distributing the work. These conclusions stymied the trademark and the deceptive-trade arguments Woods made. The court reminded ETW that Woods had been photographed countless times and that no one thought that every photograph contained an implied endorsement.[48]

Further, the majority decision was unwilling to allow Woods's right of publicity to trump free speech. Plus, it added that Rush had a right to profit from his art: "Speech is protected even though it is carried in a form that is sold for profit," adding that "even pure commercial speech is entitled to significant First Amendment protection."[49] The court quickly commented that Rush's work was not commercial speech and that the question before them was a matter of balancing Woods's rights with Rush's rights. The court acknowledged that the State of Ohio (where the lawsuit was filed) recognized the right of publicity and that the Sixth Circuit Court of Appeals had thus recognized it. But the court admitted that "there is an inherent tension" between the right of publicity and the First Amendment.[50] The Sixth Circuit majority, after a careful analysis of previous case law, concluded that "Rush's work has substantial informational and creative content which outweighs any adverse effect on ETW's market."[51] It's interesting to note that the court added that Woods made a great deal of money from golf, both from the game and from his endorsements; the court was certain that he could continue to profit from his image and was uncertain that Rush's prints would diminish Woods's value. Further, following the California Supreme Court's use of the transformative test (if the image substantively transforms reality, it is art), the majority believed Rush's print to have been just that, largely because of the message that Woods would join the other Masters of Augusta.[52]

Judge Eric Clay, writing in dissent, was convinced that Woods's right of publicity had been violated and that significant issues of fact regarding the possible trademark violations should go to trial. In the section regarding the publicity claim in his lengthy dissent, Clay stated that the majority used three different tests to balance Rush's rights versus Woods's and thus reached three different conclusions. In this, Clay has a point. The majority did mention multiple tests but found that each benefited Rush. Clay argued that the correct test in this case was the California "transformative test," which was one of the many tests the majority acknowledged. Clay, though, believed that

Rush's work failed the transformative test. The California Supreme Court had created that test in deciding a case between the company that owned the rights to The Three Stooges and a T-shirt company. The T-shirt company had made a charcoal drawing of The Three Stooges, turned it into a lithograph, and then printed the image onto T-shirts, which they sold. The image was fairly lifelike. The California court concluded that the process of reproducing the images of the Stooges did not add any "new expression, meaning, or message" to the original images of the Stooges. The court said the test was "whether and to what extent the new work is transformative."[53] Judge Clay then applied that test to the facts of Woods's case as he viewed it: Rush's work was not transformative. He noted that the serigraphs looked much like a Nike poster that had been submitted into evidence. He added that although "Rush is an adequately skilled artist," the focus of the work was Woods and the representation of Woods was too lifelike to have been transformative. Because the other figures in the print were marginalized or in the background, Clay did not consider that sufficient enough to have transformed Woods's image. He argued that the prints gained their commercial value by "exploiting the fame and celebrity status that Woods has worked to achieve."[54]

REACTION TO *JIREH*

Reaction to the Sixth Circuit's ruling was mixed. Immediately after the decision was rendered, and to no one's surprise, Rush's attorney Dennis J. Niermann crowed, "Artists and those involved in the creative profession have cause today to celebrate."[55] In an interesting twist, a different sports artist, LeRoy Neiman, disagreed with the sentiment and the verdict. He believed that celebrities, including athletes, should get a share of all artistic profits. He himself had created a serigraph of Mark McGwire hitting a home run and charged $7,500 per print. He told reporters, "We had the official approval of the team, the league, the player. Each gets a small percentage. . . . Why should an artist just looking for a hot market do something without having an arrangement? The player is entitled to a cut."[56]

Some scholars (but not the seventy-three law professors who had written on behalf of Jireh) were not particularly enthusiastic about the ruling. Legal scholar Michael J. Breslin argued that the appellate court failed to factor in the marketability of the art; he asked if Woods were replaced with another, unidentifiable golfer, would the prints have sold as well?[57] Legal scholar Sharlene A. McAvoy and actor William Windom argued that the majority was wrong to distinguish Woods's case from *Comedy III Productions v. Saderup*.

Siding with the dissent, they found the two cases quite parallel: Saderup used his own charcoal-drawn image of the Stooges as the basis of lithographs and T-shirts. The California court prohibited him from selling anything but the original charcoal drawing itself without permission from the copyright holder. The scholars believed *Saderup* to be more fair and to better balance the right of publicity for the celebrity with the First Amendment rights of the artists.[58] Other scholars suggested that the court in *Jireh* reached the proper conclusion, even if the court's means to that end were convoluted. "What we are seeing here are public figures who are attempting to control what is said about them, what is written about them, what ideas are depicted in art and in literature," argued scholars John McMillen and Rebecca Atkinson. They concluded that "under the claim of a right of publicity to control their persona, they are in the process of trampling on fundamental rights of expression."[59] One scholar praised the Sixth Circuit majority, arguing that the decision factored in the role of creativity in the production of art in distinguishing it from mere merchandizing.[60]

These criticisms have some merit: the likelihood of Rush selling his prints if the golfer were generic seems remote, but from a historical perspective Woods could not be removed from the moment. If the artwork was celebrating that moment in history, then Woods had to be in it or it would not be historical. At the same time, the line between sports merchandise and art is perilously thin. Those representing celebrities were understandably concerned that this decision might hinder their ability to sell their own faces.

LIFE AFTER LAWSUITS

Franklin Mint's loss to Woods was the beginning of a downhill slide. In 1998 one of Tiger Woods's attorneys, Mark S. Lee, represented Princess Diana's estate and her memorial fund in a lawsuit against the Franklin Mint for the unauthorized use of her image on a variety of items. The company had been producing Diana-related items since her marriage to Prince Charles in 1981 without Diana's authorization but also without her objection. The case was repeatedly dismissed by the courts, and Franklin Mint was awarded $2.3 million in attorney fees.[61] In 2002 Franklin Mint countersued both the charity and the law firm representing the charity, claiming that Franklin Mint's own lawyers' fees had topped $7 million and that the company had suffered from the memorial fund's lawsuits. The memorial fund's leaders blamed the fund's lawyers (including Lee) for encouraging them to pursue legal action, and the charity suspended charitable donations pending the outcome of the lawsuit.[62]

The parties apparently agreed in 2004 to settle for roughly $25 million, to be made as donations (as agreed upon by Franklin Mint and the charity), but a judge rejected the settlement.[63] Diana's charitable fund officially closed its doors in 2011, in part because of the financial pressures of the lawsuit.[64]

Although the Franklin Mint won that lawsuit, its efforts, along with a changing cultural landscape, cost the company. In 2003 the Mint laid off two hundred employees at its Philadelphia headquarters and announced that it would refocus its production on cast-iron cars, airplanes, and Harley-Davidson collectibles because of declining interest in figurines.[65] By the next year the company had closed all of its retail stores and its museum.[66] In 2015 the Franklin Mint operated only through an online store, selling a variety of memorabilia and collectibles.[67]

Rick Rush and Jireh Publishing survived their lawsuit with Woods in rea-sonable condition. Although his brother Don, the president of Jireh Publish-ing, died in May 2014, Rick Rush in 2014 continued his work as an artist. His Web site gave his version of his victory over ETW:

> In 1999, Rick Rush and Jireh Publishing made headlines across the globe. In a modern day David and Goliath [story], Tiger Woods's ETW Corporation sued Rick Rush for painting the golfer's likeness without permission. Despite having nowhere near the resources of a Tiger Woods, Rick Rush stood by his art as a form of free speech. Finally in 2003, the Sixth Circuit of the United States Court of Appeals decided in Rush's favor—the First Amendment protects an artist's expression as a freedom of speech over a celebrity's right of publicity.[68]

Rush was fairly accurate in his assessment. Many commentators called it a David-over-Goliath-style victory.

Life moved on for Tiger Woods after the Franklin Mint and ETW cases, and with a number of successes. Between 2003 and 2009 he won six ma-jor championships and was ranked number one in the world from 2005 to 2010. He won between $6 million and $13 million dollars per year on golf and only added to his endorsements. All that changed in November 2009, when Woods acutely understood the value of another aspect of the Warren and Brandies tort of privacy, the right to be let alone. Woods's sex life and a renewed discussion about what aspects of a celebrity's life are private burst into the American media when he was briefly hospitalized in 2009 after he drove his car into a tree. His wife of five years, Elin Nordegren, had broken one of the car windows with a golf club, and rumors were rampant about how she had chased him down the drive after learning of his infidelities. Soon after this episode, Woods posted a statement on his Web site that harked back to Warren and Brandeis's assertion that some things are too private for public consumption: "This is a private matter and I want to keep it that way," Woods posted. "Although I understand there is curiosity, the many false, unfounded and malicious rumors that are currently circulating about my family and me are irresponsible." "I appreciate all the concern and well wishes that we have received," the statement concluded, "but, I would also ask for some understanding that my family and I deserve some privacy no matter how intrusive some people can be."[69] Those pleas for privacy went largely ignored as Woods was again the object of media obsession; only this time, he and his team had less success controlling the message. A few of his sponsors dropped him (although Nike stayed with its man), and Woods lost an estimated $22 million from his previous endorsement level of $91 million.[70] His marriage to Elin ended in 2010.

Woods and his team's long-term efforts to control his image crashed, along with his car, in 2009. The scandal combined issues of sex and celebrity in ways that made the American media salivate. In a most salacious way, race re-entered the conversation, even if it was just in the sometimes-disturbing and racist posts after online stories: Woods was portrayed as a black man cheating on his white wife with white women. As cultural anthropologist Orin Starn argued, the role of race had often been a presence beneath the surface of Woods's representation, and race played at least a minor role in the national obsession with his sex life. Also at issue was the fact that the public did not really know the real Woods; it knew only his representations through the press and through carefully crafted advertisements. In fact, Starn wrote, because Woods "protected his privacy away from the game so tightly . . . most Americans knew very little about him aside from the steady stream of advertisements." Woods had, after all, named his yacht "Privacy," a clear acknowledgment of how much he wanted to control his image.[71] One indication of Woods's public slide is the change in book titles; instead of *The Chosen One*, there were titles such as *The Tiger Woods Phenomenon: Essays on the Cultural Impact of Golf's Fallible Superman*, *The Big Miss: My Years Coaching Tiger*, and *Tiger Woods: Doomed by Distraction*.[72]

Some seven years later Woods's golf game had not entirely recovered to his pre-scandal success: he did not win a major tournament after 2008 (at least through October 2015) and was plagued by a series of injuries. But to argue he did not return to his pre-scandal success indicates just how dominant he was. Despite his apparent decline, post-scandal Woods still held the number-one rank in the world for sixty weeks, ending in May 2014. Woods, however, seems to have fully recovered financially from the scandal: he was still in 2015 the ninth-highest-paid athlete in the world. According to Forbes.com, he earned about $50.6 million between June 1, 2014, and June 1, 2015. Just over half a million dollars came from winnings (he had struggled with injury for much of this time period) and appearance fees for golf; the remainder was from endorsements.[73] Although he might have lost his personal privacy, he still utilized his right of publicity to sell his name and image.

CONCLUSION

Woods stopped production of the commemorative coins on the grounds that they were commercial items, but the First Amendment still protected serigraphs and lithographs. While the appellate court's reasoning in justifying the ruling in favor of Rush and Jireh Publishing was not universally liked or respected, it moved forward the national conversation about the different standards for weighing the right of publicity against the protections of the First Amendment.

The lost *Jireh* lawsuit weighed on Woods's attorneys, particularly Mark S. Lee, who, as a partner in a large law firm in Los Angeles, specialized in intellectual property. Lee and his firm had also lost the Princess Diana charity fund lawsuit against the Franklin Mint. After these two high-profile losses, Lee published an article in the *Loyola of Los Angeles Entertainment Law Review*. He argued, "If people buy a picture of Tiger Woods predominantly because they like Tiger Woods, rather than because they are attracted to the composition of the picture, that picture should be deemed to violate Tiger Woods's right of publicity."[74] Under this predominant purpose test, Woods might have won his lawsuit against Jireh Publishing. Fortunately for Tony Twist, a retired ice hockey player, the Missouri Supreme Court later that year adopted the predominant purpose test in order to determine when art violates the right of publicity.[75] That adoption will be discussed in the next chapter.

7

WHAT'S IN A NAME?
COMIC BOOKS AND HOCKEY
DOE v. TCI CABLEVISION (2003)

Todd McFarlane was a serious sports fan and memorabilia collector. He made headlines when he purchased Mark McGwire's seventieth homerun ball for $3 million and then again when he purchased Barry Bonds's seventy-third homerun ball for $450,000.[1] For a time he owned a small share of the Edmonton Oilers of the National Hockey League (NHL).[2] McFarlane was also a successful comic-book creator, and his love of comics and sports intersected when he named a character in his comic book *Spawn* after an NHL player, Tony Twist. That intersection of sport and comics cost him millions of dollars after the real Tony Twist sued him for appropriation of Twist's name. The case resulted in a fascinating debate in the Missouri state courts about whether the First Amendment rights of an artist transcend the publicity rights of a celebrity athlete. In the end the Missouri Supreme Court adopted a "predominant purpose test" originally articulated by one of Tiger Woods's attorneys and then ruled that the use of the name Tony Twist was commercial speech and thus not protected by the First Amendment. The road to that opinion and the characters involved make the story even more convoluted than the court's ruling.

TODD MCFARLANE'S LIFE

Todd McFarlane's background foreshadowed his eventual mix of Tony Twist and his comic book, *Spawn*. Born in Calgary, Alberta, on March 16, 1961, McFarlane's family moved to Southern California while he was still young, but they returned to Calgary, where his father was a printer, when McFarlane was fourteen years old. As a youth, he enjoyed playing Little League Baseball and reading comic books. He continued to combine the two in college: he moved first to Spokane, Washington, hoping to earn a baseball scholarship to Gonzaga University, but after he failed to earn a scholarship, he enrolled for a year at Spokane Falls Community College. Subsequently, he earned a baseball scholarship to Eastern Washington University (EWU), where he majored in general studies with a concentration in graphic arts. While at EWU, he worked part-time at a comic book shop to subsidize his education and living expenses. In his free time, McFarlane sketched comic books and comic strips, hoping that should his professional baseball dreams fail, he might be able to work in comics. In the summers, he played semi-professional baseball for a team in Kamloops, British Columbia, but after his college eligibility ended, so did his baseball career.[3] In later years McFarlane would credit some of his success to the ethics he learned as an athlete: "Maybe that is where I get my drive and competitiveness. . . . Every single day, it's me winning at life. You cannot let it beat you. I guess I am too much of a farmer boy: You put in a hard day's work for a hard day's pay and play."[4]

During his last semester at EWU, McFarlane struggled to get hired in the comic-book industry. He sent applications and samples of his artwork to dozens of companies, collecting seven hundred rejection letters before signing on as an artist with Marvel/Epic Comics just before his graduation in 1984. A year later he married a fellow student, Wanda, whose name McFarlane would later bestow on a character in *Spawn*.[5]

While working at Marvel, McFarlane become something of a cult hero among comic-book fans. After several years with Marvel, he began working on "The Amazing Spider-Man" comic. He redesigned the popular character, making him less mainstream: "I wanted to emphasize the 'spider' in the word 'Spider-Man,'" McFarlane said. He worked on that comic book for several years and was named favorite "cover artist and penciler" for two years in a row by the Comics Buyer's Guide readers' poll. McFarlane's version of Spider-Man was so popular that Marvel made him a writer and artist on a new series, titled simply "Spider-Man." McFarlane struggled to put energy on the page and to fill each frame with action and motion. His work was rewarded when the first issue sold nearly three million copies in the summer of 1990 to become the bestselling comic book in the history of the United States.[6] By comparison, the bestselling comic book issue of 1989, "Legends of the Dark Knight," sold about eight hundred thousand copies.[7]

In February 1992, McFarlane and seven other artists and writers left Marvel Comics. They formed a new company, Imagine Comics, which was loosely associated with the Malibu Graphics Publishing Group, the fourth-largest publisher of U.S. comic books. Imagine was different from Marvel largely because with Imagine the artists owned the characters they created, and they controlled and profited from the merchandizing of those characters. At Marvel, the company owned all characters the artists drew or created and had complete creative and financial control over the merchandizing of those characters.[8] Concerning the reasons he and the other artists left Marvel, McFarlane said, "We were trying to get an acknowledgement that we were important to the process. . . . They [Marvel executives] thought we were interchangeable. We're not."[9] Within four years Imagine grew large enough to compete with Marvel and D.C. Comics as one of the most dominant comic book companies in the country.[10]

The creation of Imagine and McFarlane's departure from Marvel made him a rich man and a leader in the entertainment business. In 1995 his comics brought in $2 million in sales. Sales from licensed toys, video games, television shows, and apparel netted another $35 million. McFarlane took home $5 million.[11] In 1996, *Forbes* magazine recognized McFarlane as one of the top in his business and estimated his net worth at about $75 million.[12] By 1998 that value had grown to $130 million.[13]

The McFarlane empire's foundation was laid in May 1992 when Imagine released a highly touted new character, Spawn, created and drawn by McFarlane. Spawn became the focal point of the comic-book series bearing his name.[14] The comic book drew advance sales of $1.7 million.[15] Once released, the comic book was a critical and commercial success; one columnist named it rookie of the year.[16] The sales of the comic book itself made McFarlane wealthy. Ultimately, *Spawn* was spun off into toys, video games, an animated television series for HBO, and a live-action film. McFarlane himself built on *Spawn*'s success and later used that capital to diversify his work and his businesses.

The comic book *Spawn*, the center of the McFarlane empire and of the lawsuit to come, was a new kind of comic book for the era. Previous comic book heroes were just that, heroic, but the character of Spawn was something of an anti-hero. McFarlane later explained, "One of the reasons that I quit Marvel is that everything revolved around their icons. So I created my own ugly icon, not a heroic icon, and gave it a life around the world."[17]

The story begins with Al Simmons, a former U.S. Marine and former assassin who died and went to Hell. In Hell, he makes a deal with the Devil; he will return to the land of the living to work for the Devil so that he can spend time with his wife, Wanda, whom he dearly loved and regretted not spending more time with. When he returns, however, he discovers that he is very large, very disfigured from burns, and that five years have passed since his death. Wanda has remarried his best friend. Angered by what Spawn sees as a broken deal, he reneges on his agreement with the Devil and commits himself to battling and killing evildoers. He has a wide range of powers, including teleporting and shape-shifting. Spawn is also one of the first and, at the time, few African American comic book heroes.[18]

In 1994 McFarlane started a merchandising company to sell collectible action figures of the *Spawn* characters,[19] and in just three months more than 2.2 million Spawns were shipped nationwide.[20] The toy company had its own complicated history. Originally called Todd Toys, it was renamed McFarlane Toys after Mattel sent a cease-and-desist letter to McFarlane claiming that Todd Toys was confusing because Mattel had a toy in the Barbie line named Todd. McFarlane agreed to change the name, despite the fact that the Mattel Todd was a clean-cut, white, all-American character, while Spawn was a large, African American anti-hero returned from Hell.[21] Although the initial production lines focused on figures from McFarlane's own comic books, it quickly expanded and created action-figure versions of popular culture icons, such as the rock stars in the band KISS,[22] characters from cult movies such as the *Texas Chainsaw Massacre*, and television programs like *The X-Files*. Eventually, the company licensed the images of sports figures also, such as professional football player Terrell Owens. McFarlane himself diversified and worked on various projects as well: for example, he drew an album cover, directed a Grammy-winning animated video, and was also the animation producer for the 2002 film *The Dangerous Lives of Altar Boys*.[23]

In 1997 *Spawn* appeared as an animated series on cable television's Home Box Office (HBO), and that summer the live-action film version was released nationwide.[24] McFarlane maintained creative control over both versions; he was the executive producer of the film, which cost some $50 million to produce and included award-winning actor Martin Sheen. The film had a gross income of about $100 million from the theatrical release that summer.[25]

The toy company, the HBO series, and the film all reflected the themes of control and profit that resonated throughout McFarlane's professional life. He originally left Marvel comics to have greater control over his characters and the subsequent profit they generated. He founded his merchandizing company when existing toy companies such as Hasbro refused to give him the power and percentage of the profits he wanted. Before he agreed to work with HBO on the animated *Spawn*, he insisted on a great deal of control. When Columbia Pictures tried to buy the rights to a live-action film version of *Spawn*, McFarlane rejected the deal because Columbia wanted to control the film; instead, he signed with independent New Line.[26] McFarlane had worried that a larger production company would insist on changing the characters to maximize cross-promotional items and tie-ins. McFarlane insisted he wanted integrity in the marketing of the film as well as consistency with the comic book characters: he did not want Spawn softened, to be marketed with something like children's meals at a fast-food restaurant.[27]

Despite McFarlane's independent streak as an entrepreneur, he showed strong loyalty to his friends and his family, including his wife and three children. He claimed to have diversified his entertainment empire not just for his own profit but because, as he said, "I need to do this because if I am wrong about Spawn, I can still employ the people that have been loyal to me."[28] He repeatedly asserted in various interviews that his family was the single most important thing in his life: "I don't work weekends. I run an empire, but I quit at five p.m. every day. I've been with my wife for twenty years between dating and marriage, and we do a lot of family outings. I'd burn this whole company in a heartbeat if I thought it would interfere with my family."[29]

McFarlane's loyalty to family and friends was reflected in his comic book *Spawn*; he named characters after those most important to him. "The simple thing is that (Spawn) wants to get back to his wife, and his wife in the movie is named Wanda," he said in an interview. "And my wife is named Wanda. So it's not a coincidence that this man, in the blink of an eye, when he died, traded his soul to see his wife for a second."[30] Another character was named after his eldest daughter, Cyan,[31] and the lead character's dog had the same name, Shanna, as McFarlane's dog.[32] The title character in *Spawn* was named Al Simmons before becoming Spawn; Al Simmons was McFarlane's best friend in real life, who appeared as Spawn at promotional events.[33]

McFarlane's love of sport, though, never left him, despite his work in entertainment. He became a collector, and, in October 1992, his sports memorabilia received national attention after he bought the baseball uniform Madonna wore in the movie *A League of Their Own* for $9,000.[34] This was one of his cheaper memorabilia purchases. In 1998, joining a group of thirty-six investors, McFarlane bought a 2 percent share of the Edmonton Oilers. He did so, he said, because he felt that too many Canadian teams had been moved to the United States, and he did not want to see the Oilers move as well.[35]

In 1999 he anonymously purchased Mark McGwire's record-setting seventieth homerun ball from the 1998 season at auction for $3 million. A few weeks after the auction, McFarlane held a press conference to confirm that he was the buyer. Always the promoter, the press conference was held at the annual Toy Fair in New York, and McFarlane stood in front of a banner with "Todd McFarlane Productions" spelled out 103 times. There he reported that he had just been to a Major League Baseball fantasy camp and added that "sports make you forget death, taxes and politics, and all the other garbage that goes on in life," emphasizing that even for a man who made his fortune drawing comic books and selling toys, sports played a special, romanticized role in life.[36] He admitted the price was "crazy" and noted that "right now, I'm the idiot who spent $3 million on the crown jewel of sports memorabilia." "If the record falls, I'm the idiot who spent $3 million on a $5 ball." But when Barry Bonds broke McGwire's record with seventy-three homeruns in 2001, McFarlane bought that ball for the relatively bargain price of $450,000.[37] He claimed the cost of the balls took all his personal savings.[38]

At the McGwire-ball press conference, McFarlane said he bought the ball to keep it from being locked up in a collector's vault, and he announced that in separate deals totaling about $300,000, he had also bought McGwire's first, sixty-seventh, sixty-eighth, and sixty-ninth homerun balls from that season and Sammy Sosa's thirty-third, sixty-first, and sixty-sixth homerun balls. He planned to call the group of balls the McFarlane Collection, a name he said sounded better than "The Guy Who Has More Money Than Brains Collection."[39]

The McFarlane Collection toured Major League Baseball cities throughout the 1999 season, with all proceeds benefiting the ALS Association, a charity dedicated to fighting Lou Gehrig's Disease (amyotrophic lateral sclerosis). The McFarlane Collection did not charge a fee to the estimated six hundred thousand viewers who attended that event, but it accepted donations totaling about $60,000 (or about ten cents per visitor) for the ALS society. McFarlane himself paid for the exhibit and its moving expenses, and, in exchange for the exhibit, McFarlane asked for and received permission to take twenty pregame practice swings with every home team, something he felt helped to make up for never making the Major Leagues as a player.[40] McFarlane's rewards for the exhibit seem to have outweighed those received by the ALS Association. He offered to loan the exhibit to the Baseball Hall of Fame in Cooperstown, New York, but the organization said it would accept it only as a donation and not as a temporary exhibit, so the balls have not yet made it to Cooperstown.[41]

Given Todd McFarlane's love of sport, his commitment to his comic book, and his tendency to name his characters after those individuals he loved and admired, his introduction of a new *Spawn* character named Antonio "Tony Twist" Twistelli in November 1993 seemed almost inevitable. The character was a mafia-type figure who committed a number of immoral and illegal acts, such as murder and child abductions. He was a minor character who had appeared in only about 0.5 percent of the total panels of the comic book by 1997. In a September 1994 issue of *Spawn*, in the back of the comic book where he responded to fans' letters, McFarlane wrote "whenever I choose a name I try to have a little bit of play on it . . . I am a big hockey fan and a lot of my characters have been named for current NHL hockey players. For example, Antonio Twistelli, a/k/a Tony Twist, is actually the name of a hockey player of the Quebec Nordiques."[42] The real life Tony Twist did not find the naming an honor, and in 1997 he filed a lawsuit against McFarlane and his various companies.[43] Given the real-life Tony Twist's background, this lawsuit should not have been surprising.

TONY TWIST'S LIFE

Tony Twist was born in Saskatchewan on May 9, 1968. His grandparents may have bequeathed some of their athletic prowess to him. His paternal grandfather, Harry, boxed as a welterweight under the name Harry Runcorn and once held the Western Canada title for his weight class. In 1923 one of his opponents died from his injuries after the match, and Harry retired to become an officer with the Royal Canadian Mounted Police and to train fighters as a hobby. Twist's grandmother Ethel, whom newspapers nicknamed "Dirty Andy" as a player, was enshrined in the British Columbia Lacrosse Hall of Fame for her field hockey skill. As a fifteen-year-old midget player, Twist was not a fighter, but the next year as a junior hockey player, his coach noted his size and strength—he had been weight training since he was thirteen years old—and encouraged him to become an enforcer on the ice. He embraced the role and was drafted into the NHL in 1988.[44]

Enforcers in ice hockey play a very specific role. They are not expected to make goals or assists or even to be strong stick handlers or skaters. But they are expected to be excellent fighters and to log a large number of penalty minutes for fighting. Enforcers fight for a number of reasons: they retaliate against a player who has been perceived as taking a cheap shot at one of their teammates; they fight to change the momentum of a game—especially when their team is losing; and they fight to establish a level of intimidation. The idea is that the game is played more fairly and that opposing players give a wider berth to skilled players for fear that the enforcer will come and literally beat them up. In theory, enforcers follow a specific but unwritten "code" and try to avoid sucker punches, hits from behind, fights with smaller players (unless they've behaved egregiously by hockey standards), and fights with players who are tired, injured, or at the end of their shifts. Off the ice, enforcers are often decent human beings who are loved by their teammates and respected by their peers. They have been known to visit their opponents in the hospital even after their fists caused the injury.[45] Prior to rule changes in 2005, almost every team carried at least one enforcer on the roster, and most carried several.[46]

On the ice, Tony Twist made his career as an enforcer. He stood 6'1½" and weighed about 240 pounds. From the beginning of his professional career, he was physically dominant and tough; in 1990, after being briefly demoted to the the Peoria Rivermen, an American Hockey League team, Twist knocked the Milwaukee Admirals' goalie Steve McKichan unconscious with a hard check after the whistle had blown. McKichan's neck injury from the incident shortened his career, and he sued Twist and the Blues for the injuries he sustained. Although a jury awarded him $175,000, the court reversed the ruling on appeal, concluding that professional hockey is a violent sport and injuries are part of the game.[47] In the NHL Twist was regarded as one of the biggest punchers and most effective enforcers in the game. He spent more than 1,120 minutes in the penalty box between 1989 and 1999, mostly for fighting. In 1995 he punched Rob Ray, the Buffalo Sabres' enforcer, so hard that he fractured Ray's orbital bone.[48] Twist himself reported that he studied films of other enforcers fighting to prepare for his own fights. He claimed also to have "fought with malice, meaning I didn't just fight to fight. I fought to win, and I wanted to hurt my opponent. My objective was to put my fist through the back of that guy's skull."[49]

Although drafted initially by the St. Louis Blues, Twist spent several seasons with the Quebec Nordiques until he returned by trade to the Blues in 1994. In St. Louis, Twist became a fan favorite, with a popular, high-selling jersey and a weekly television show. Off the ice, Twist was a father of two and active with a number of charities. He hosted a five-day Harley Davidson Ride to support the Head First Foundation, which raised money to find ways to prevent head injuries.[50] He also hosted the annual Tony Twist Invitational Golf Tournament to benefit the St. Louis Society, which serves people with physical disabilities.[51] He was a celebrity in the St. Louis metro area and was recognized within the world of the NHL. He was in a severe motorcycle accident in August 1999, breaking his pelvis and tearing knee ligaments and cartilage. Although he had spent the previous season with the St. Louis Blues, he was, at the time of the accident, an unrestricted free agent; the Blues had ended their negotiations with him just hours before the accident.[52] Tony Twist's NHL career was over.

THE INITIAL TRIAL

In 1997 Twist filed a lawsuit against Todd McFarlane personally, Todd McFarlane Productions Inc., and McFarlane's various toy companies. Twist also named Imagine Comics, HBO, TCI Cablevision, Blockbuster Entertainment, and Hollywood Video in the lawsuit.[53] The latter two were named for renting or selling *Spawn* videos, and TCI was named for airing those videos.[54] Wizard Press was also named in the suit after publishing the Wizard Spawn Tribute (which reported that the Twist character was based on the "real life persona" of Tony Twist).[55] The lawsuit alleged that McFarlane had appropriated Twist's name by using it without Twist's permission and that Twist had been defamed because the comic book character was so despicable.[56] One of his points of complaint was that in the HBO version of *Spawn* the Twist character wore pink G-string underwear.[57] Twist testified that he had heard about the character only after his mother called him from British Columbia. She was disturbed by the character to whom she was introduced when some children stopped by her home to show her some of the items that were based on the fictional Tony Twist.[58] When Twist filed the lawsuit, he did so as John Doe in order to keep publicity to a minimum.[59]

At the first trial in June 2000, Twist's lawyer argued that the real Twist had a positive pubic image as a volunteer for children's groups, and that the fictional Twist harmed his reputation and diminished his earning potential. McFarlane's lawyers argued that the Twist character was fictional and nothing like the real man; they noted further that the real Tony Twist had only once earned more than $20,000 in income outside of hockey and that he had not played hockey since his motorcycle accident the year before.[60] Sports agent Rocky Arceneaux testified that Twist deserved 20 percent of the estimated $123 million in gross revenue from Spawn-related sales.[61] Marketing professor Brian Till of Saint Louis University testified that Twist deserved 15 percent of the revenue from the comic book and the first season of the animated HBO series as damages for the use of his name. Till testified that the evilness of the character hurt the real Twist's ability to gain outside endorsements,[62] and a vice president of EAS (Experimental and Applied Sciences Inc.), a company that makes and sells dietary supplements designed for athletes, confirmed Till's testimony via videotape, saying that even after Twist's motorcycle accident, he intended to hire Twist as an endorser but withdrew the offer after learning about the *Spawn* character of the same name.[63] Twist admitted on the stand that this was probably the only endorsement that he lost because of the character and confirmed that none of the charities he worked with had severed their relationship with him. At the initial trial Twist explained his reaction to discovering the character: "I felt that the negative impact on me was going to be substantial," he told jurors. "My unwilling participation in this infuriated me."[64]

The jury in 2000 was asked to decide whether McFarlane had appropriated Twist's name, and if so, what financial damages should be awarded. The jury instructions said the verdict should be for Twist if they found that McFarlane had intentionally used Twist's name, that McFarlane benefited from that use, that Twist suffered harm from that use, that Twist did not consent to the use of his name, and that, if as a result of the use, Twist suffered damages.[65] Later, McFarlane said that after hearing the jury instructions, "I would have voted against myself. And I like me."[66]

McFarlane lost the initial trial, and the St. Louis jury awarded Twist $24.5 million in compensatory damages, a figure just under twenty percent of the gross revenue of *Spawn* and its related industries. McFarlane's case was hurt in part by his testimony about how he came up with the name of the character. At the initial trial, McFarlane was vague about the source of the character's name, despite his previous admission in his own comic book that the character was named for the hockey player. At the trial McFarlane, in fact, suggested he might have named the character for an old mob figure named "Kid Twist," even though he admitted knowing who Tony Twist was. Twist also may have benefited from a home ice advantage: he had been and was still a popular sports figure in St. Louis, and after learning the verdict, he signed autographs for some of the jurors. One juror shook his hand after the verdict and confirmed that the jury felt that Twist's name had been used intentionally and without his consent, making him due some compensation.[67]

The jurors' decision, however, was just round one of what would be a long legal fight. The next step came quickly on November 1, 2000, when St. Louis Circuit Judge Robert H. Dierker Jr., who presided over the initial trial, reversed the jury's verdict and award. He wrote that he "must in good conscience hold that the verdicts in this case are against the manifest weight of the evidence." He added that "no rational person could believe that the use of plaintiff's name as the nom de guerre of a swarthy Mafioso in a comic-book series, having absolutely nothing to do with hockey, either benefited defendants or injured plaintiff in any way, except perhaps in plaintiff's imagination."[68] Dierker did not doubt that the comic-book character was named after Twist, but he believed that "the question is not whether the use of plaintiff's name caused injury, the question is whether the defendants intended to cause such injury by using plaintiff's name." "On this record," he said, "that evidence is wholly lacking."[69] In the event his opinion was overruled on appeal, he ordered a retrial on the grounds that his instructions to the jurors had been erroneous and that some of the expert testimony regarding the damages was inadmissible.[70] The issue of what the legal question actually was and what the appropriate test for that legal question should be was the basis for the subsequent multiple appeals and extensive debate in the legal community.

Judge Dierker's conclusion reflected the sentiments of the general public in St. Louis. The local newspaper published several letters to the editor on the topic, and none supported Twist; in fact they seemed to believe that Twist's role as goon on the ice did more to harm his reputation than the character in the comic book did. One man wrote that the original jury verdict was "yet another example of what is wrong with the world. The Tony Twist lawsuit is all about greed. This suit wasn't filed because some comic book reader came up to Tony Twist and said, 'Hey, aren't you the evil mobster from Spawn.' It was filed because the NHL no longer condones goon tactics and someone is out of a job."[71] Another questioned how the jurors reached the verdict amount, asking "exactly when and how do these delusional jurors think Twist is going to earn $24 million? After a year off, is Tony going to suddenly have his break-out season in the National Hockey League? He is setting quite the pace with his one-goal-a-year average. It's ironic that Twist is suing someone for damaging his 'good name' after all those years of being a paid thug."[72] A third felt that the character helped Twist: "Outside of St. Louis, no advertisers were knocking down Twist's door when he was active to sell their products, so how could he have been hurt by the use of his 'cool' name in a comic book? If anything, it might possibly enhance his bottom line having the name out in public."[73] Tony Twist and his lawyers disagreed with the judge and the locals, and they appealed Judge Dierker's decision.

THE MISSOURI APPELLATE COURT

On appeal, Judge James R. Dowd wrote for a unanimous three-judge panel of the Missouri Court of Appeals, affirming the trial judge's decision in favor of McFarlane but for different reasons. Twist had appealed on the grounds that the trial court had been wrong to change the elements of an appropriation-of-name claim after the trial to include an intent to harm the plaintiff. Twist argued also that his experts had established that $24.5 million was an appropriate judgment and that further use of his name should be prohibited until he gave his consent.[74]

Judge Dowd noted that although Twist's original complaint had stated appropriation of name as grounds for his lawsuit, the case was really a matter of Twist's right of publicity. Missouri courts had in previous cases prohibited the use of a person's identity for purely commercial purposes, but those cases had not addressed situations where only a public figure's name had been used. Dowd noted that in other states, courts had refused to say that using only one's name was sufficient to raise an appropriation-of-name or right-of-publicity claim. Although Twist's lawyers argued that the use of his name plus the public identification of Twist as the inspiration for the name resulted in the appropriation of his identity, the court disagreed.[75]

Dowd wrote that because Twist wanted to restrict the use of his name in a publication, the real question was whether *Spawn* was protected under the First Amendment. Because Twist asked the court to ban any use of his name without his permission, Dowd said he was asking for content-based restriction of speech, a request of which the Supreme Court has historically been leery. Twist argued that his case was analogous to that of *Zacchini v. Scripps-Howard Broadcasting Co.* in 1977, a case in which the Supreme Court ruled that a local television station was wrong to broadcast, without his consent, the entire fifteen-second act of a human being shot out of a cannon.[76] The Missouri Court of Appeals did not agree with Twist's reading of *Zacchini*, as the judges believed that case had not carved a right-of-publicity exception to the First Amendment but rather had been a matter of right of performance. Dowd also rejected Twist's claim that comic books did not have First Amendment protection, writing that "comic books continue to be a legitimate and important part of the American artistic and literary landscape."[77]

Dowd then expanded on the significance of Twist's status as a celebrity in an American culture obsessed with celebrities. He wrote that the "ability to use Twist's name . . . is important in a society such as ours, where so much of social life and discourse revolves around celebrities."[78] He added that extending the right of publicity "to allow a celebrity to control the use of his or her identity in a work of fiction would grant them power to suppress ideas."[79] Thus the only way Twist could win his case, Dowd said, was to establish that the Twist character in *Spawn* was not just vaguely about the real Twist but was "of and concerning" the real Twist. If Twist could prove that, he then needed to meet the actual malice standard as a public figure and to prove that the use of his identity was false or in reckless disregard of the truth. But Dowd completely rejected the idea that the character was "of and concerning" the man: he wrote that "no intelligent person could believe that the fictional Tony Twist's actions are those of the plaintiff."[80] He further concluded that when McFarlane wrote and spoke about how he named his characters, he was not advertising the product but simply reporting information truthfully, thus making it news. The court ruled, therefore, that the First Amendment protected *Spawn* and ruled against Twist.[81] Twist appealed the case to the Missouri Supreme Court.

THE MISSOURI SUPREME COURT DECISION

Judge Stephen N. Limbaugh Jr., a cousin of conservative commentator Rush Limbaugh, wrote for a unanimous Missouri Supreme Court which overturned the appellate court's decision and sent Missouri speech law in a different direction than that in the rest of the country. Limbaugh began his opinion agreeing with the Court of Appeals that the case was about Twist's right of publicity rather than a case of appropriation of name. While the two torts are similar, the judge noted that to succeed in a right-of-publicity case, the plaintiff needed to establish that the defendant used the name to incur a "*commercial* advantage" (italics in original). Thus, for Twist to win, he needed to establish that McFarlane used Twist's name as a "symbol of his identity" and that the name was used without consent with the "intent to obtain a commercial advantage."[82]

Although the trial judge had concluded that Twist did not establish that McFarlane had used his name as a symbol of his identity, the Missouri Supreme Court disagreed. Limbaugh wrote that even though the fictional Twist did not physically resemble and was not meant to mirror the real Twist (writing that the only similarity was that each had an "'enforcer' or tough guy image"),[83] the link between the name and the enforcer role was enough to "create an unmistakable correlation" between the two. Because McFarlane explained that he used Twist's name intentionally, that correlation was confirmed.[84] The trial court judge had also concluded that no evidence proved that Twist's marketability had been harmed, that McFarlane had capitalized on the recognition of the name, or that McFarlane had directly profited from using Twist's name. Limbaugh stated that the trial court had used the wrong criteria: all Twist had to prove was that McFarlane had capitalized on the use of Twist's name. Limbaugh argued that McFarlane had done just that by first using Twist's name and then by marketing *Spawn* products at hockey games, the very site of Twist's fame.[85]

Judge Limbaugh next addressed the question of whether the First Amendment protected McFarlane from this right-of-publicity claim, as the appellate court had concluded. Limbaugh argued that the appellate court's interpretation of *Zacchini v. Scripps Howard Broadcasting Co.* was wrong and that *Zacchini* did not establish that actual malice needed to be proved in rights-of-publicity cases. Instead, Limbaugh maintained, the question was whether McFarlane had used Twist's name for "expressive" purposes or for purely commercial speech. If the former, the First Amendment protected McFarlane; but if the later, McFarlane received no protection. Limbaugh noted that two methods for distinguishing expressive and commercial speech had been articulated. One was the "relatedness test" articulated by the Restatement of Unfair Competition, which protected the use of a person's name and identity in matters related to that person, such as news reports and entertainment. California state courts have also used a parallel test called the "transformative test," which protects the use of names and identities if they have been sufficiently transformed into something more than a mere likeness or imitation. Limbaugh argued that neither test was useful because they did not account for the fact that the use of the identity could be both expressive and commercial simultaneously; instead, he utilized a balancing test that asked what the predominant purpose of the use was. A Los Angeles intellectual-property lawyer named Mark S. Lee, who included Tiger Woods among his clients, had recently articulated the "predominant use test" in a law-review article.[86] In applying the test, Judge Limbaugh wrote that the primary purpose of the use of Twist's name was "a ploy to sell comic books and related products," and thus the First Amendment did not protect McFarlane's use. Limbaugh ordered a new trial using the standard for rights-of-publicity cases, which he had articulated.[87]

McFarlane appealed to the United States Supreme Court, and his appeal was joined by a number of high-profile writers and Hollywood actors/directors, including Michael Crichton (creator of television's *E.R.*), bestselling mystery writer Elmore Leonard, and Ron Shelton (writer and director of *Bull Durham*). The writers feared that because of nationwide distribution of media materials, the Missouri Supreme Court's ruling could ultimately have implications for their work, even if they were not writing in Missouri.[88] They feared that if the Missouri decision stood, it would reduce the artistic freedom of artists across the nation.[89] When the United States Supreme Court declined to hear the case, it returned to the trial court level.

THE RETRIAL AND ITS AFTERMATH

When Twist's case returned to the trial-court level, St. Louis Circuit Judge Steven Ohmer presided over the retrial.[90] After a four-week trial, the jury ruled that McFarlane and his comic book company, Todd McFarlane Productions Inc., had violated Twist's right of publicity and awarded Twist $15 million.[91] At the retrial, both sides changed tactics from the original trial. Twist's lawyers focused on establishing that McFarlane and his companies gained a commercial advantage by using Twist's name and identity without his permission. McFarlane's co-defendants, including some of the companies of which he owned pieces, devoted more time to separating themselves from McFarlane personally—which resulted in only one company and McFarlane himself being held liable. Each of the other defendants, McFarlane Productions International, Todd McFarlane Entertainment, and Imagine Comics, had its own attorney, which also allowed each to make a separate closing statement and to provide his or her own instructions to the jury.[92] The strategy suggested that McFarlane's lawyers feared that they could not win under the test the state supreme court had articulated and, given that they could not win, they tried to protect as much of McFarlane's assets as they could. The tactic worked.

Just as after the first verdict, the amount of the second verdict stunned some in the community of sport. One sports columnist in Philadelphia wrote, "If you need proof that the world has gone completely mad, look no further than the case involving former St. Louis Blues enforcer Tony Twist and 'Spawn' comic-book creator Todd McFarlane."[93]

With this second verdict against him, McFarlane's legal team took two approaches: they appealed, and they filed for bankruptcy. After unsuccessfully asking the trial judge to overturn the jury's verdict, McFarlane appealed the verdict again to the Missouri Court of Appeals, but that court did not reach a decision until 2006.[94] Just five months after the jury verdict, though, Todd McFarlane Productions Inc. filed for bankruptcy protection under Chapter 11 in an Arizona Bankruptcy Court. By filing, the company continued to operate and reorganize its finances without being sued by creditors. In 2003 McFarlane reported that his seven companies had annual sales of over $50 million,[95] but bankruptcy court documents showed that in 2004, Todd McFarlane Productions Inc. had revenue of only $1.3 million. After the second verdict, Twist's attorneys had garnished the assets of both the company and McFarlane personally, taking more than $50,000 from the company. The Chapter 11 filing stopped future garnishment from the company but did nothing to protect McFarlane personally.[96] The bankruptcy filing resulted in multiple appearances before bankruptcy judges as Twist fought to collect his verdict from McFarlane and his insurance companies. That battle dragged on for years.[97]

Finally, in 2006, a three-judge panel of Missouri Appellate Court unanimously affirmed the jury's second verdict.[98] McFarlane had argued that the trial court erred, in that the evidence demonstrated that McFarlane's use of Twist's name was predominantly commercial and thus not protected under the First Amendment. For each of McFarlane's arguments, the court pointed to the Missouri Supreme Court's decision in 2003 and affirmed the trial court. Although McFarlane provided evidence from two English professors and writers about the challenges of finding character names who also suggested possible alternative reasons for using the name Tony Twist,[99] ultimately McFarlane was doomed because, prior to the original trial in his own magazine, he had cited the real Tony Twist as the inspiration for the name. The court concluded that based on the evidence and the ruling of the Missouri Supreme Court that McFarlane selected the name predominantly to sell comic books,[100] despite McFarlane's regular use of names of family, friends, and other athletes as a form of homage. The court also rejected McFarlane's claims of error based on admission of expert testimony that led to the dollar value of the verdict.[101]

On December 19, 2006, the Missouri Supreme Court refused to hear McFarlane's appeal, and in 2007 a bankruptcy court in Arizona approved a $5 million settlement for Twist. McFarlane apparently did not want to settle and instead repeated that he wanted to continue the appeal process and ask the United States Supreme Court to hear the case. Conversely, the insurance companies that represented Todd McFarlane Productions Inc. chose to make the settlement to avoid further litigation and any increased liability. Because the company was in Chapter 11 bankruptcy protection, McFarlane's objections were overruled when the court allowed the settlement, ending any appeal. The bankruptcy court ordered that Twist and his first wife divide almost $2.6 million equally, and the remainder was for Twist's attorneys.[102] In 2007 Todd McFarlane Productions Inc. reached a settlement with its insurance company, reorganized, and emerged from Chapter 11 bankruptcy protection after generating income of $638,659 in 2006.[103]

REACTION TO THE DECISIONS

Legal scholars were caught off guard by the Missouri Supreme Court's decision and were not particularly enthusiastic about it.[104] Missouri was now the first state to rely on the predominant-purpose test, and some worried that this test would have a chilling effect on artistic expression while giving a great deal of protection to celebrities' controlling their names and images.[105] At least one author changed her approach to naming characters after the verdict: author Colette Shaw wrote a novel about a music executive who worked with her in the 1970s (with the rock group KISS), and although the work and the main character were fictional, after the *Twist* ruling, she and the lawyers at her publishing house decided that she needed to get permission from band members to include their names and characters in the book.[106]

Because the United States Supreme Court has traditionally given greater protection to speech deemed to be newsworthy and to artistic expression than it has to commercial speech, determining what is commercial expression, rather than artistic expression, is critical. The Court has not created a clear test to define the category of speech, leaving various jurisdictions to adopt their own kind of balancing test. The Restatement of Unfair Competition maintains that a person's name or identity can legally be used if it is in a work that is "related to that person." It gives the following illustration of acceptable circumstances:

> The use of a person's name or likeness in news reporting, whether in newspapers, magazines, or broadcast news . . . use in entertainment and other creative works, including both fiction and nonfiction . . . use of a celebrity's name or photograph as part of an article published in a fan magazine or in a feature story broadcast on an entertainment program . . . dissemination of an unauthorized print or broadcast biography . . . [and] use of another's identity in a novel, play, or motion picture.[107]

McFarlane likely would have won his case if the Missouri Supreme Court had used this test, assuming that the court had classified a comic book as similar to a novel, play, or movie.

Another test is the transformative test—that is, when the artist or writer adds enough fictional elements to a real identity that the real person is transformed into a fictional character. For example, DC Comics published a five-volume mini-series in which the Autumn brothers appeared. The Autumn brothers were half-worm, half-human villains in the story; they had blonde hair, pale faces, and red eyes, and one brother wore a stove-pipe hat. Johnny and Edgar Winters, musicians from Texas, sued DC Comics for appropriation of image, claiming that the Autumn brothers were based on their identities. The Winter brothers were also blonde, pale, and had some albino characteristics, and one brother frequently wore a stove-pipe hat. The California Supreme Court rejected their claim on the grounds that the identity of the

Winter brothers had been sufficiently transformed (presumably by being made half worms) into fictional characters, noting "the right of publicity cannot, consistent with the First Amendment, be a right to control the celebrity's image by censoring disagreeable portrayals."[108] McFarlane would likely have been successful under this test given that his version of Tony Twist was caricature of a mob member who looked nothing like the real Tony Twist.[109]

The Missouri Supreme Court, however, became the first state supreme court to adopt the predominant-purpose test, and legal scholars were worried about how far the test would tread into First Amendment rights. One author called the predominant-purpose test "a clear showing of concern for protecting actors' and other artists' rights" by rejecting the more First Amendment–friendly relatedness or transformative tests.[110] Another law-review article noted that because of the limited defenses and the lack of consistency in standards for publicity cases, McFarlane might have been better off claiming his fictional Tony Twist was a parody of the real man and then fighting a defamation suit. Further, the authors found the predominant-purpose test to be severely flawed, arguing, "Virtually all published speech has both an expressive and a commercial component, so this test would in effect give a court carte blanche to censor speech at the behest of a celebrity, based solely on the court's personal view of the relative value of the speech."[111] Mark Sableman, a lawyer, wrote that the predominant-purpose test "appears to put artists in a near-impossible dilemma when they seek to use any cultural content that may implicate the right of publicity."[112] The *Harvard Law Review* reported, "It is disconcerting that the Missouri test poorly distinguishes commercial from expressive works; it is more disconcerting that this flaw permits a court to impose liability on creators of expressive works."[113] It seems that no legal scholars were happy with the Missouri court's decision, and most questioned if the predominant-purpose test was fair to artists.

The predominant-purpose test in Missouri did not become quite the slam-dunk that celebrities might have hoped. In 2006 a federal district court in Missouri ruled that no violation of the rights of publicity of Major League Baseball (MLB) players occurred when the CBC Distribution and Marketing Corporation used the names and statistics of real players in their for-profit online fantasy baseball leagues. The judge concluded that the use of the names and historical facts (their baseball statistics) did not mean that their identities were used for a commercial purpose under the predominant use test. Even if the identities of the players were used, the judge wrote, the First Amendment protected CBC's use of the names.[114] On appeal, the Eighth Circuit Court of Appeals affirmed that decision but on very different grounds. Chief Judge Morris S. Arnold, writing for the majority, believed that the identities of the players were, in fact, being used for commercial purposes, but that the CBC's First Amendment rights trumped the players' publicity rights. The appellate court used the elements of the right of publicity that the Missouri Supreme Court articulated in the Twist case, but the court concluded that because the information CBC used was publicly available, because CBC's use of their identities did not stop the players from making large amounts of money, and because the use of the names did not imply any endorsement, the First Amendment protected the online gaming company.[115] The court did not explain how the facts of this case differed from those of Tony Twist's. Under the standards as articulated by the Eighth Circuit, Todd McFarlane likely would have been protected: Twist's name was public knowledge; no court established that, in using the name, the real Twist lost money; and the use of Twist's name did not seem to imply any endorsement. The *Twist* case, however, was judged under different standards.

CONCLUSION

The lawsuit, which spanned ten years, brought together an interesting cast of characters, each of whom was deeply vested in the outcome. Tony Twist and Todd McFarlane had similarities: they were sports-loving Canadians with ties to British Columbia, but the strongest similarity, that each loved a good fight, possibly contributed to their long, drawn-out battle. McFarlane once said that his epitaph should read: "He died free. I will never understand why people want to control others,"[116] and Tony Twist would probably agree. Twist described the lawsuit as "a war, a battle. . . . It hasn't been a drain on me. If it's an emotional drain to go to battle, don't do it, because you're probably not cut out for the job." The reporter who quoted Twist added, "He's referring to the McFarlane case, but he could be describing numerous aspects of his post-hockey life. . . . [U]nder different circumstances, they [Twist and McFarlane] might have become fast friends."[117]

Just prior to the 2006 settlement to which McFarlane's insurance companies agreed, Twist lived with his second wife outside of St. Louis, Missouri. His two teenaged children by his first wife lived with him as well. The family owned and operated four bars in surrounding communities, and Twist still had a reputation as a tough guy. Several people had filed restraining orders against him, and one filed a civil suit, claiming that Twist had punched him in the face—although all charges and lawsuits were eventually dropped or dismissed.[118] In 2014 Twist continued to be a St. Louis public figure, co-hosting a local radio show.

Todd McFarlane's Facebook page and Web site in 2014 reported that he still lived in Arizona with his wife and three children, that he was happy but busy balancing all of his interests, and that Todd McFarlane Productions Inc. was still publishing *Spawn* as well as other comic books. No mention was made anywhere about the lawsuit or the company's stint in bankruptcy.[119]

This case has interesting ties both to other rights-of-publicity cases and to the entertainment world. McFarlane's lead counsel throughout the case, Michael Kahn, had a vested interest in protecting the rights of an artist: Kahn is the author of a number of mystery novels.[120] The basis of the Missouri Supreme Court's predominant-purpose test, which ultimately ended McFarlane's hopes of victory, was a law-review article written by Mark S. Lee. Lee was a partner in a large law firm in Los Angeles who specialized in intellectual property, and he had represented Tiger Woods in at least two of Woods's lawsuits to protect the golfer's image. Although Woods and Lee lost the lawsuit against Rick Rush, Lee then published his influential article in 2003. In the article he referred to the Woods lawsuit: "If people buy a picture of Tiger Woods predominantly because they like Tiger Woods, rather than because they are attracted to the composition of the picture, that picture should be deemed to violate Tiger Woods's right of publicity."[121] Under the predominant-purpose test that thus he articulated (and that the Missouri court adopted), Woods might have won the lawsuit of *ETW v. Jireh Publishing*. The predominant-purpose test appears to make the state of Missouri the state most friendly to celebrities' rights of publicity cases. Although the district court in *C.B.C. v. MLB Advanced Media* seemed to narrow the definition of identity by saying that use of a name and statistics did not constitute identity, the Eighth Circuit Court of Appeals broadened the district court's definition but still offered more First Amendment protections than the *Twist* case. The Eighth Circuit seems to have narrowed the impact of a problematic Missouri Supreme Court decision, but the Missouri Supreme Court's decision and its reliance on the predominant-purpose test in *Twist* still applies in the state of Missouri.

CONCLUSION

The legal cases presented in this book, like the long line of precedent in which they fit, are essentially about identity, control, and money. Each of the sporting celebrities highlighted in the preceding chapters wanted to control his identity, image, and reputation; when he lost control of those basic parts of humanity, he turned, with varying degrees of success, to the court system. The struggle to determine who the world sees you as and who profits from you continues. The six legal cases in this book are links in the ongoing evolution of the laws of reputation, and they are the story of how celebrities struggle to control how they are viewed. Together the cases provide a window into how the law protects our right of expression as a nation in the context of or in balance with our rights of reputation as individuals.

REVIEWING EVOLUTION

The right of privacy has evolved from a right of protecting one's image and reputation to a pecuniary right of protecting the financial value of one's image, and that evolution is reflected in the cases presented in this book. Legal scholar Samantha Barbas argued that the creation of the right of privacy (protecting one's reputation) and the convoluted path it took to the right of publicity (protecting one's finances) was a reflection of the evolution of American society to a celebrity and consumer culture. She asserted that the invention of the photograph and the advancing technologies of image reproduction and mass communication increased the financial value of celebrities' faces and thus increased celebrities' desire to protect their profit-making ability over their dignity.[1]

Accepting Barbas's premise, the lawsuits described in this book show that such development was not a smooth and linear progression. The motivations of Wally Butts, Warren Spahn, and Don Newcombe fall into the category of protecting one's dignity more than one's financial interests. Butts had been accused of conspiring to throw a football game—and not just any football game: he was accused of trying to help one of the archrivals of the University of Georgia beat a team that he himself had coached for years and still supervised as athletic director. For a football man who had spent his entire life involved in the sport, this was an attack on his reputation, impugning his honor and his dignity. He sued the *Saturday Evening Post* for financial damages, but financial damages were practically all he could ask for in the United States legal system at that time. In this and in many of these cases, if it had been possible, the plaintiff might have preferred an older form of retribution, such as a duel or horsewhipping.

Like Butts, Warren Spahn seemed less concerned about money. Spahn succeeded in stopping publication of a biography because it placed him in too positive a false light.[2] His lawyer's primary argument was that the book said he had won a military honor that Spahn himself did not claim. Spahn's motivation seems to have been to protect not so much his reputation as the reputation of the soldiers who fought and died in World War II with him, the soldiers he believed were the real heroes.

Similarly, Don Newcombe sued Coors Brewing because, as a recovering alcoholic who had devoted much of his public life after becoming sober to helping others do the same, he was fundamentally appalled by the use of his image in an advertisement for beer. The man believed that he had failed to maximize his athletic potential, had ruined marriages, and had lost his spot in the Baseball Hall of Fame because of alcohol, and he saw himself being used to sell it. His lawsuit can be interpreted as a battle to save his reputation, to be remembered as the man who bested beer, not hawked it.

The other three celebrity athletes involved in lawsuits presented in this book seem to have been motived by pecuniary interests, although intuiting motives behind a lawsuit is suspect, as all motives are incredibly complicated. Joe Montana's reputation seemed unharmed by his appearance on yet another poster celebrating his football success. What Montana stood to lose was, potentially, money, either from his fans purchasing the *San Jose Mercury News* poster with his image or a loss of his exclusive control of his likeness. He may also have been motivated by his longstanding issues with the press generally (which had not always portrayed him in the most favorable or fair light) and the *San Jose Mercury News* specifically (which had also implied

Montana used drugs). Montana, though, lost this lawsuit in 1995.³ Similarly, Tiger Woods's unsuccessful lawsuit in 2000 against Jireh Publishing also seems to have been financially motivated. Rick Rush's portrayal of the young golfer was flattering in that it placed him in the same category as the legends of the sport. Unlike Warren Spahn, nothing in Woods's lawsuit suggests that he was worried about protecting the reputation of the real masters of Augusta. The ETW Corporation was focused, understandably so, on protecting Woods's financial interests. The Tony Twist lawsuit of 2003 showed how intertwined the motives of protecting one's reputation and protecting one's financial opportunities could be. Twist argued that his lawsuit against Todd MacFarlane's companies was because of the negative spin of his namesake character; he feared being mistaken for the villainous character. He made reference to his mother's being upset when she saw the comic version with her son's name: that is a matter of dignity. He argued also that he had lost other endorsements because of the comic-book character, which was a matter of protecting his financial image even more than his personal reputation. Yet Twist asked for and was awarded damages that many found beyond belief: $15 million. While Twist, like all plaintiffs, was limited to asking only for financial damages, rather than a duel or horsewhipping, the sheer amount of what he won implies a significant pecuniary interest in the outcome of the case.

Chronologically, these cases do not quite fit an even evolution of the right of privacy to publicity as linked to the history of celebrity and consumerism. All came after cameras and celebrity endorsements were common, and, as in many other lawsuits, the attorneys representing these sporting celebrities relied on any law or claim that might work. As a result, each contributes to the changes in the laws surrounding reputation in different ways, with some having a more significant, immediate effect than others. But one thing we can know from law is that no decision is meaningless; in time, a dissent in a case can later become controlling law.⁴

The first case in this book and one of the first lawsuits involving sporting figures to be heard by the Supreme Court was that of Wally Butts. The Supreme Court's decision in *Butts* in 1967 was significant because it established that sporting figures were celebrities. This case laid the foundation for all future sporting celebrity lawsuits, including the other five explored in this book, regarding reputation and financial interests.⁵

The final published decision for Warren Spahn was also delivered in 1967 in an era when Spahn did have endorsements and did profit from his image,⁶ but his motivation for filing the lawsuit seems not to have been money.

From a legal perspective, Spahn's lawsuit is, in many ways, a dead end. New York and several other states have dropped the false-light category from the tort of privacy because its protections overlap with defamation and it, more than the other privacy torts, seems to imperil the First Amendment freedom of expression.[7] The First Amendment allows someone to assert that Warren Spahn is an American hero, despite his opposition to that belief, although it is worth noting that Spahn won his case because of the inaccurate "facts" presented in the book. Today, Spahn would not win his claim from that perspective; he would have to argue that he had somehow been defamed, which would be a challenge, as no one was likely to think less of him after reading the biography.

Joe Montana's lawsuit in 1995 was in some ways a reflection of the era of increased endorsement power and consumerism. Although Montana seems to have been motivated largely by the financial interests in limiting the use of his photo to authorized posters, he lost his case; but in pursuing it, he challenged the press's right to profit in perpetuity from his photo. The court in the *Montana* cased argued that Montana would forever be a celebrity and that his newsworthy photos, owned by the newspaper, would always be newsworthy. Forever, though, is a long time, and another court may someday conclude that the statute of limitations on Montana's newsworthiness has ended.

The final decision in Don Newcombe's case was in 1998, when being a celebrity athlete for many meant cashing in on as many endorsements as possible. The Ninth Circuit, the final arbiter of the case, essentially decided the matter on the right-of-publicity grounds. Newcombe's image was recognizable, he had not consented to its use, and Coors stood to profit from its use; the court rejected Newcombe's claim that he had been defamed because he had failed to establish that his reputation had been harmed in the eyes of a third party. Newcombe's dignity might have been damaged and he might have felt humiliated, but defamation requires that a third party think less of the plaintiff because of the communication. Perhaps as a tribute to Newcombe's strong reputation at that point in his life, he could not establish that his actual reputation had been damaged. The combined complaints show Newcombe's motivation (protecting his reputation) and the evolution of law (the court's protecting his right to profit form his image). Legally, the *Newcombe* decision strengthened the celebrity sporting figure's rights of publicity.[8]

Like *Montana*, Woods's lawsuit pushed the boundaries in asking the court where the line between the right of publicity and the First Amendment's freedom of expression lay.[9] This question of how to balance the individual's right to profit from his or her image and the public's right to know about newsworthy events and to produce art and communication under the First Amendment remains largely unanswered. Although Woods lost his lawsuit, his loss was Tony Twist's gain when the Missouri Supreme Court relied on Woods's attorney's law-review article articulating a test for the right of publicity.

As with the *Spahn* case, the legal implications of the *Twist* decision seem to have been limited. Almost no other courts have adopted the flawed predominant-purpose test, which an attorney to celebrities proposed. For artists and scholars this is important; the *Twist* decision warns of a day when a celebrity can control every aspect and every use of his or her name and image, which could signal a shift for the entire country from principles, like the First Amendment, to consumerism and profit. The predominant-use test could have profound impact on the ability of artists and scholars to use the names and images of celebrities in their own work.

The struggle to define the limits of the right of publicity against the First Amendment and freedom of speech has continued without any nationwide standard being applied. Although Joe Montana and Don Newcombe each relied on the tort of appropriation to protect their rights, neither was challenging the right of an artist to create under the First Amendment. Montana lost his case because of the First Amendment; the court determined that his photos were originally newsworthy and remained so, an exception to all limitations of publication. "Newsworthy" has never been clearly defined, and thus is determined on a case-by-case basis. Newcombe won his case, but because the advertisement was not art but literally commercial speech, the Coors company could not rely on the First Amendment for the same degree of protection. Coors argued instead that Newcombe's image was not recognizable and therefore could not have been appropriated. They lost that argument, but had an artist used that rendition of Newcombe on a T-shirt or as a print, an argument about the limitations of freedom of speech against the right of publicity would have been appropriate. And that would have required a test.

As has been discussed, courts have used, discarded, critiqued, and returned to myriad tests, from the transformative test described in the *Woods* case to the predominant-purpose test utilized in the *Twist* case. The transformative test requires that the art "substantively" alters the original image by adding some unique artistic expression, making the piece uniquely the artist's. Further, the sale of the product must be driven by something other than merely the fame of the celebrity. The predominant-purpose test, as articulated by a plaintiff's attorney, asks if the subject of the alleged art is being exploited.

Even if there is artistic or expressive value in the alleged speech, if the product being sold predominantly relies on the commercial value of an individual's image or identity, the subject has a right of publicity that outweighs the artist's freedom of speech rights.[10] Other courts in other cases have relied on other tests. For example, the relatedness test presumes that the work in question is expressive and that the right of publicity will not bar the use of a celebrity's image unless the use is unrelated to the work or the use is obviously an attempt to disguise the implication of endorsement. So, essentially, as long as the work does not suggest that the celebrity supports the product, it is protected under the First Amendment. The actual-malice test suggests that the plaintiff must prove that the defendant who used the celebrity's image or name knew or should have known that use of the image or name was misleading. Another example of a test is a kind of balancing test in which the court determines, on a case-by-case basis, if the economic implications or loss to the plaintiff outweighed the metaphorical costs of limiting the First Amendment. The transformative test seems to be, in 2014, the most popular test across jurisdictions.[11]

THE CURRENT STATE OF THE RIGHT OF PUBLICITY

Two subsequent decisions have added to the evolution of the legal rights for athletes and sporting figures to protect their dignity or at least their financial interests. In 2012 the Third Circuit Court of Appeals ruled that Electronic Arts Inc. (EA) had violated the rights of publicity of Ryan Hart, a former college football player, by using his image in a videogame.[12] In 2013 the Ninth Circuit Court of Appeals ruled in favor of college athletes in a similar action against EA.[13] In both cases, the vote was 2–1, and in each case the majority relied on the transformative-use test to render its verdict. Judge Joseph A. Greenaway Jr. was the author of the Third Circuit majority decision. The case involved Hart, a very successful quarterback at Rutgers University from 2002 to 2005, who was included in a version of an online video game about NCAA football, in which a video gamer uses avatars of real college players, including Hart, to play virtual versions of football. The video franchise focused on realism, and the avatars closely matched their real-life inspiration, the same physical characteristics, jersey numbers, team uniforms, hometowns, and ages. Judge Greenaway began with the assumption that video games were protected forms of speech under the First Amendment and that Hart had rights of publicity. To evaluate the relationship between the two, Greenaway considered the existing modern tests, specifically the predominant-use test and the transformative-use test. EA had argued that the *Twist* decision describing the predominant-use test was the best option, but Greenaway disagreed, writing, "By our reading, the Predominant Use Test is subjective at best, arbitrary at worst, and in either case calls upon judges to act as both impartial jurists and discerning art critics."[14] Instead, Greenaway utilized the transformative-use test because "it provides courts with a flexible—yet uniformly applicable—analytical framework."[15] Greenaway then concluded that EA had insufficiently transformed Hart's image in the game for the company's First Amendment rights to outweigh the player's right of publicity. The court specifically noted that the default Hart avatar looked like, had the same name, had the same history, and had all the same statistics of the real Hart. Although the gamer had the power to change certain things about the Hart avatar such as hairstyle, facial hair, and accessories, the court did not think these alterations were sufficient to transform the avatar enough for full First Amendment protection.

Dissenting Judge Thomas L. Ambro disagreed. He acknowledged that part of the basic problem of the case, the reason that it seemed so unfair to Hart, was that the rules of the NCAA prohibited Hart from accepting compensation from EA for the use of his avatar. He, too, felt that there was something inequitable about the situation, but that the case was about law. He agreed that the transformative-use test was the appropriate test but disagreed with the majority's application. Ambro argued that EA's use of the avatar was the use of a character, much like in books and in movies, and further he concluded that the use of the changeable avatar in invented and historical games was a kind of fiction. Even the digital transformation of Hart into an avatar contributed to a transformative use, according to Ambro.[16]

In the parallel case in the Ninth Circuit the following year, the court followed the same patterns in the decision of the Third Circuit. Judge Jay S. Bybee began his majority decision for the Ninth Circuit with a description of the man at the center of the case. The lead plaintiff for the NCAA athletes, Sam Keller, had been a starting quarterback for Arizona State University in 2005 and for the University of Nebraska in 2007. Bybee, like Greenaway, noted that EA tried to replicate teams and players as realistically and accurately as possible. His majority opinion, just as the Third Circuit's did, relied on the transformative-use test, and he rejected EA's demand for protection under the First Amendment because the company "literally recreates Keller in the very setting in which he has achieved renown."[17] Judge Sidney R. Thomas, however, disagreed. Similar to his Third Circuit counterpart, he agreed that the transformative-use test was the appropriate test for the situation, but he too believed his majority had misapplied the facts to the test. He, like Judge Ambro, believed that the video game was a kind of "interactive historical fiction" and that the ability of the gamer to control the weight, fitness, and actions of the avatar athlete was transformative.[18]

With the adoption of the transformative-use test by both the Third and Ninth Circuits, this test seems to be the most commonly used test for rights of publicity, but as the split decisions indicate, interpreting the test is not going to be a simple or uniform matter. One critique of these two decisions is that they seemed limited by the default visual similarity between the athletes and their avatars; one scholar argued that art was more than just re-creation with transformation, noting that Andy Warhol simply changed the color schemes of the Campbell soup cans, which arguably was not a transformative use of the cans.[19]

PERSONAL ISSUES

If I were writing a law-review article, I would be offering my own test for balancing the rights of the First Amendment with the rights of publicity, and while I have no answer, I do have a stake in the outcome. Some scholars have argued that in the twenty-first century all of us are celebrities and all of us have rights of publicity.[20] By my own and by any general definition, I am not a celebrity. No one has ever stolen my visual image to advertise products or put my avatar into a video game, because my image has limited value. Of course, like most Americans, my image is on the internet on both public and private sites, and my professional, and probably some personal, details are also available. Almost all of my university employers and many of my alma maters have used my name or image to advertise the institution, but they all did so with my implicit, if not always explicit, consent. Perhaps, someday, I will be a celebrity and have a practical need to apply the rights of publicity to my own life. For now, I, like everyone in the twenty-first century, struggle to control my private facts, but unlike many of my fellow citizens, I fight to keep my virtual profile limited.

For now, though, I am just a scholar who tells the stories of other people's lives without ever getting their permission to do so, and this project has forced me to think about the potential irony of what I am doing. I do not expect to get rich from this book, although I am not averse to that proposition, so I do not really expect to profit monetarily from telling these stories, but I do expect that this book will benefit me professionally. Should I have contacted the subjects of these lawsuits or their estates to ask for their permission?

Am I doing something fundamentally different from putting their images on a T-shirt and selling that shirt? Legally, this book is protected under the First Amendment because it is a history based on public documents. If any of the people or companies in this book are unhappy with my representation of them, any one of them can create their own counternarratives, and I would expect that Tiger Woods's autobiography will sell much better than this work. Morally, though, I am less certain of my position, as I have some ambivalence about being the subject of other people's scholarship and art.

Image, reputation, and identity are all intensely personal things, and no matter how much we share publicly, we all want to control that image, whether it be to protect our dignity, our self-image, or our financial interests. We all want to control the truth of ourselves. In the world of the twenty-first century, however, our reputation, our identity, maybe even ourselves are often mediated by something, be it a magazine, a biography, a poster, an advertisement, a portrait, a comic book, or a scholarly monograph. I believe that histories and law are intriguing because of the stories that they relate,[21] and I have tried to respect the stories of the individuals in these lawsuits. In the end, though, if we are frustrated with how others use our image, we must turn to the courts and trust that they will find the balance between the First Amendment and our individual rights of reputation.

NOTES

PREFACE

1. Barry Smart, *The Sport Star: Modern Sport and the Cultural Economy of Sporting Celebrity* (London: Sage, 2005), 1.

2. Marianne Engle, "Sports and Kids: Pathway to Healthy Development or to Unhealthy Competition," *NYU Child Study Center: Giving Children Back Their Childhood*, accessed July 6, 2014, http://www.aboutourkids.org/articles/sports_kids_pathway _healthy_development_or_unhealthy_competition.

3. "How $194.64 Billion is Spent in Sports," *Street and Smith's SportBusiness Journal*, accessed July 6, 2014, http://www.sportsbusinessjournal.com/images/random/ SportsIndustry.pdf.

4. Sara Bibel, "Super Bowl XLVII on FOX Is Most Watched Television Show Is U.S. History," *TV by the Numbers*, last modified February 3, 2014, http://tvbythenumbers .zap2it.com/2014/02/03/super-bowl-xlviii-on-fox-is-most-watched-television-show -in-u-s-history/234089.

5. For a detailed discussion of the intertwining of sport and the media, see Lawrence Wenner, ed., *MediaSport* (London: Routledge, 1998) and David Rowe, *Sport, Culture and the Media*, 2nd ed. (Berkshire, Eng.: McGraw-Hill, 2004).

6. Yalda T. Uhls and Patricia Greenfield, "The Value of Fame: Preadolescent Perceptions of Popular Media and their Relationships to Future Aspirations," *Developmental Psychology* 48 (2012): 315–26.

7. Dara Greenwood, Christopher R. Long, and Sonya Dal Cin, "Fame and the Social Self: The Need to Belong, Narcissism, and Relatedness Predict the Appeal of Fame," *Personality and Individual Differences* 55 (2013): 490–95.

8. Lawrence M. Friedman, *Guarding Life's Dark Secrets: Legal and Social Controls over Reputation, Propriety, and Privacy* (Stanford, Calif.: Stanford University Press, 2007).

9. Andrew Parker, "Sport, Celebrity and Identity: A Socio-Legal Analysis," in *Sport and Social Identities*, edited by John Harris and Andrew Parker (London: Palgrave MacMillian, 2009), 155.

10. *Butts v. Curtis Publishing Company*, 225 F. Supp. 916 (N.D. Ga. 1964), *aff'd*, 351 F.2d 702 (5th Cir. 1965), *aff'd*, 388 U.S. 130 (1967).

11. General Edwin A. Walker (ret.) had sued the Associated Press for defamation after the AP issued a report saying he had led an angry crowd protesting the admission of an African American student to the University of Mississippi. Because this book focuses on sporting figures and their lawsuits, Walker's case will not be discussed.

12. *Spahn v. Julian Messner, Inc.*, 250 N.Y.S.2d 529 (N.Y. Sup. Ct. 1964), *aff'd*, 260 N.Y.S.2d 451 (N.Y. App. Div. 1965), *aff'd*, 221 N.E.2d 543, 544 (N.Y., 1966), *vacated by*, 387 U.S. 239 (1967), *on remand at, adhered to*, 233 N.E.2d 840 (N.Y., 1967).

13. Milton J. Shapiro, *The Warren Spahn Story* (New York: Messner, 1958).

14. *Montana v. San Jose Mercury News*, 40 Cal. Rptr. 2d 639 (Cal. Ct. App. 1995).

15. *Newcombe v. Adolf Coors, Co.*, 157 F.3d 686 (9th Cir. 1998).

16. *ETW v. Jireh Publishing Co.*, 99 F. Supp. 2d 829 (N.D. Ohio 2000), *aff'd*, 332 F.3d 915 (6th Cir. 2003).

17. *Doe v. TCI Cablevision*, No. ED78785, 2002 Mo. App. LEXIS 1577 (Mo. Ct. App. July 23, 2002), *aff'd in part, rev'd in part*, 110 S.W.3d 363 (Mo. 2003).

18. "Athletes," *Forbes.com*, accessed June 29, 2015, http://www.forbes.com/athletes.

19. The research on women's reputation in sport is extensive; for just a few examples see Margaret Carlisle Duncan and Michael A. Messner, "The Media Image of Sport and Gender," in Wenner, *MediaSport*, 170–85, and Mary Jo Kane, Nicole M. LaVoi, and Janet S. Fink, "Exploring Elite Female Athletes' Interpretations of Sport Media Images: A Window into the Construction of Social Identity and 'Selling Sex' in Women's Sports," *Communication and Sport* 1 (2013): 269–98.

CHAPTER 1. THE HISTORY OF CELEBRITY AND THE LAWS OF REPUTATION AND SPEECH

1. Friedman, *Guarding Life's Dark Secrets*, 259.

2. Daniel J. Boorstin, *The Image; or, What Happened to the American Dream* (New York: Atheneum, 1961), reprint: *The Image: A Guide to Pseudo-Events in America* (New York: Atheneum, 1972), 57 (page citations are to the reprint edition).

3. As technology and fame are both fleeting elements, a brief historical overview is necessary. In 2015 Wikipedia was a free, Web-based encyclopedia with entries written and edited by anyone in the general public, including the subject of an entry. Facebook was an online social networking site. Twitter was a social networking system that allowed its users to send 140-character messages, or "tweets," to anyone signed up as a "follower" of that user. Athletes used tweets to announce everything from signing contact extensions to their feelings about other celebrities. Instagram was an online photo-sharing site. Tiger refers to golfer Tiger Woods; LeBron to LeBron James, a National Basketball Association player; and Serena, to tennis star Serena Williams,

each of whom was a highly successful athlete who at times was both famous and infamous in the early twenty-first century.

4. "LeBron James' 'Decision' Watched by Nearly 10 Million Viewers," *USA Today*, last modified July 11, 2010, http://usatoday30.usatoday.com/sports/basketball/nba/heat/2010-07-11-lebron-decision-tv-viewers_N.htm. Four years later, when James signed a new contract returning him to Cleveland, he announced this decision via an article in *Sports Illustrated* posted online. LeBron James (as told to Lee Jenkins), "I'm Coming Home," *Sports Illustrated*, last modified July 11, 2014, http://www.si.com/nba/2014/07/11/lebron-james-cleveland-cavaliers.

5. James Monaco, ed., *Celebrity: The Media as Image Makers* (New York: Delta, 1978), 10–11.

6. In 1978 when Monaco published this definition, he listed Ralph Nader as a hero, presumably because of Nader's consumer-advocacy work in that decade. More than twenty years and two failed presidential runs later, Nader probably would no longer be Monaco's example of a heroic celebrity.

7. Boorstin, *The Image*, 76.

8. Chris Rojek, *Celebrity* (London: Reaktion, 2001), 18.

9. John Harris and Ben Clayton, "Femininity, Masculinity, Physicality and the English Tabloid Press: The Case of Anna Kournikova," *International Review for the Sociology of Sport* 37 (2002): 397–413.

10. Ellis Cashmore, *Celebrity/Culture* (New York: Routledge, 2006), 4.

11. Richard Sandomir, "In Endorsements, No Athlete Is a Sure Thing," *New York Times*, last modified August 1, 2007, http://www.nytimes.com/2007/08/01/sports/football/01sandomir.html. For a thorough discussion of athletes who have lost endorsements after questionable behavior, see Lawrence A. Wenner, ed., *Fallen Sports Heroes, Media, and Celebrity Culture* (New York: Peter Lang, 2013).

12. For an analysis of Jordan commercials, see Mary G. McDonald, "Michael Jordan's Family Values: Marketing, Meaning, and Post-Reagan America," *Sociology of Sport Journal* 13 (December 1996): 344–65.

13. Cashmore, *Celebrity/Culture*, 14.

14. David L. Andrews and Steven J. Jackson, *Sport Stars: The Cultural Politics of Sporting Celebrity* (New York: Routledge, 2001), 9.

15. For an analysis of the stalking phenomenon, see J. Reid Meloy, Lorraine Sheridan, and Jens Hoffmann, eds., *Stalking, Threatening, and Attacking Public Figures: A Psychological and Behavioral Analysis* (New York: Oxford University Press, 2008).

16. Charles Edwardes, "The New Football Mania," in *The Faber Book of Soccer*, edited by Ian Hamilton (London: Faber and Faber, 1992), 8.

17. Smart, *Sport Star*, 39.

18. Tom Spousta, "Wie's Pro Debut Comes with a Price," *USA Today*, October 13, 2005.

19. P. David Marshall, *Celebrity and Power: Fame in Contemporary Culture* (Minneapolis: University of Minnesota Press, 1997), x.

20. See Elliott J. Gorn, ed., *Muhammad Ali: The People's Champ* (Urbana: University of Illinois Press, 1995) and Samuel O. Regalado, *"Clay, aka Ali v. United States* (1971): Muhammad Ali, Precedent, and the Burger Court," in *Sport and the Law: Historical and Cultural Intersections* (Fayetteville: University of Arkansas Press, 2014), 3–18.

21. William C. Rhoden, "Sport of the Times: Jordan Finds a New Arena to Play In," *New York Times*, last modified February 12, 2000, http://www.nytimes.com/2000/02/12/sports/sports-of-the-times-jordan-finds-a-new-arena-to-play-in.html.

22. Sean Gregory, "Why Athletes Won't Stay Silent Anymore," *Time*, last modified December 19, 2014, http://time.com/3638006/lebron-icantbreathe-obama-garner-ferguson.

23. Rojek, *Celebrity*, 11.

24. U.S. Constitution, Amendment I.

25. See Roger K. Newman, *Hugo Black: A Biography* (New York: Pantheon, 1994).

26. *Schenck v. United States*, 249 U.S. 47 (1919), 52.

27. *Whitney v. California*, 274 U.S. 357 (1927) (Brandeis concurrence), 375.

28. *Schenck*, 52.

29. *Brandenburg v. Ohio*, 395 U.S. 444 (1967), 447.

30. Sir William Blackstone, *Commentaries on the Laws of England*, Book 4 (Oxford: Clarendon, 1766), 151–52, quoted in David M. O'Brien, *Privacy, Law, and Public Policy* (New York: Praeger, 1979), 140.

31. *Valentine v. Chrestensen*, 316 U.S. 52 (1942).

32. *Virginia State Board of Pharmacy v. Virginia Citizens Consumer Council, Inc.*, 425 U.S. 748 (1976).

33. For a discussion of the history of commercial speech and the Supreme Court, see Andrew J. Wolf, "Commercial Speech: What Pharmaceutical Marketing Reveals about Bans on Commercial Speech," *William and Mary Bill of Rights Journal* 21 (2013): 1291–323. Note as well that the Roberts Supreme Court of 2014 has expanded rights to corporations, and this expansion could in theory reach commercial speech as well.

34. See Zechariah Chafee, *Free Speech in the United States* (Cambridge: Harvard University Press, 1941; reprint New York: Atheneum, 1969); page citations are to the reprint edition.

35. Chafee, *Free Speech*, 17.

36. For an introduction to defamation, see Jerome A. Barron and C. Thomas Dienes, *First Amendment Law in a Nutshell*, 4th ed. (St. Paul, Minn.: West, 2008).

37. J. H. Baker, *An Introduction to English Legal History*, 2nd ed. (Boston: Butterworth, 1979), 364.

38. For a discussion of the history of the Star Chamber and an argument that it was not a secretive or restrictive as portrayed in many histories, see Daniel L. Vande Zande, "Coercive Power and the Demise of the Star Chamber," *American Journal of Legal History* 50 (July 2008–2010): 326–49.

39. Norman L. Rosenberg, *Protecting the Best Men: An Interpretive History of the Law of Libel* (Chapel Hill: University of North Carolina Press, 1986), 4–6.

40. Ibid, 27.

41. Ibid, 59.

42. Quoted in Rosenberg, *Protecting the Best Men*, 61.

43. Rosenberg, *Protecting the Best Men*, 121–27.

44. *Cantwell v. Connecticut*, 310 U.S. 296 (1940), 309–10.

45. *Chaplinsky v. New Hampshire*, 315 U.S. 568 (1942), 571–72.

46. *New York Times v. Sullivan*, 376 U.S. 254 (1964), 269.

47. Samuel Warren and Louis Brandeis, "The Right to Privacy," *Harvard Law Review* 4 (1890): 193–247. Note that tort law is a branch of civil law that requires someone who causes injury to a plaintiff to pay cash damages to the plaintiff for those injuries. Torts are not crimes.

48. Ibid., 193.

49. Ibid., 198.

50. Ibid., 196.

51. Ibid., 215–16.

52. Alpheus Thomas Mason, *Brandeis: A Free Man's Life* (New York: Viking, 1946), 70.

53. Don R. Pember, *Privacy and the Press: The Law, the Mass Media, and the First Amendment* (Seattle: University of Washington Press, 1972), 39–41.

54. Ibid., 1–22.

55. Warren and Brandeis, "The Right to Privacy," 196.

56. Melvin M. Nimmer, "The Right of Publicity," *Law and Contemporary Problems* 19 (1954): 203–23, quotation on 204.

57. William L. Prosser, "Privacy," *California Law Review* 48 (1960): 383–423. Prosser included this definition of privacy in the Restatement (Second) of Torts § 652 (1977).

58. See *Time, Inc. v. Hill*, 385 U.S. 374 (1967).

59. Restatement (Second) of Torts § 652 (1977).

60. *Pavesich v. New England Life Insurance Co.*, 50 S.E. 68 (Ga. 1905), 69, 73, and 74.

CHAPTER 2. LIES, LIBEL, AND FOOTBALL: COACHES AS PUBLIC FIGURES

1. *Butts v. Curtis Publishing*, 225 F. Supp. 916 (N.D. Ga., 1964), *aff'd* 242 F. Supp. 390 (N.D. Ga., 1964), *aff'd* 351 F.2d 702 (5th Cir., 1965), *aff'd* 388 U.S. 130 (1967). Hereinafter *Butts*, 225 F. Supp. 916 will be *Butts I*; *Butts*, 242 F. Supp. 390 will be *Butts II*; *Butts*, 351 F. 2d 702 will be *Butts III*, and *Butts*, 388 U.S. 130 will be *Butts IV*.

2. See Gardner Linn, "Wally Butts," in *The New Georgia Encyclopedia*, last modified August 21, 2013, http://www.georgiaencyclopedia.org/articles/sports-outdoor-recreation/wally-butts-1905-1973, and "Wally Butts Dies," *Chicago Tribune* December 18, 1973. For a comprehensive description of the Butts's years at UGA, see Ed Thilenius and Jim Koger, *No Ifs, No Ands, a Lot of Butts: 21 Years of Georgia Football* (Atlanta: Foote and Davies, 1960).

3. Robert Emrich, "The Forties," *Sports Illustrated*, last modified October 6, 2007, http://sportsillustrated.cnn.com/vault/2007/10/03/100793501/the-forties.

4. Bob Considine, "On the Line with Considine," *Washington Post*, December 9, 1942.

5. "Frosh Rule Dropped in S.E. Conference," *Washington Post*, September 19, 1942.

6. "Georgia Will Play Own Navy Eleven," *New York Times*, July 4, 1943.

7. "Butts, Georgia Coach Weighs Lions' Offer," *Chicago Daily News*, January 27, 1948. Average salary for Americans in 1946 was about $3,000. "Income of Nonfarm Families and Individuals: 1946," Department of Commerce, January 28, 1948, http://www2.census.gov/prod2/popscan/p60-001.pdf.

8. William Fay, "When Grid Fellows Get Together," *Chicago Daily Tribune*, October 26, 1947. Butts was a popular speaker as early as 1941; the *Washington Post* reported he would be the principal speaker at the annual Touchdown Club banquet in January 1942. "Georgia Coach Heads Speakers at Banquet," *Washington Post*, December 18, 1941.

9. Bob Considine, "On the Line with Considine," *Washington Post*, October 22, 1941.

10. Shirley Povich, "This Morning with Shirley Povich," *Washington Post*, December 31, 1946.

11. "Scorecard: They Said It," *Sports Illustrated*, October 23, 1961, 15.

12. Ray Cave, "High Tide in Alabama," *Sports Illustrated*, last modified September 26, 1960, http://www.si.com/vault/1960/09/26/589399/high-tide-in-alabama.

13. "Wally Butts Quits as Coach," *Chicago Daily Tribune*, December 24, 1960.

14. James Kirby, *Fumble: Bear Bryant, Wally Butts, and the Great College Football Scandal* (New York: Harcourt, Brace, Jovanovich, 1986), 19–21.

15. Ibid., 26–33.

16. Howard Ector, Georgia Tech Athletic Association, to President Edwin Harrison, GA Tech, June 1, 1959, Records of the Office of the President, 1949–66, box 9, Athletic Association Correspondence, June–July 9, 1959, Georgia Tech Archives. Thanks to Ronald A. Smith for this reference.

17. John S. Watterson, *College Football: History, Spectacle, Controversy* (Baltimore, Md.: Johns Hopkins University Press, 2002), 293–95.

18. For a discussion of Wolfson and Fortas, see Laura Kalman, *Abe Fortas: A Biography* (New Haven, Conn.: Yale University Press, 1990).

19. Kirby, *Fumble*, 26–33.

20. Ibid., 32–34.

21. For a complete examination of Bryant's life, see Allen Barra, *The Last Coach: A Life of Paul "Bear" Bryant* (New York: Norton, 2005).

22. B. J. Phillips and Peter Ainslie, "Football's Supercoach," *Time*, last modified September 29, 1980, http://content.time.com/time/magazine/article/0,9171,952802,00.html.

23. "Sport: A Bear at 'Bama," *Time*, last modified November 17, 1961, http://content.time.com/time/magazine/article/0,9171,939336,00.html.

24. Barra, *Last Coach*, 250–54.

25. Andrew Doyle, "An Atheist in Alabama Is Someone Who Doesn't Believe in Bear Bryant: A Symbol for an Embattled South," in *The Sporting World of the Modern South*, edited by Patrick B. Miller (Champaign: University of Illinois Press, 2002), 261.

26. Paul Bryant and John Underwood, "Black Days after a Black Charge," *Sports Illustrated*, September 5, 1966, 28.

27. Otto Friedrich, *Decline and Fall* (New York: Ballantine, 1971), 7–13.

28. Ibid., 37. Friedrich maintains that the lawsuit was the beginning of the end for the magazine because it "had lost a dangerously large part of its reputation for accuracy and responsibility." Ibid., 44–48.

29. Kirby, *Fumble*, 41–47. Burnett's notes on the phone call reflect Butts's chronic mispronunciation (and misspelling) of the names (Brigham) Woodward and (Ray) Rissmiller as "Woodard" and "Reismueller/Reismuller." Burnett's own misspellings of these names in his hasty transcription of the conversation adds further veracity to his claim of having overheard the exchange between Bryant and Butts.

30. "Football: All-Time Football Results," *Crimson Tide*, accessed July 14, 2014, http://www.rolltide.com/sports/m-footbl/archive/m-footbl-results-archive.html; "Football 1962 Schedule," *Georgia Dogs*, accessed July 15, 2014, http://www.georgia dogs.com/sports/m-footbl/spec-rel/1962-schedule.html.

31. "Georgia Denies Report of Butts Resigning," *Washington Post*, February 13, 1963. A year earlier Butts had been rumored to be a candidate for the head coaching position at the NFL franchise Chicago Cardinals. Shirley Povich, "This Morning with Shirley Povich," *Washington Post*, February 18, 1962.

32. Kirby, *Fumble*, 48–54.

33. Frank Graham Jr., *A Farewell to Heroes* (New York: Viking, 1981). See also Dan Jenkins, "A Debatable Football Scandal in the Southeast," *Sports Illustrated*, last modified March 25, 1963, http://www.si.com/vault/1963/03/25/606263/a-debatable -football-scandal-in-the-southeast.

34. Graham, *Farewell to Heroes*, 282–84.

35. Roger Kahn, "Frank Graham Jr.'s Autobiography: Father and Son, Butts and Bryant," Booktalk, *Sports Illustrated*, last modified November 16, 1981, http://www .si.com/vault/1981/11/16/826117/booktalk-frank-graham-jrs-autobiography-father -and-son-butts-and-bryant.

36. Graham, *Farewell to Heroes*, 279–88.

37. Kirby, *Fumble*, 231.

38. *Butts I*, at 917–18.

39. Jenkins, "A Debatable Football Scandal in the Southeast."

40. Red Smith, "Unkept Secret: Red Smith's Column . . .," *Washington Post*, March 19, 1963.

41. "19th Hole: The Readers Take Over," *Sports Illustrated*, last modified April 8, 1963, http://www.si.com/vault/1963/04/08/593593/19th-hole-the-readers-take-over.

42. "19th Hole: The Readers Take Over," *Sports Illustrated*, last modified April 29, 1963, http://www.si.com/vault/1963/04/29/593063/19th-hole-the-readers-take-over.

43. Wilbur L. Bradbury, "Georgians Find Butts Case Confusing," *New York Times*, April 4, 1963, 62.

44. "Butts's Calls to Gamblers Are Revealed," *Chicago Tribune*, March 28, 1963.

45. "Butts, Scoby Tie Is Business," *Chicago Tribune*, April 6, 1963.

46. "Scorecard," *Sports Illustrated*, last modified April 15,1963, http://www.si.com/vault/1963/04/15/618751/scorecard.

47. Dan Jenkins, "A Trial That Has the South Seething," *Sports Illustrated*, last modified August, 5, 1963, available at http://www.si.com/vault/1963/08/05/595704/a-trial-that-has-the-south-seething.

48. John Sibley, "Georgia Football Coach Is Sure Plays Were Leaked to Alabama," *New York Times*, August 7, 1963.

49. John Sibley, "Butts Tearfully Denies Fix," *New York Times*, August 13, 1963.

50. Kirby, *Fumble*, 115.

51. Robert Boyle, "'It's Not the Money, It's the Vindication,'" *Sports Illustrated*, last modified September 2, 1963, http://www.si.com/vault/1963/09/02/596491/its-not-the-money-its-the-vindication. Butts's gravestone in Oconee Hill Cemetery bears no epitaph.

52. Ibid.

53. Kirby, *Fumble*, 112–13.

54. Quote from Frank Graham Jr., "The Story of a College Football Fix," *Saturday Evening Post*, reprinted in Kirby, *Fumble*, 241–42. Reference to deposition in *Butts III* at 714.

55. Boyle, "'It's Not the Money.'"

56. Kirby, *Fumble*, 148.

57. Ibid., 229.

58. Ibid., 121. Kirby, however, is not without his biases. He is not a Bear Bryant fan, but he was an unabashed fan of SEC football, arguing that big-time college football "helps to support university academic programs." Ibid., 83.

59. Barra, *Last Coach*, 298–307.

60. *Butts I*, 919.

61. Ibid., 920, 922.

62. *New York Times v. Sullivan*, 376 U.S. 254 (1964). The ad itself ("Heed Their Rising Voices," *New York Times*, March 29, 1960) can be seen at https://research.archives.gov/id/2641477.

63. See Jerome A. Barron and C. Thomas Dienes, *First Amendment Law in a Nutshell* (Minneapolis: West, 1993): 116–18.

64. *Butts II*, 394–95.

65. *Butts III*, 710–13.

66. Original case was *Associated Press v. Walker*, 393 S.W.2d 671 (Tex. Civ. App. 1965).

67. Report quoted in *Walker*, 393 S.W.2d. at 674.

68. For a discussion of Edwin A. Walker and his role in this era, see Clive Webb, *Rabble Rousers: The American Far Right in the Civil Rights Era* (Athens: University of Georgia Press, 2010).

69. *Butts IV*, 134.

70. Ibid., 136.

71. Ibid., 155–56. Harlan concluded though that Walker had not met that burden.

72. Ibid., 162–63 (Warren concurrence).

73. Ibid., 164 (Warren concurrence).

74. Ibid., 171 (Black dissent).

75. Ibid., 173–74 (Brennan dissent).

76. Chief Justice Warren writing alone, Brennan joined by White, and Hugo Black joined by William Douglas applied the *Sullivan* test to public figures.

77. Quoted in Dennis J. Hutchinson, "Tribute: The Man Who Once Was Whizzer White," *Yale Law Journal* 103 (1993): 46.

78. Dennis J. Hutchinson, *The Man Who Once Was Whizzer White: A Portrait of Justice Byron R. White* (New York: Free Press, 1998), 11–122.

79. Harry Kalven Jr., "The Reasonable Man and the First Amendment: Hill, Butts, and Walker," *Supreme Court Review* (1967) 1967: 307.

80. *Rosenbloom v. Metromedia*, 403 U.S. 29, 32 (1971).

81. *Gertz v. Robert Walsh Inc.*, 418 U.S. 323 (1974).

82. See Pamela C. Laucella and Barbara Osborne, "Libel and College Coaches," *Journal of Legal Aspects of Sport* 12 (2002): 183–204, for a discussion of coaching and public figures.

83. *Silvester v. American Broadcasting Companies, Inc.*, 839 F.2d 1491 (11th Cir. 1988).

84. *Daubenmire v. Sommers*, 805 N.E.2d 571 (11th Cir. 2004).

85. *Abbott v. Harris Publications, Inc.*, No. 97 Civ. 7648, 2000 U.S. Dist. LEXIS 9384 (S.D. NY July 7, 2000).

86. *M. G. v. Time Warner, Inc.*, 107 Cal Rptr. 2d 504 (Cal. Ct. App. 2001).

87. *Wilson v. The Daily Gazette Company*, 588 S.E.2d 197 (W. Va. 2003).

88. *Holt v. Cox Enterprises*, 590 F. Supp. 408 (N.D. Ga., 1984).

89. "Wally Butts Carves Out a New Career," *Washington Post*, March 9, 1966. This article also claimed he had moved to Atlanta to live with his wife Nancy and her two children. However, two years later the *Post* reported that Butts lived in Athens with his wife Winnie (his first and perhaps only marriage was to Winnie). "Butts Finds He Misses Coaching," *Washington Post*, December 15, 1968. Butts and Winnie had three daughters. Whether the 1966 *Post* article was inaccurate or if he had moved in with another woman is unclear.

90. Kirby, *Fumble*, 216.

91. "Wally Butts Dies," *Chicago Tribune*, December 18, 1973.

92. Quoted in Kirby, *Fumble*, 216.

93. Ivan Maisel, "College Football Report: Butts Is Famous, Thanks to a Kinder, Gentler Era," *Sporting News*, February 10, 1997.

94. Kirby, *Fumble*, 165, reports the settlement was for $320,000, but Allen Barra in his biography places the figure at $360,000. Barra, *Last Coach*, 294.

95. Bryant and Underwood, "Black Days."

96. Ibid.

97. Barra, *Last Coach*, 292–94.

98. Phillips and Ainslie, "Football's Supercoach."

99. "About the *Saturday Evening Post*," accessed June 29, 2015, http://www.saturday eveningpost.com/about.

100. "Campus Paper Warned," *New York Times*, November 14, 1953.

101. Doyle, "Atheist in Alabama," 271.

102. Drew Pearson, "A Libel Jury Polled," *Washington Post*, March 5, 1967.

CHAPTER 3. STOP THE PRESS: A BASEBALL LEGEND AND BIOGRAPHY

1. Shapiro, *Warren Spahn Story* (New York: Messner, 1958). As will be discussed later, whether or not Spahn won a Bronze Star is complicated, but I believe that he did not win the award during World War II.

2. Al Silverman, *Warren Spahn: Immortal Southpaw* (New York: Bartholomew, 1961), 26; Silverman is one of the only writers to mention Spahn's mother by name.

3. Joe MacKay, *The Great Shutout Pitchers: Twenty Profiles of a Vanishing Breed* (Jefferson, N.C.: MacFarland, 2004), 62–63. Showing the power of the Shapiro article, MacKay reported that Spahn had injured his shoulder. The court wrote that Spahn's elbow was injured. *Spahn v. Julian Messner, Inc.* 250 N.Y.S.2d 529, 539 (N.Y.Sup.Ct., 1964) [hereinafter *Spahn I*].

4. LoRene's name has been published as both Lorene and LoRene. I utilize LoRene because that is the spelling in Oklahoma newspapers. See Bryan Painter, "Memories of a Legend and a Father," *The Oklahoman*, last modified March 16, 2008, http://newsok.com/memories-of-a-legend-and-a-father/article/3216734.

5. See *Baseball Almanac*, "1956 Milwaukee Braves Roster, accessed November 24, 2014, http://www.baseball-almanac.com/teamstats/roster.php?y=1956&t=MLN.

6. Gary Caruso, *The Braves Encyclopedia* (Philadelphia: Temple University Press, 1995), 72. Silverman, *Warren Spahn*, 67, claimed the phrase was "Spahn and Sain and two days of rain."

7. Robert Creamer, "Are Lefties Human?" *Sports Illustrated*, last modified June 25, 1956, http://www.si.com/vault/1956/06/25/615983/are-lefties-human.

8. Roy Terrell, "A Mean Hand with a Rock," *Sports Illustrated*, last modified October 21, 1957, http://www.si.com/vault/1957/10/21/605515/a-mean-hand-with-a-rock.

9. Warren N. Wilbert, *What Makes an Elite Pitcher?* (Jefferson, N.C.: MacFarland, 2003), 201.

10. Al Hirshberg, *Sport Magazine*, quoted in Silverman, *Warren Spahn*, 53–55.

11. Shapiro, *Warren Spahn Story*.

12. Milton J. Shapiro, *Jackie Robinson of the Brooklyn Dodgers* and *The Sal Maglie Story* (New York: Messner, 1957).

13. "Books and Authors," *New York Times Book Review*, September 17, 1933. In 1958 the press was run by Kathryn G. Messner.

14. "Mrs. Kathryn G. Messner, 61, Chief of Publishing House, Dies," *New York Times*, August 6, 1964.

15. Margalit Fox, "Leona Nevler, Editor, 79; Shepherded 'Peyton Place,'" *New York Times*, December 15, 2005.

16. *Spahn I*, 538.

17. Shapiro, *Warren Spahn Story*, 40–45.

18. Ibid., 16–32.

19. Ibid., 65.

20. Ibid., 9–10.

21. Ibid., 68.

22. Robert E. Tomasson, "Spahn Institutes $175,000 Suit Over 'Fictionalized' Image," *New York Times*, January 25, 1964.

23. *Spahn I*, 31.

24. *Roberson v. Rochester Folding Box Co.*, 64 N.E. 442, 443 (N.Y., 1902).

25. Quoted in *Spahn I*, 531n1.

26. *Spahn I*, 537.

27. Ibid., 539.

28. Ibid., 538. Shapiro, *Warren Spahn Story*, 65, simply states Spahn won the award, without describing what he had allegedly done. Shapiro spent far more time describing his vision of Spahn's experience at Remagen.

29. *Spahn I*, 538–41.

30. The Purple Heart is awarded to any service member injured or killed in combat with an enemy. An injury is defined in part as a wound treated and recorded by a medical officer. "Military Awards," Army Regulations 600-8-22, June 24, 2013, 20–21.

31. Shapiro, *Warren Spahn Story*, 65–66.

32. Ibid., 14.

33. *Spahn I*, 539.

34. Ibid., 542.

35. Ibid., 543–43.

36. *Spahn v. Julian Messner, Inc.*, 260 N.Y.S.2d 451,452 (N.Y. App. Div., 1965) [hereinafter *Spahn II*].

37. Ibid., 456.

38. Ibid., 456.

39. Unlike the federal court system and most state courts, the highest court in New York is the Court of Appeals. The Supreme Court of New York is below the Court of Appeals and is parallel to the circuit or district courts in other states' legal systems.

40. *Spahn v. Julian Messner, Inc.*, 221 N.E.2d 543, 544 (N.Y., 1966) [hereinafter *Spahn III*].

41. *Spahn III*, 545.

42. *Time Inc. v. Hill*, 385 U.S. 374 (1967).

43. *Julian Messner, Inc. v. Spahn*, 387 U.S. 239 (1967). No opinion was offered; the decision was simply vacated and the case remanded.

44. *Spahn v. Julian Messner, Inc.*, 233 N.E.2d 840, 843 (N.Y., 1967) [hereinafter *Spahn IV*].

45. Ibid., 843, unnumbered footnote.

46. *Julian Messner, Inc. v. Spahn*, 393 U.S. 1046 (1969).

47. Provided of course that the Missouri courts never heard the case: see chapter 7 about Tony Twist.

48. Jonathan Kahn, "Bringing Dignity Back to the Light: Publicity Rights and the Eclipse of the Tort of Appropriation of Identity," *Cardozo Arts and Entertainment Law Journal* 17 (1999): 213–72, n286.

49. Isidore Silver, "Privacy and the First Amendment," *Fordham Law Review* 34 (1966): 558.

50. Ibid., 563.

51. Ibid., 366.

52. Diane Leenheer Zimmerman, "False Light Invasion of Privacy: The Light That Failed," *New York University Law Review* 64 (1989): 364–453.

53. Michael C. Hartmere, "Comment: Defining New York's Statutory Right of Privacy: A Case Comment on *Messenger v. Gruner + Jahr Printing and Publishing*," *Fordham Intellectual Property, Media and Entertainment Law Journal* 10 (2000): 905–31. Some scholars believe the New York courts have erred in not overturning *Spahn*. See F. Jay Dougherty, "All the World's Not a Stooge: The "Transformativeness" Test for Analyzing a First Amendment Defense to a Right of Publicity Claim against Distribution of a Work of Art," *Columbia Journal of Law and the Arts* 27 (2003): 1–78, n32.

54. Gary T. Schwartz, "Explaining and Justifying a Limited Tort of False Light Invasion of Privacy," *Case Western Reserve Law Review* 41 (1991): 885–919.

55. Silverman, *Warren Spahn*.

56. "Messner Bought by Pocket Books," *New York Times*, December 31, 1964.

57. Morris Kaplan, "Drysdale, Aaron, Mathews Sue to Stop 'Distorted' Biographies," *New York Times*, June 30, 1967.

58. "Three Baseball Players Fail to Halt Biographies," *New York Times*, August 17, 1967.

59. Myron Cope, "El Spahnie of Los Tigres," *Sports Illustrated*, July 4, 1966, 26–31.

60. Ray Yasser, "Warren Spahn's Legacy: The Right to Be Free from False Praise," *Seton Hall Journal of Sports and Entertainment Law* 18 (2008), 58n67.

61. Shapiro, *Warren Spahn Story*, 60.

62. Mark Feeney, "Warren Spahn," *Boston Globe*, November 25, 2003 (also claimed Spahn won a Bronze Star).

63. Roger Kahn, "Mind over Batter: No One Had a Better Head for Pitching than Warren Spahn," *Sports Illustrated*, last modified December 8, 2003, http://www.si.com/vault/2003/12/08/355740/mind-over-batter-no-one-had-a-better-head-for-pitching-than-warren-spahn. Caruso, *Braves Encyclopedia*, 240, repeated this story.

64. Feeney, "Warren Spahn."

65. Caruso, *Braves Encyclopedia*, 242, reported Spahn enlisted and does not report Spahn's winning a Bronze Star.

66. For those reports that Spahn was drafted, see Rich Westcott, *Winningest Pitchers: Baseball's 300 Game Winners* (Philadelphia: Temple University Press, 2002), 112 (also reports Spahn won Bronze Star), but Westcott reported something slightly different in his book *Splendor on the Diamond: Interviews with 35 Stars of Baseball's Past* (Gainesville: University of Florida Press, 2000), writing on p. 99 that Spahn "entered the Army" and making no mention of the Bronze Star; Joe MacKay, *The Great Shutout Pitchers: Twenty Profiles of a Vanishing Breed* (Jefferson, N.C.: MacFarland, 2004), 63 (adding that Spahn was awarded the Bronze Star); Shapiro, *Warren Spahn Story*, 60; Warren N. Wilbert, *What Makes an Elite Pitcher?* (Jefferson, N.C.: MacFarland, 2003), 201 (including that Spahn won the Bronze Star).

67. Shapiro, *Warren Spahn Story*, 65.

68. Ibid.

69. Yasser, "Warren Spahn's Legacy," 53n27.

70. Email from Jamila Porter to the author, July 20, 2014.

71. Email from Jamila Porter to the author, August 8, 2014.

72. *Spahn IV*, 843, unnumbered footnote.

73. "Military Awards," Army Regulation 600-8-22, Bronze Star 3-15(b), June 24, 2013, 42.

74. Ibid., 3-15(d)(2), 42.

75. Ibid., 3-15(d)(3), 42.

76. Jim Kaplan, "Warren Spahn," accessed June 21, 2015, http://sabr.org/bioproj/person/16b7b87d.

77. Kahn, "Mind Over Batter"; Guy Curtright, "Warren Spahn: 1921–2003: A Special Delivery," *Atlanta Journal Constitution*, November 25, 2003; and "The Hall of Famers: Warren Spahn," accessed November 24, 2014, http://baseballhall.org/hof/spahn-warren.

CHAPTER 4. SUPER BOWL ICON OR MARKETING TOOL?

1. A Google search on November 28, 2014, for "Joe Montana best quarterback ever" resulted in more than 408,000 hits.

2. Juliet Chung, "Where Joe Montana Kicks Back," *Wall Street Journal*, November 6, 2009.

3. Ken Horowitz, "Behind the Design: Joe Montana Football," last modified November 20, 2007, http://www.sega-16.com/2007/11/behind-the-design-joe-montana-football/. Joe Montana Football was one of the top five (in sales) video games of 1991 and netted Montana $3.5 million in royalties over five years.

4. Thomas R. King, "BVD Hopes Regular Guys Sell Skivvies," *Wall Street Journal*, November 2, 1990.

5. Joe Montana with Dick Schaap, *Montana* (Atlanta: Turner, 1995), 17.

6. Brian Kilmeade, *It's How You Play the Game: The Powerful Sports Moments That Taught Lasting Values to America's Finest* (New York: Harper Collins, 2007), 353–54.

7. Joe Montana and Bob Raissman, *Audibles: My Life in Football* (New York: Morrow, 1986), 89–107.

8. Montana, *Audibles*, 41.

9. Paul Zimmerman, "The Ultimate Winner," *Sports Illustrated*, last modified August 13, 1990, 72–78.

10. Montana, *Audibles*, 60.

11. Because the NFL season begins in one calendar year and ends with a championship in the next calendar year, citing seasons in the NFL is confusing. The general understanding is the season is defined as the calendar year in which the regular season was played. Thus the 1981 season began in September 1981 and ended in January 1982. This chapter will follow that convention.

12. David Harris, *The Genius: How Bill Walsh Reinvented Football and Created an NFL Dynasty* (New York: Random House, 2008), 175.

13. Ibid., 177–88.

14. Zimmerman, "Ultimate Winner," 72–78.

15. Ibid.

16. Harris, *Genius*, 246.

17. Ibid., 307–39.

18. Ibid., 14–15.

19. Ibid., 114–15.

20. Mark Purdy, "Montana Calls the Wrong Signal for 49ers Fans," *Sporting News*, May 3, 1993, 8.

21. Paul Zimmerman, "Born to Be a Quarterback," *Sports Illustrated*, August 6, 1990, 62–76.

22. Zimmerman, "Ultimate Winner," 72–78.

23. Bill Walsh with Glenn Dickey, *Building a Champion: On Football and the Making of the 49ers* (New York: St. Martin's, 1990): 81.

24. Montana, *Audibles*, 127; see also Zimmerman, "Ultimate Winner."

25. Gary Wayne Dunn, "Early San Jose Journalists and Their Newspapers" (master's thesis, San Jose State University, 1977), 18.

26. Ibid., 33–57.

27. "Two Papers from Early Days Survive," *San Jose Evening News*, December 31, 1941.

28. "Retired Publisher Buried at San Jose," *Spokane Daily Chronicle*, September 1, 1948.

29. "Exception Report for the Chronological Indexes of the United States Newspapers Available at the Library of Congress: 1940–1989," accessed December 14, 2014, http://www.loc.gov/rr/news/chronological/exception_report.html.

30. "Joseph Ridder Was Publisher for 25 Years," *Pittsburgh Post-Gazette*, January 26, 1989.

31. Michael Shapiro, "The Newspaper That *Almost* Seized the Future," *Columbia Journalism Review* (November/December 2011): 64–80.

32. *Montana v. San Jose Mercury News*, 40 Cal. Rptr. 2d 639 (Cal. Ct. App. 1995), 640.

33. *Montana*, 640. The California statute was Civ. Code § 3344.

34. Eric Farber, "Publicity Rights in Entertainment: From Second-Life to the Afterlife; U-La-La, What's Happened to Our California Right of Publicity?" *Chapman Law Review* 11 (2008): 449–63.

35. *Montana*, 640, quoting CA Civ. Code § 3344 (d).

36. Associated Press, "Court Upholds Paper's Right to Put Joe Montana Photo on Poster," last modified August 21, 1995, www.lexisnexis.com.

37. *Montana*, 640.

38. Ibid., 640, quoting *Dora v. Frontline Video Inc.*, 18 Cal Rptr. 2d 790 (1993).

39. *Montana*, 640, quoting Civ. Code § 3344, subd. (d).

40. *Montana*, 641 (emphasis in the original).

41. See *Dora v. Frontline Video, Inc.*, 18 Cal Rptr. 2d 790 (1993).

42. Mark Kriegel, *Namath* (New York: Viking, 2004), 358.

43. *Namath v. Sports Illustrated*, 363 N.Y.S.2d 276 (N.Y. App. Term), *aff'd* 48 A.D. 487 (N.Y. App. Div. 1975).

44. Kriegel, *Namath*, 247–48.

45. Ibid., 292–96.

46. Ibid., 298–99.

47. Ibid., 358.

48. Ibid.

49. Ibid., 359–60.

50. *Namath v. Sports Illustrated*, 363 N.Y.S.2d 276 (N.Y. App. Term), 278.

51. *Namath v. Sports Illustrated*, 48 A.D. 487 (N.Y. App. Div. 1975).

52. *Namath v. Sports Illustrated*, 352 N.E.2d 584 (NY 1976).

53. *Montana*, 642.

54. Jim Carleton, "Once Money in the Bank, Now It's a Face Only His Mother Can Love," *Wall Street Journal*, July 16, 1991.

55. Leah R. Vande Berg, "The Sports Hero Meets the Mediated Celebrity," in Wenner, *MediaSport*, 140–41.

56. Mark Purdy, "Montana Calls the Wrong Signal for 49ers Fans," *Sporting News*, May 3, 1993, 8.

57. Ibid.

58. "Montana Will Pass on Praise: Family Tops Fame in 49er's Fortunes," *San Jose Mercury News*, last modified July 28, 1985, article ID: 8501150823, http://www.mercury news.com/archive-search.

59. "Montana: A Legendary Performance, Clutch Passes Amaze Teammates," *San Jose Mercury News*, last modified January 23, 1989, article ID: 8901070265, and "Montana is Still the Biggest Star," *San Jose Mercury News*, last modified January 21, 1989, article ID: 8901050936, http://www.mercurynews.com/archive-search.

60. "Montana on the Defensive: Drug-Use Rumors Return," *San Jose Mercury News*, January 26, 1990, article ID: 9001080286, http://www.mercurynews.com/archive -search.

61. David Tan, "Beyond Trademark Law: What the Right of Publicity Can Learn from Cultural Studies," *Cardozo Arts and Entertainment Law Journal* 25 (2008): 961.

62. "Montana Sues Manufacturer of Poster," *San Francisco Chronicle*, December 25, 1991. No further public record of this suit exists.

63. "Montana's Suit Rejected Atherton Neighbors," *San Jose Mercury News*, March 18, 1995.

64. "Joe Montana Sues Maker of Video Game," *San Jose Mercury News*, July 15, 1997.

65. "Joe Montana Loses Right of Publicity Lawsuit against *San Jose Mercury News* Seeking Compensation for Newspaper's Sale of Poster Reproductions of Its Pages Bearing His Name and Likeness," *Entertainment Law Reporter* 17, no. 3 (August 1995).

66. Darren F. Farrington, "Should the First Amendment Protect against Right of Publicity Infringement Actions Where the Media Is the Merchandiser? Say It Ain't So, Joe," *Fordham Intellectual Property, Media, and Entertainment Law Journal* 7 (1997): 779–820.

67. W. Mack Webner and Leigh Anne Lindquist, "Transformation: The Bright Line between Commercial Publicity Rights and the First Amendment," *Akron Law Review* 37 (1994): 190.

68. *Martin Luther King Jr., Center for Social Change, Inc. v. American Heritage Products, Inc.*, 296 S.E.2d 697 (Ga. 1982); see "Battles Flare on the King Legacy, Just as Lucrative as It Is Lasting," *New York Times*, January 15, 1997.

69. F. Jay Dougherty, "All the World's Not a Stooge: The 'Transformativeness' Test for Analyzing a First Amendment Defense to a Right of Publicity Claim against Distribution of a Work of Art," *Columbia Journal of Law and Arts* 27 (2003): 1–78.

70. Tailia Baron, "Joe Montana Blitzes Mercury Again," *(San Jose) Business Journal*, last modified January 3, 1994, 1, http://www.lexis-nexis.com.

71. Purdy, "Wrong Signal," 8.

72. Silver, M., "All Hail the King: The Legendary Joe Montana Is Finally Ready to Rest on his Laurels," *Sports Illustrated*, April 24, 1995, 16–23.

73. Joe Montana and Tom Mitchell, *The Winning Spirit: 16 Timeless Principles that Drive Performance Excellence* (New York: Ballantine, 2005).

74. "Joint Juice Commercial Starring Joe Montana," accessed August 8, 2014, https:// www.youtube.com/watch?v=WFwnbgIbfHI.

75. "Skechers Shape Ups," accessed August 27, 2010, http://www.skechers.com/ info/joe_montana_shape-ups.

76. "Hass Avocados Taps Joe Montana for Big Game Promo," progressivegrocer.com, last modified December 20, 2009, http://www.lexis-nexis.com.

77. Mike Rosenberg, "Joe Montana Rewarded after Making 'Old Woman Happy' at Meeting," *San Jose Mercury-News*, last modified February 12, 2014, http://www .lexis-nexis.com.

78. "Not Your Average Joe," *Grand Rapids (Michigan) Press,* August 15, 2010; and Mike Huguenin, "Tanner Lee Wins Tulane QB Job over Nick Montana," last modified August 12, 2014, http://www.nfl.com/news/story/0ap3000000376913/article/tanner -lee-wins-tulane-qb-job-over-nick-montana.

79. Rosenberg, "Joe Montana Rewarded."

80. Sam Whiting, "S.F.'s Favorite Niner Makes City His Home," *San Francisco Chronicle,* July 6, 2010.

81. Eliana Dockterman, "This Is the Real Story behind *Kill the Messenger,*" *Time,* last modified October 14, 2014, www.ebscohost.com.

82. Shapiro, "Newspaper," 64–80.

83. Bob Egelko, "Hearst, MediaNews Group Settle Reilly Suit," last modified April 25, 2007, http://www.sfgate.com/business/article/Hearst-MediaNews-Group-settle -Reilly-suit-2599576.php.

84. "MediaNews Group and 21st Century Media Transaction Has Been Finalized," last modified December 30, 2013, http://www.digitalfirstmedia.com/category/press.

85. "Black Monday at the Merc," *Save the Merc,* accessed August 30, 2010, www .savethemerc.com.

86. Pete Carey, "Mercury News Announces Move to Downtown San Jose," *San Jose Mercury News,* last modified June 12, 2014, http://www.mercurynews.com/business/ ci_25951487/mercury-news-announces-move-downtown.

87. *Namath v. Sports Illustrated,* 352 N.E. 2d 584 (N.Y. 1976).

88. The former publisher of the *Mercury News* addressed the tension between profit and journalism in Jay Harris, "The Bottom Line: Profits and Journalism in Newspapering," *Press/Politics* 6(4) (2001): 106–12.

89. See, Restatement (Third) of Unfair Competition § 47 (1995) ("The name, like-ness, and other indicia of a person's identity are used 'for purposes of trade' . . . if they are used in advertising the user's goods or service, or are placed on merchandise marketed by the user, or are used in connection with services rendered by the user"). See also *Brinkley v. Casablancas,* 438 N.Y.S.2d 1004, 1008 (App. Div. 1981) (holding that the sale of a poster of her was a sale for "trade purposes" within the New York privacy statute).

CHAPTER 5. OWNING A FACE: PUBLICITY AND ADVERTISING

1. *Newcombe v. Adolf Coors Company,* 157 F.3d 686 (9th Cir. 1998).

2. Ibid.

3. Robert Creamer, "Subject: Don Newcombe," *Sports Illustrated,* August 22, 1955, 28.

4. Peter Golenbock, *Bums: An Oral History of the Brooklyn Dodgers* (New York: Putnam's, 1984), 233–35.

5. Kelly D. Patterson, "Baseball Great Portrays Struggle to Make It Big," *Arlington (Texas) Morning News,* June 13, 1998.

6. Some reports claimed that the league president threatened to shut the league down if Campanella and Newcombe played. See Patterson, "Baseball Great." Other

sources suggest that the team president, a friend of Rickey's, was concerned about the reaction of the town of Danville. Scott C. Roper and Stephanie Abbot Roper, "'We're Going to Give All We Have for This Grand Little Town': Baseball Integration and the 1946 Nashua Dodgers," *Historical New Hampshire* 53(1/2) (1998): 2–19.

7. Quoted in Roper and Roper "'Give All We Have,'" 10.

8. Quoted in Ibid., 11.

9. Quoted in Ibid., 12.

10. Roper and Roper "'Give All We Have,'" 15.

11. "Montreal Halts Newark," *New York Times*, April 24, 1948.

12. "Dodgers Buy Newcombe from Montreal Farm," *New York Times*, May 14, 1949.

13. "Newcombe, Sievers Gain Top Awards," *New York Times*, October 24, 1949. This was the first time that a representative from both the National League and the American League were selected for the award. Previously only one player was named. The award is now named after Jackie Robinson, who was the first African American to be named Rookie of the Year.

14. Lew Freedman, *African American Pioneers of Baseball: A Biographical Encyclopedia* (Westport, Conn.: Greenwood, 2007), 99–108.

15. Walter Haight, "Newcombe Here as Referee, Expects Raise—Not $50,000," *Washington Post*, Jan. 11, 1950.

16. Jim Reisler, *Black Writers/Black Baseball: An Anthology of Articles from Black Sportswriters Who Covered the Negro Leagues* (Jefferson, N.C.: McFarland, 1994), 27–30.

17. See Roscoe McGowen, "Dodger Ace Faces Another Physical," *New York Times*, November 8, 1951, and "Army Rules Tuesday on Newcombe's Case," *New York Times*, November 10, 1951.

18. Creamer, "Subject: Don Newcombe," 28.

19. "Don Newcombe," *BaseballReference.com*, accessed August 24, 2014, http://www.baseball-reference.com/players/n/newcodo01.shtml?redir.

20. Freedman, *African American Pioneers*, 103–4.

21. Ibid., 105.

22. Golenbock, *Bums*, 240.

23. "Matthew Fagan, Judge, Dies at 55," *New York Times*, July 3, 1966.

24. "Don Newcombe Disappears," *Montreal Gazette*, October 11, 1956.

25. Arthur Daley, "Sports of the Times," *New York Times*, June 17, 1958.

26. Ibid.

27. See "Don Newcombe Has $300 Night on the Town," *New York Times*, June 1, 1958, and Daley, "Sport of the Times," June 17, 1958.

28. David Condon, "In the Wake of the News," *Chicago Daily Tribune*, June 18, 1958.

29. "3 Newcombes Indicted," *New York Times*, October 29, 1958.

30. "All Charges Dropped," *Washington Post*, December 10, 1958.

31. "Don Newcombe Learned that Fast Balls and Highballs Don't Mix," *People*, last modified December 1, 1975, http://www.people.com/people/archive/article/0,20065910,00.html.

32. Daley, "Sports of the Times," February 19, 1962.

33. "Don Newcombe Turned Down on Home Bid," *Chicago Daily Tribune*, January 6, 1963.

34. "Ex-Pitcher Pleads Bankrupt," *New York Times*, September 28, 1967.

35. Freedman, *African American Pioneers*, 104.

36. Ibid., 106–8.

37. Dave Anderson, "Big Newk Is Winning the Big One," *New York Times*, November 6, 1975.

38. "Newcombe Found Booze Was a Long Trip Nowhere," *Chicago Tribune*, February 23, 1975.

39. Jay Horning, "Pitcher Broke Race, Alcohol Barriers," *St. Petersburg (Florida) Times*, April 18, 1993.

40. Robert Fachet, "Newcombe Delivers People to Dodgers," *Washington Post*, June 9, 1972.

41. Jim Kaplan, "Alcohol Was Bob Welch's Problem," *Sports Illustrated*, last modified March 29, 1982, http://si.com/vault/article/magazine/MAG1125341/index.htm.

42. Freedman, *African American Pioneers*, 106–7.

43. For an early history of Coors, see William Kostka, *The Pre-Prohibition History of the Adolph Coors Company, 1873–1933* (Golden, Colo.: Adolph Coors Company, 1973).

44. "Coors Brewery," accessed December 8, 2014, http://www.golden.com/coors-brewery.htm.

45. Scott Hume, "Killian Caps Coors' National Goal," *Advertising Age*, March 14, 1988, 79.

46. Tom McGhee, "Coors Drafts Strategy," *Denver Post*, last modified September 14, 2006, http://www.denverpost.com/News/Local/Colorado/ci_4333235/Coors-drafts-strategy.

47. See Dan Baum, *Citizen Coors: An American Dynasty* (New York: Morrow, 2000).

48. Ibid.

49. "Don Newcombe Seeking $100 Million for Use of His Likeness," *Los Angeles Sentinel*, March 17, 1994.

50. Advertisement, *Sports Illustrated*, February 14, 1994, 137.

51. "Killian's Ad Called Foul," *Adweek*, last modified March 21, 1994, http://www.lexis-nexis.com.

52. "Don Newcombe Seeking $100 Million for Use of His Likeness."

53. "Ex-Dodger Don Newcombe Headed to Court against Coors Brewery," *Jet*, October 12, 1998, 50.

54. Ibid.

55. Ibid.

56. *O'Brien v. Pabst Sales Co.*, 124 F.2d 167 (5th Cir. 1941).

57. Ibid.

58. Ibid., 169.

59. Ibid., 168.

60. Ibid., 168–69.

61. Ibid., 170.

62. Ibid.

63. Ibid., 171.

64. Ibid., 170.

65. *O'Bannon v. National Collegiate Athletic Association*, 7 F. Supp. 3d 955, 1007 (N.D. Cal., 2014). See Steve Berkowitz, "Judge Releases Verdict on O'Bannon Case: NCAA Loses," *USA Today*, last modified August 8, 2014, and Daniel A. Nathan, "'A Matter of Basic Fairness:' Ed O'Bannon Takes the NCAA to Court," in *Sport and the Law: Historical and Cultural Intersections*, edited by Samuel O. Regalado and Sarah K. Fields (Fayetteville: University of Arkansas Press, 2014), 135–53, for a discussion of the O'Bannon case.

66. "*Edward O'Bannon, Jr. v. NCAA*," United States Court of Appeals for the Ninth Circuit, last modified September 30, 2015, http://www.ca9.uscourts.gov/content/view .php?pk_id=0000000757.

67. Martin Donell Kohout, "O'Brien, Robert David [Davey]," accessed January 10, 2014, *Handbook of Texas Online*, http://www.tshaonline.org/handbook/online/ articles/fob15.

68. *Haelan Laboratories, Inc. v. Topps Chewing Gum, Inc.*, 202 F.2d 866 (2nd Cir. 1953).

69. *Kimbrough v. Coca-Cola*, 521 S.W.2d 719 (Tex. App. 1975).

70. "John Kimbrough," accessed January 10, 2014, http://www.b-westerns.com/ kimbrough.htm.

71. Quoted in Ed Sherman, "Elroy 'Crazylegs' Hirsch 1923–2004: Great Receiver Had a Great Nickname," *Chicago Tribune*, last modified January 29, 2004, http:// articles.chicagotribune.com/2004-01-29/sports/0401290324_1_hirsch-was-general -manager-great-lakes-naval-station-elroy-hirsch.

72. *Hirsch v. S. C. Johnson & Son, Inc.*, 280 N.W.2d 129 (Wis. 1979).

73. Ibid.

74. Adam Mertz, "UW Icon 'Crazylegs' Hirsch Dies," last modified January 28, 2004, http://host.madison.com/archives/obits/uw-icon-crazylegs-hirsch-dies/article _1999d308-9642-11e2-858a-0019bb2963f4.html.

75. "Judge Rejects Don Newcombe's Charges against Coors Brewery," *Los Angeles Sentinel*, December 28, 1994.

76. Ibid.

77. *Eastwood v. Superior Court of Los Angeles County*, 198 Cal. Rpt. 342 (Ct. App. 1983).

78. *Newcombe*. For a detailed summary of the case see Nairi Chakalian, "Intellectual Property: *Newcombe v. Adolf Coors Co.*," *Golden Gate University Law Review* 29 (1999): 131–38.

79. See California Civ. Code § 334(b)(1).

80. *Newcombe*, 690.

81. Ibid., 693.

82. Ibid., 694.

83. Ibid., 695.

84. Erika T. Olander, "Stop the Presses! First Amendment Limitations on Professional Athletes' Publicity Rights," *Marquette Sports Law Review* 12, no. 2 (2002): 885–905.

85. Gary Khermouch, "Killian's Bulls Ahead with Import Cues," *Brandweek*, April 5, 1999, 14.

86. McGhee, "Coors Drafts Strategy."

87. "Coors Brewery."

88. Matt Nesvisky, "How Did the Miller-Coors Merger Affect the U.S. Beer Industry?" *NBER Digest*, last modified December 2013, http://go.galegroup.com/ps/i.do?id=GALE%7CA356039618&v=2.1&u=auraria_main&it=r&p=ITOF&sw=w&asid=e8332138065a3e454329da902287c4ed.

89. "Coors Brewery."

90. "Dodgers: Don Newcombe, Special Advisor to the Chairman," accessed January 10, 2014, http://mlb.mlb.com/la/community/executives/newcombe.html.

CHAPTER 6. ART VERSUS IMAGE: THE FIRST AMENDMENT VERSUS THE RIGHT OF PUBLICITY

1. An OCLC WorldCat search on July 30, 2014, for "Tiger Woods" limited to English language books (but excluding theses and dissertations) resulted in 560 hits. The same search on Amazon.com resulted in 3,815 hits.

2. Tim Rosaforte, *Tiger Woods: The Makings of a Champion* (New York: St. Martin's, 1997), xiv.

3. Judy Polumbaum and Stephen G. Weiting, "Stories of Sport and the Moral Order: Unraveling the Cultural Construction of Tiger Woods," *Journalism and Communication Monographs* 1 (1999), 106.

4. Andrew C. Billings, "Portraying Tiger Woods: Characterizations of a 'Black' Athlete in a 'White' Sport," *Howard Journal of Communications* 14 (2003): 29–37.

5. I rely on four major sources for information about Woods's life: his own representation on www.tigerwoods.com; Lawrence J. Londino, *Tiger Woods: A Biography*, 2nd ed. (Santa Barbara, Calif.: Greenwood, 2010) (this book is one of the more academic biographies of the golfer); Rosaforte, *Tiger Woods* (although unauthorized, this is a highly laudatory biography by a sports writer); and David Owen, *The Chosen One: Tiger Woods and the Dilemma of Greatness* (New York: Simon and Schuster, 2001) (as the title indicates, this is not the most critical of the biographies).

6. See Londino, *Tiger Woods*, for a discussion of the military courses.

7. See Rosaforte, *Tiger Woods*, for a detailed discussion of Woods's career.

8. Ibid., 84.

9. Stanford University, "Stanford Bulletin, 1995–96," 33, accessed July 30, 2014, http://sul-derivatives.stanford.edu/derivative?CSNID=00002191&mediaType=application/pdf.

10. Rosaforte, *Tiger Woods*, 147.

11. See Londino, *Tiger Woods,* and Rosaforte, *Tiger Woods*, for discussions of NCAA issues.

12. Londino, *Tiger Woods*, 89.

13. "Tiger Woods, Hello World," accessed July 31, 2014, https://www.youtube.com/watch?v=qSRzdXshLow.

14. Londino, *Tiger Woods*, 98.

15. "About Tiger: Chronology," accessed July 31, 2014, http://www.tigerwoods.com/about-tiger.

16. CNN Library, "Tiger Woods Fast Facts," last modified December 13, 2013, http://www.cnn.com/2013/05/30/us/tiger-woods-fast-facts.

17. Brad D. Carlson and D. Todd Donavan, "Concerning the Effect of Athlete Endorsements on Brand and Team-Related Intentions," *Sport Marketing Quarterly* 17 (2008): 154.

18. Kevin YC Chung, Timothy P. Derdenger, and Kannan Srinivasan, "Economic Value of Celebrity Endorsements: Tiger Woods' Impact on Sales of Nike Golf Balls," *Marketing Science* 32 (2013): 271–93.

19. Rosaforte, *Tiger Woods*, xv.

20. Ibid.

21. John Feinstein, *The First Coming: Tiger Woods, Master or Martyr* (New York: Ballantine, 1998).

22. David Owen, *The Chosen One: Tiger Woods and the Dilemma of Greatness* (New York: Simon and Schuster, 2001).

23. Sharlene A. McEvoy and William Windom, "A Tale of Two Cases: Right of Publicity Versus the First Amendment," *Communications and the Law* 25 (August 2003): 31–46.

24. Laura Lee Stapleton and Matt McMurphy, "The Professional Athlete's Right of Publicity," *Marquette Sports Law Review* 10 (1999): 23–68.

25. Rick Reilly, "Stroke of Genius," *Sports Illustrated*, originally published April 21, 1997, last modified February 22, 2008, http://www.golf.com/special-features/strokes-genius.

26. Dave Ivey, "Franklin Mint Cashes in on Collectibles," *Bangor [Maine] Daily News*, January 17, 1996.

27. Marcia Chambers, "Golf: Lawsuit Pits Artists' Rights vs. Athletes,'" *New York Times*, February 16, 1999.

28. "Teed-off Tiger Wins a Mint in Medal Lawsuit," *Daily Telegraph* (Sidney, Australia), April 17, 1998, 124.

29. *Woods v. The Franklin Mint*, No. 97CV4393, 1997 WL 33306646 (C.D. Cal., July 3, 1997).

30. Chambers, "Golf"; Allan Hall, "Aiming to Make a Mint out of Franklin," *Evening Standard* (London), August 13, 1998.

31. "Tiger Settles Lawsuit," *Courier Mail* (Queensland, Australia), April 17, 1998.

32. "Teed-off Tiger," 124.

33. "Rick Rush," accessed August 1, 2014, http://rickrushart.com/index.php?main_page=page&id=1&chapter=1.

34. The image of the print can be seen at Rush's homepage, accessed December 9, 2014, http://www.rickrushart.com/new-products-2.

35. *ETW Corporation v. Jireh Publishing, Inc.*, 99 F. Supp.2d 829 (2000), hereinafter *ETW I*.

36. Stephanie Hoops, "Local Artist Masters Tiger," *Tuscaloosa [Alabama] News*, June 21, 2003.

37. Chambers, "Golf."

38. McEvoy and Windom, "A Tale of Two Cases."

39. *ETW I*, 832–33.

40. *Pirone v. MacMillan, Inc.*, 894 F.2d 579 (2nd Cir. 1990). Quoted in *ETW I*, 833.

41. *ETW I*, 835.

42. See Mark Tushnet, "Art and the First Amendment," *Columbia Journal of Law and the Arts* 35 (2012): 169–220; and George Dickie, "Defining Art," *American Philosophical Quarterly* 6 (1969): 253–56.

43. Marcia Chambers, "Artists vs. Icons, with Woods in the Middle," *New York Times*, last modified July 3, 2002, http://www.nytimes.com/2002/07/03/sports/golf/03GOLF.html.

44. Ibid.

45. Ibid.

46. *ETW Corp. v. Jireh Publishing*, 332 F.3d 915, 922 (2003), hereinafter *ETW II*.

47. *ETW II*, 920–21.

48. Ibid., 923.

49. Ibid., 925.

50. Ibid., 931.

51. Ibid., 937.

52. Ibid., 938.

53. *Comedy III Productions v. Saderup, Inc.*, 21 P.3d 797 (Cal. 2001), 808.

54. *ETW II*, 960 (dissent). Tiger's motion for the entire court to hear the appeal was denied. *ETW Corp. v. Jireh Publ., Inc.*, 2003 U.S. App. LEXIS 19044 (Sixth Cir., Sept. 8, 2003).

55. Chambers, "Golf."

56. Robert DeWitt, "Tiger Woods' Lawyers Suing Local Company Over Print," *Tuscaloosa [Alabama] News*, February 18, 1999.

57. Michael J. Breslin, "Note: *ETW Corp. v. Jireh Publishing, Inc.*: Turning an Athlete's Publicity over to the Public," *Journal of Intellectual Property Law* 11 (2004): 369–94.

58. McEvoy and Windom, "A Tale of Two Cases."

59. John McMillen and Rebecca Atkinson, "Artists and Athletes: Balancing the First Amendment and the Right of Publicity in Sport Celebrity Portraits," *Journal of Legal Aspects of Sport* 12 (2004): 117–44.

60. John Grady, "Right of Publicity and Trademark Case: Implications for Marketing Professional Athletes," *Sport Marketing Quarterly* 13 (2004): 59–60.

61. *Cairns v. Franklin Mint Company*, 292 F.3d 1139 (9th Cir. 2002).

62. Marius Meland, "Princess Diana Fund, Franklin Mint Settle Trademark Dispute," *Law360*, last modified November 11, 2004, http://www.law360.com/articles/2540/princess-diana-fund-franklin-mint-settle-trademark-dispute.

63. Bloomberg News, "Franklin Mint Case Settlement Is Rejected," *Los Angeles Times*, last modified July 19, 2005, http://articles.latimes.com/2005/jul/19/business/fi-franklin19.

64. Rebecca English and Deborah Sherwood, "Controversial Diana Memorial Fund to Close after 14 Years," *MailOnline*, last modified July 20, 2011, http://www.dailymail.co.uk/news/article-2016638/Diana-memorial-fund-close-14-years.html.

65. "Franklin Mint Plans Layoffs and Product Changes," *New York Times*, last modified November 14, 2003, http://www.nytimes.com/2003/11/14/business/company-news-franklin-mint-plans-layoffs-and-product-changes.html?module=Search&mabReward=relbias%3Ar%2C%7B%221%22%3A%22RI%3A1%22%7D.

66. Wendy Tanaka, "Franklin Mint Shuts Doors of Retail Stores, Museum," *The [Philadelphia] Inquirer*, last modified February 13, 2004, http://articles.philly.com/2004-02-13/business/25375666_1_franklin-mint-prussia-mall-auction-collectibles.

67. See www.franklinmint.com, accessed June 24, 2015.

68. "Biography on Rick Rush," accessed August 3, 2014, http://rickrushart.com/index.php?main_page=page&id=1&chapter=1.

69. Quoted in "Tiger Woods' Injuries Sideline Him for Golf Tournament," *FoxNews.com*, last modified December 1, 2009, http://www.foxnews.com/us/2009/12/01/tiger-woods-injuries-sideline-golf-tournament.

70. Will Wei, "Tiger Woods Lost $22 Million in Endorsements in 2010," *Business Insider*, last modified July 21, 2010, http://www.businessinsider.com/tiger-woods-lost-22-million-in-2010-endorsements-2010-7.

71. Orin Starn, *The Passion of Tiger Woods: An Anthropologist Reports on Golf, Race, and Celebrity Scandal* (Durham, N.C.: Duke University Press, 2011), 34.

72. Donna J. Barbie, ed., *The Tiger Woods Phenomenon: Essays on the Cultural Impact of Golf's Fallible Superman* (Jefferson, N.C.: McFarland, 2010); Hank Haney, *The Big Miss: My Years of Coaching Tiger* (New York: Three Rivers, 2012); and Michael Essany, *Tiger Woods: Doomed by Distraction* ([Amazon] Kindle e-book, 2012).

73. "The World's Highest Paid Athletes," *Forbes.com*, accessed July 2, 2015, http://www.forbes.com/athletes.

74. Mark S. Lee, "Agents of Chaos: Judicial Confusion in Defining the Right of Publicity-Free Speech Interface," *Loyola of Los Angeles Entertainment Law Review* 23 (2003): 500.

75. *Doe v. TCI Cablevision*, 110 S.W.3d 363, 369, *cert. denied sub nom. McFarlane v. Twist*, 540 U.S. 1106 (2004).

CHAPTER 7. WHAT'S IN A NAME: COMIC BOOKS AND HOCKEY

1. Richard Wilner, "'Spawn' Creator's Biz, Long Balls Losing Value," *New York Post*, December 21, 2004.

2. Sherry Ross, "Oil's Well: Cartoonist Todd McFarlane Helps Save Edmonton, Adds to His Empire," *New York Daily News*, December 10, 2000.

3. "Todd McFarlane Complete Biography," accessed October 5, 2014, http://www.spawn.com/info/todd/bio.long.aspx. Additional information from Jim Kershner, "'Spawn' Storm," *Spokesman Review* (Spokane, Wash.), June 3,1997.

4. Joseph Szadkowski, "An 'Ugly' Icon Helps Spawn McFarlane's Business Success," *Washington Times*, July 4, 1998.

5. "Todd McFarlane Complete Biography." Additional information from Kershner, "'Spawn' Storm."

6. Paul Geitner, "From Baseball Hopeful to Comic Book Artist," *Associated Press Wire*, last modified August 13, 1990, http://www.lexis-nexis.com.

7. Paul Geitner, "Move Over Tracy, Back Off Bart; Spider-Man Is Here," *Associated Press Wire*, last modified July 30, 1990, http://www.lexis-nexis.com.

8. "Another Blow for Marvel," *New York Times*, February 20, 1992.

9. Kerbi Brenner, "New Superheroes Vie for Comic Book Fans," *[Portland] Oregonian*, May 29, 1992.

10. Frank Green, "Imagine Comic Is Quick on the Draw," *San Diego Union-Tribune*, November 22, 1994.

11. "Unconventional Millionaires," *San Jose Mercury News*, May 12, 1996.

12. Kershner, "'Spawn' Storm."

13. David Holthouse, "Comic Book Mogul Finally Makes the Big Leagues," *Phoenix New Times*, last modified July 15, 1999, http://www.lexis-nexis.com.

14. Jim Bullard, "Comic Book News," *St. Petersburg [Florida] Times*, May 1, 1992.

15. Brenner, "New Superheroes."

16. Jim Bullard, "Comics Were Jumping," *St. Petersburg [Florida] Times*, December 18, 1992.

17. Szadkowski, "'Ugly' Icon."

18. Joseph Szadkowski, "Spawn and Batman Meet," *Washington Times*, March 12, 1994.

19. Paul Davis, "Toy Firms See Stars in Their Future," *Providence [R.I.] Journal-Bulletin*, February 20, 1994.

20. Bette Harrison, "Comic Book Spawns a Hot New Toy," *Atlanta Journal Constitution*, December 6, 1994.

21. Joseph Szadkowski, "Disney Cards Lead the Pack," *Washington Times*, July 22, 1995.

22. Paula Spin, "Small Wonders at World Toy Fair," *[Greensboro, N.C.] News and Record*, March 1, 1997.

23. "Rolling Stones' Tour Stall by Bug That Strikes Jagger," *Cleveland Plain Dealer*, February 2, 1999.

24. Ray Richmond, "Toons Tune to Adult Auds," *Variety*, October 7–13, 1996, 37.

25. Michael Grunwald, "He's Having a Ball, for $3 Million," *Washington Post*, February 9, 1999.

26. Eric Deggans, "Spawning a New Breed of Hero," *St. Petersburg [Florida] Times*, May 16, 1997.

27. David Holthouse, "The Devil and Todd McFarlane: Spawn's Creator Revolutionized the Comic-Book Industry, but Did He Survive Hollywood with His Soul Intact?" *Phoenix New Times*, last modified July 31, 1997, http://www.lexis-nexis.com.

28. Ibid.

29. Kershner, "'Spawn' Storm."

30. Avis L. Weathersbee, "At the Controls of 'Spawn,'" *Chicago Sun-Times*, August 5, 1997.

31. Szadkowski, "'Ugly' Icon."

32. Rebecca Rolwing, "Rebel Comic Artist Spawns Success," *Business Journal-Phoenix and the Valley of the Sun*, June 7, 1996. McFarlane in "The Spawning Ground" (letters to readers section) of *Spawn* no. 24, September 1994, reports that not only is the dog named after his but is physically similar.

33. Holthouse, "Devil and Todd McFarlane." Holthouse says that McFarlane and Simmons played minor league baseball together. Other sources state that the two were roommates at Eastern Washington University. Ophelia Johnson, "Variety Will Be Show's Spice," *Richmond Times-Dispatch*, July 31, 1997. In the letters to readers section ("The Spawning Ground"), Todd McFarlane described the real Al Simmons as his college roommate. *Spawn* no. 24, May 1994.

34. "People in Sports," *Houston Chronicle*, October 7, 1992.

35. Ross, "Oil's Well," 75.

36. Ronald Blum, "Comic Book Creator Has McGwire Ball," *Associated Press Online*, February 9, 1999, www.lexis-nexis.com.

37. Wilner, "'Spawn' Creator's Biz."

38. Goldman, "Blowing a Wad, Having a Ball, Who Spent $3 Million for a Piece of Baseball History? Mystery Solved," *Philadelphia Inquirer*, February 9, 1999.

39. Grunwald, "He's Having a Ball."

40. Holthouse, "Comic Book Mogul."

41. Kevin Kernan, "Wonderball," *New York Post*, December 26, 1999.

42. *Doe v. TCI Cablevision*, No. ED78785, 2002 Mo. App. LEXIS 1577 at *51 (Mo. Ct. App. July 23, 2002 [henceforth *Doe I*].

43. Tim Bryant, "Tony Twist Takes Aim at Comic Villain as Trial Opens," *St. Louis Post-Dispatch*, June 20, 2000.

44. Austin Murphy, "Fighting for a Living," *Sports Illustrated*, March 16, 1988, 42–45.

45. Tony Twist had such a reputation as a nice guy that this collegiality was apparent during his interactions with Todd McFarlane during the first trial. According to the local beat reporter, Twist and McFarlane frequently "chatted amiably . . . outside the courtroom during a break" in the initial trial proceedings. Tim Bryant, "Professor Says Twist Deserves Revenue from 'Spawn' for Use of Name," *St. Louis Post-Dispatch*, June 23, 2000.

46. For a detailed description of the code and its history in hockey, see Ross Bernstein, *The Code: The Unwritten Rules of Fighting and Retaliation in the NHL* (Chicago: Triumph, 2006).

47. Ben Westhoff, "Twist of Fate," *[St. Louis] Riverfront Times*, last modified October 4, 2006, http://www.lexis-nexis.com. See also *McKichan v. St. Louis Hockey Club*, 867 S.W.2d 209 (Mo. Ct. App., 1998).

48. Murphy, "Fighting for a Living," 42.

49. Bernstein, *Code*, xiii–xiv.

50. Murphy, "Fighting for a Living," 43.

51. Bernie Miklasz, "Let's Hope the Blues Keep Their Wallet Open," *St. Louis Post-Dispatch*, July 8, 2000.

52. Bryant, "Tony Twist Takes Aim."

53. HBO reached an undisclosed settlement with Twist during the first trial and thus was not involved in any of the subsequent trials and appeals. Tim Bryant, "Jury Awards Tony Twist $24.5 Million in Suit Over Use of His Name," *St. Louis Post-Dispatch*, July 6, 2000.

54. The trial court dismissed these defendants because they were "passive distributors" of the comic books and related paraphernalia. *Doe I*, *9 n6.

55. Wizard Press also settled with Twist prior to the verdict. *Doe I*, *6 n4.

56. Fred Faust, "Blues Player Sues," *St. Louis Post-Dispatch*, January 26, 1998.

57. Bryant, "Tony Twist Takes Aim."

58. Tim Bryant, "Twist Tells Jury His Mother First Told Him His Name Was Being Used for Comic," *St. Louis Post-Dispatch*, June 27, 2000.

59. Faust, "Blues Player Sues."

60. Tim Bryant, "Twist's Lawyer Says Portrayal Harms Player's Good Image," *St. Louis Post-Dispatch*, June 21, 2000.

61. *Doe I*, *11.

62. Bryant, "Professor Says."

63. Tim Bryant, "Jurors Watch 'Spawn' Episodes," *St. Louis Post-Dispatch*, June 24, 2000.

64. Bryant, "Twist Tells Jury."

65. *Doe I*, *12.

66. Bryant, "Jury Awards."

67. Ibid.

68. Tim Bryant, "Judge Overrules Damages Awarded to Twist," *St. Louis Post-Dispatch*, November 1, 2000.

69. "Judge Overturns Verdict Awarding Former St. Louis Blues Player Tony Twist $24.5 Million," Sports News, *Associated Press*, last modified November 2, 2000, http://www.lexis-nexis.

70. *Doe I*, *13.

71. "Sound Off," *St. Louis Post-Dispatch*, July 9, 2000.

72. "Letters to the Editor," *St. Louis Post-Dispatch*, July 7, 2000.

73. "Sound Off," *St. Louis Post-Dispatch*, July 16, 2000.

74. *Doe I*, *15.

75. Ibid., *18–24

76. 433 U.S. 562 (1977).

77. Ibid., *28–30, quotation at 35.

78. Ibid., *38.

79. Ibid., *40.

80. Ibid., *46–48, quotation at *48.

81. Ibid., *54–59.

82. *Doe v. TCI Cablevision*, 110 S.W.3d 363, 369, *cert. denied sub nom. McFarlane v. Twist*, 540 U.S. 1106 (2004) [hereinafter *Doe II*].

83. *Doe II*, 366.

84. Ibid., 370.

85. Ibid., 371.

86. See Mark S. Lee, "Agents of Chaos: Judicial Confusion in Defining the Right of Publicity-Free Speech Interface," *Loyola of Los Angeles Entertainment Law Review* 23 (2003): 471–501. How Limbaugh knew of this particular article is unclear, but most likely it was cited in the briefs presented on Twist's behalf. Any of the Missouri Supreme Court justices or their clerks may also have read the article independently.

87. *Doe II*, 374–76.

88. Gina Holland, "High Court Urged to Hear Comic Book Case," *Associated Press Online*, last modified November 27, 2003, http://www.lexis-nexis.

89. "Brief of Amici Curiae writers Michael Crichton, Larry David, Jeremiah Healy, Elmore Leonard, Harry Shearer, Ron Shelton, Scott Turow, Paul Weitz, and the Authors Guild, Inc. In Support of the Petitioners," On Petition for Writ of Certiorari No. 03–615, November 23, 2003 (unpublished document on file with the author).

90. Deb Peterson, "KMOX Grabs KTRS' Harris to Fill Void Left by Milhaven," *St. Louis Post-Dispatch*, June 25, 2004, http://www.lexis-nexis.com.

91. Peter Hinkle, "Tony Twist Wins $15 Million Verdict," *St. Louis Post-Dispatch*, July 10, 2004.

92. Geri L. Dreiling, "Retrial of Twist Lawsuit Results in $15M Verdict," *Missouri Lawyers Weekly*, last modified July 19, 2004, http://www.lexis-nexis.com.

93. Tom Mahon, "'W' Dazzles Classmate," *Philadelphia Daily News*, July 12, 2004.

94. *Doe v. McFarlane*, 207 S.W.3d 52 (2006) [hereinafter *Doe III*].

95. "'Spawn' Publisher in Bankruptcy Court," *Associated Press Online*, last modified December 18, 2004, http://www.lexis-nexis.com.

96. Heather Cole, "Lawyers of St. Louis Blues Hockey Player's Firecracker Lawsuit Fight over Who Gets Paid What," *Missouri Lawyers Weekly*, last modified February 26, 2007, http://www.lexis-nexis.com.

97. See *Hanover Ins. Co. v. TMP International, Inc.*, 2000 U.S. Dist. LEXIS 34970 (US Bank. ED Mo. December 21, 2005); *Hanover Ins. Co. v. TMP Int'l, Inc.*, 2006 U.S. Dist. LEXIS 47 (E.D. Mo., January 3, 2006); *Hanover Ins. Co. v. TMP Int'l, Inc.*, 2006 U.S. Dist. LEXIS 341 (E.D. Mo., January 6, 2006); *Hanover Ins. Co. v. TMP Int'l, Inc.*, 2006 U.S. Dist. LEXIS 2502 (E.D. Mo., January 24, 2006); and *Hanover Ins. Co. v. TMP Int'l*, 2006 U.S. Dist. LEXIS 59083 (E.D., Mo., August 26, 2006). In the final decision by the Eastern District of Missouri, the United States District Court judge sent the whole matter to the bankruptcy court in Arizona. That judge ruled that the insurance companies were not liable for the full award. *In re* Todd McFarlane Productions, Inc., 2007 Bankr. LEXIS 2327 (Bankr. Ariz., July 5, 2007).

98. None of the members of the appellate court who ruled on the first jury trial was a member of the second panel.

99. One of those English professors was my father, Wayne Fields, who told me about the case and provided his notes after his deposition.

100. *Doe III*, 59–61.

101. Ibid., 61–76.

102. Donna Walter, "Final Twist," *St. Louis Daily Record*, February 16, 2007, http://www.lexis-nexis.com. Twist's lawyers themselves then began arguing over how the fees would be divided and McFarlane had threatened to sue the insurance companies for the over $5 million in legal fees he expended. Cole, "Lawyers."

103. Jamie Mason, "Spawn Creditors to be Paid in Full," *Daily Deal*, last modified October 11, 2007, http://www.lexis-nexis.com.

104. See Michael S. Kruse, "Note: Missouri's Interfacing of the First Amendment and the Right of Publicity: Is the 'Predominant Purpose' Test Really That Desirable?" *Missouri Law Review* 69 (2004): 799–816, for a contextualization of the case.

105. John Grady, Steve McKelvey, and Annie Clement, "A New 'Twist' for 'The Home Run Guys'?" An Analysis of the Right of Publicity versus Parady," *Journal of the Legal Aspects of Sport* 15 (2005): 263–93; Steve McKelvey, "Sport Celebrities and the Right of Publicity Take a New Twist," *Sports Marketing Quarterly* 14 (2005): 188–90; and Joy Simmons, "Right of Publicity Suits in Missouri May Increase Due to the Property Suit of Hockey Player," *Missouri Lawyers Weekly*, last modified June 26, 2006, http://www.lexis-nexis.com.

106. Carla Di Fonzo, "The Sweet KISS of Success," *[Lancaster, Penn.] Intelligencer Journal*, April 26, 2005. KISS agreed. Colette Shaw, *Won't Get Fooled Again* (Lancaster, Penn.: Loose Slips, 2005). See also "Colette Shaw Is Living the Fantasy," accessed June 26, 2008, http://www.kissfiction.com.

107. Restatement (Third) of Unfair Competition 47, cmt. c (1995).

108. *Winter v. DC Comics*, 69 P.3d 473, 478 (Cal. 2003).

109. See Cecilia Chung, "Comment: Preservation of First Amendment Rights: Finding the Proper Balance between Expression and Exploitation in Works of Art," *Santa Clara Law Review* 46 (2006): 889–919 (arguing that the transformative test is the best of the available tests).

110. Joel Anderson, "Note and Comment: What's Wrong with This Picture? Dead or Alive; Protecting Actors in the Age of Virtual Reanimation," *Loyola of Lost Angeles Entertainment Law Review* 25 (2004/2005): 183.

111. David S. Welkowitz and Tyler T. Ochoa, "The Terminator as Eraser: How Arnold Schwarzenegger Used the Right of Publicity to Terminate Non-Defamatory Political Speech," *Santa Clara Law Review*, 45 (2005): 657, 670. Twist actually listed defamation as a cause of action in his complaint, but the trial court dismissed it because the judge felt that the elements of defamation had not been met in the complaint. The court agreed with the defense that no reasonable person would believe that any element of the character was an assertion of fact. *Doe I*, *9.

112. Mark Sableman, "Artistic Expression Today: Can Artists Use the Language of Our Culture?" *Saint Louis University Law Journal* 52 (2007): 213.

113. "RECENT CASE: First Amendment—Right of Publicity—Missouri Supreme Court Creates 'Predominant Purpose' Test for First Amendment Defenses to Publicity Right Claims," *Harvard Law Review* 117 (2004): 1281.

114. *C.B.C. Distribution and Marketing v. Major League Baseball Advanced Media*, 443 F. Supp. 2d 1077 (E.D. Mo. 2006). For a complete analysis of this case, see Gabriel Grossman, "Comment: Switch Hitting: How *C.B.C. v. MLB Advanced Media* Redefined the Right of Publicity," *UCLA Entertainment Law Review* 14 (2007): 285–313. Compare to Daniel Mead, "Note: *C.B.C. Distribution and Marketing, Inc. v. Major League Baseball Advanced Media, LP*: Why Major League Baseball Struck Out and Won't Have Better Luck in Its Next Trip to the Plate," *Minnesota Journal of Law, Science and Technology* 8 (2007): 715–36.

115. *C.B.C. Distribution and Marketing v. Major League Baseball Advanced Media*, 505 F.3d 818 (8th Cir. 2007), *cert. denied*, 2008 U.S. LEXIS 4574 (U.S., June 2, 2008).

116. Szadkowski, "'Ugly' Icon."

117. Westhoff, "Twist of Fate."

118. Ibid.

119. "Todd McFarlane: Complete Biography" and "Todd McFarlane Productions, Inc.: Company Profile," accessed October 5, 2014, www.spawn.com.

120. Bill McClellan, "Michael Kahn Is at It Again, but as Michael Barron," *St. Louis Post-Dispatch*, May 2, 2005.

121. Lee, "Agents of Chaos," 500.

CONCLUSION

1. Samantha Barbas, "From Privacy to Publicity: The Tort of Appropriation in the Age of Mass Consumption," *Buffalo Law Review* 61 (2013): 1119–89.

2. *Spahn v. Julian Messner, Inc.*, 250 N.Y.S.2d 529 (N.Y. Sup. Ct. 1964), *aff'd*, 260 N.Y.S.2d 451(N.Y. App. Div. 1965), *aff'd*, 221 N.E.2d 543, 544 (N.Y., 1966), *vacated by*, 387 U.S. 239 (1967), *on remand at, adhered to*, 233 N.E.2d 840 (N.Y., 1967).

3. *Montana v. San Jose Mercury News*, 40 Cal. Rptr. 2d 639 (Cal. Ct. App. 1995).

4. Consider *Brown v. Board of Education*, 347 U.S. 483 (1954), in which the Supreme Court deemed racial segregation in public schools unconstitutional. That opinion overruled *Plessy v. Ferguson*, 163 U.S. 537 (1896). Justice John Marshall Harlan wrote the only dissent to *Plessy*.

5. *Butts v. Curtis Publishing*, 225 F. Supp. 916 (N.D. Ga., 1964), *aff'd* 242 F. Supp. 390 (N.D. Ga., 1964), *aff'd* 351 F.2d 702 (5th Cir., 1965), *aff'd* 388 U.S. 130 (1967).

6. Spahn endorsed Camel cigarettes: "1956 Camel Cigarettes Ad," accessed December 17, 2014, http://www.atticpaper.com/proddetail.php?prod=1956-camel-cigarettes-ad-baseball-players&cat=65; games; "1958 Warren Spahn Whirly Bird Game in Original Box," accessed December 17, 2014, http://www.grandoldtoys.com/toydb_Detail.php?id=1018; and Gillette razors, "Pinterest," accessed December 17, 2014, https://www.pinterest.com/pin/498492252475123665. He likely had other endorsements as well.

7. For a fuller discussion of the weaknesses of false light, see Neil M. Richards and Daniel J. Solove, "Prosser's Privacy Law: A Mixed Legacy," *California Law Review* 98 (2010): 1887–924.

8. *Newcombe v. Adolf Coors Co.*, 157 F.3d 686 (9th Cir. 1998).

9. *ETW v. Jireh Publishing Co.*, 99 F. Supp. 2d 829 (N.D. Ohio 2000), *aff'd*, 332 F.3d 915 (6th Cir. 2003).

10. *Doe v. TCI Cablevision*, 110 S.W.3d 363 (Mo. 2003).

11. Kyle D. Simcox, "Comment: Selling Your Soul at the Crossroads; The Need for a Harmonized Standard Limiting the Publicity Rights of Professional Athletes," *DePaul Law Review* 63 (2013): 87–121. See also Lindsay Korokin, "Finding Reality in the Right of Publicity," *Cardozo Law Review De Novo* 2013 (2013): 268–313.

12. *Hart v. Electronic Arts, Inc.*, 717 F.3d 141 (3rd Cir. 2012), *cert. denied*, 2014 U.S. LEXIS 4896 (U.S., Sept. 30, 2014).

13. *In Re: NCAA Student-Athlete Name & Likeness Licensing Litigation v. Electronic Arts*, 724 F.3d 1268, (9th Cir. 2013). This version of the case is often called *Keller v. EA* because Samuel Michael Keller was the lead plaintiff prior to consolidation of similar lawsuits. This specific decision did not resolve the case; it resolved a motion by the defendants to dismiss under state law.

14. *Hart*, 154.

15. Ibid., 163.

16. Ibid., 173–75 (Ambro dissent).

17. *In Re: NCAA Student Athletes*, 1271.

18. Ibid., 1285–290, quote on 1285.

19. Thomas E. Kadri, "Comment: Fumbling the First Amendment: The Right of Publicity Goes 200 against Freedom of Expression," *Michigan Law Review* 112 (2014): 1519–31.

20. Korokin, "Finding Reality in the Right of Publicity," 268.

21. See Stephen Paskey, "The Law Is Made of Stories: Erasing the False Dichotomy between Stories and Legal Rules," *Legal Communication and Rhetoric: JALWD* 11 (2014): 51–82.

INDEX

SARAH K. FIELDS is an associate professor in communication at the University of Colorado–Denver. She is author of *Female Gladiators: Gender, Law, and Contact Sport in America.*

SPORT AND SOCIETY

Team Chemistry: The History of Drugs and Alcohol
    in Major League Baseball   *Nathan Michael Corzine*
Wounded Lions: Joe Paterno, Jerry Sandusky, and the Crises
    in Penn State Athletics   *Ronald A. Smith*
Sex Testing: Gender Policing in Women's Sports   *Lindsay Parks Pieper*
Cold War Games: Propaganda, the Olympics,
    and U.S. Foreign Policy   *Toby C. Rider*
Games Faces: Sport Celebrity and the Laws of Reputation   *Sarah K. Fields*

REPRINT EDITIONS
The Nazi Olympics   *Richard D. Mandell*
Sports in the Western World (2d ed.)   *William J. Baker*
Jesse Owens: An American Life   *William J. Baker*

The University of Illinois Press
is a founding member of the
Association of American University Presses.

_____

Composed in 10.5/13 Adobe Minion Pro
by Lisa Connery
at the University of Illinois Press
Manufactured by Cushing-Malloy, Inc.

University of Illinois Press
1325 South Oak Street
Champaign, IL 61820-6903
www.press.uillinois.edu